Falkland Islands

THE BRADT TRAVEL GUIDE

THE BRADT STORY

The first Bradt travel guide was written by Hilary and George Bradt in 1974 on a river barge floating down a tributary of the Amazon in Bolivia. From their base in Boston, Massachusetts, they went on to write and publish four other backpacking guides to the Americas and one to Africa.

In the 1980s Hilary continued to develop the Bradt list in England, and also established herself as a travel writer and tour leader. The company's publishing emphasis evolved towards broader-based guides to new destinations – usually the first to be published on those countries – complemented by hiking, rail and wildlife guides.

Since winning *The Sunday Times* Small Publisher of the Year Award in 1997, we have continued to fill the demand for detailed, well-written guides to unusual destinations, while maintaining the company's original ethos of low-impact travel.

Travel guides are by their nature continuously evolving. If you experience anything which you would like to share with us, or if you have any amendments to make to this guide, please write; all your letters are read and passed on to the author. Most importantly, do remember to travel with an open mind and to respect the customs of your hosts – it will add immeasurably to your enjoyment.

Happy travelling!

Hilary Bradt

19 High Street, Chalfont St Peter, Bucks SL9 9QE, England
Tel: 01753 893444 Fax: 01753 892333
Email: info@bradt-travelguides.com
Web: www.bradt-travelguides.com

Falkland Islands

THE BRADT TRAVEL GUIDE

William Wagstaff

Bradt Travel Guides Ltd, UK
The Globe Pequot Press Inc, USA

First published in 2001 by Bradt Travel Guides Ltd,
19 High Street, Chalfont St Peter, Bucks SL9 9QE, England
web: www.bradt-travelguides.com
Published in the USA by The Globe Pequot Press Inc, 246 Goose Lane,
PO Box 480, Guilford, Connecticut 06437-0480

The author and publishers have made every effort to ensure the accuracy of the information in this book at the time of going to press. However, they cannot accept any responsibility for any loss, injury or inconvenience resulting from the use of information contained in this guide.

British Library Cataloguing in Publication Data
A catalogue record for this book is available from the British Library
ISBN 1 84162 037 8

Library of Congress Cataloging-in-Publication Data
Wagstaff, William
        Falkland Islands : the Bradt travel guide / William Wagstaff.
            p.cm
        Includes bibliographical references and index.
        ISBN 1-84162-037-8
        1. Falkland Islands—Guidebooks. 2. Falkland Islands —Description
        and travel. I. Title.
F3031.W34 2001
919.7'11042—dc21

2001033148

Photographs
Front cover Gentoo penguins on the beach, New Island (Hilary Bradt)
Text Hilary Bradt (HB), Will Wagstaff (WW)

Illustrations Dan Powell
Maps Alan Whitaker

Typeset from the author's disc by Wakewing
Printed and bound in Italy by Legoprint SpA, Trento

Author

William Wagstaff was born in Cardiff, South Wales in 1960. Having graduated with a BSc Joint Honours in Biology and Geology, he settled in the Isles of Scilly in 1981. His main passion has always been ornithology, but over the years his interests have encompassed all aspects of wildlife. In the Isles of Scilly he has worked as a tour leader and as the first Conservation Officer of the Isles of Scilly Environmental Trust. Since leaving the Environmental Trust to set up his own business, Island Wildlife Tours, he has been able to share his love of the islands with many hundreds of visitors who stay in Scilly. His regular contributions to wildlife programmes on radio and on television have also helped him foster interest in the islands. A regular agenda of walks, talks and boat excursions throughout the summer keeps him very busy but leaves him free to lead tours all over the world during the winter months. The Falkland Islands have been the most frequently visited location, but he has journeyed to the Galápagos Islands, the Seychelles, Nepal, Gambia, Senegal, North America and to several countries in southern Europe. His journeys abroad usually involve leading groups and so he has been able to communicate his love of wildlife to many.

Contents

Acknowledgements

Firstly my thanks must go to Amanda Martin, on the Isles of Scilly, for all her work in helping me with this book. Thanks must go to John Fowler in the Falkland Islands and also to Robin Woods in the UK for answering my many queries. Thanks also go to those in Falkland and in the UK who have patiently answered any other queries I have had. I am very grateful to Libby Weir-Breen of Island Holidays for sending me to the Falkland Islands so often. Long may it continue!

DEDICATION

This book is dedicated to the memory of Robin Lee, a true Falkland gentleman, who shared his love of the islands with so many people.

Introduction

Like many people in Britain I watched the television coverage of the 1982 war, little realising that I would one day visit those far-away islands. My chance came out of the blue one Saturday afternoon in January 1994. I had led some tours here on the Isles of Scilly for Libby of Island Holidays and had said that I should be pleased to lead tours elsewhere. She rang that afternoon to say 'You know you said you'd like to go to the Falkland Islands? Could you go on Monday?'

Well, to cut a long story short, a few phone calls later it was all sorted and I was ready to go. The only trouble was that I could not get off the Isles of Scilly until that very Monday and, after an anxious trip to Brize Norton, met a rather surprised group, which was still expecting the original leader. Thankfully we had the services for a few days of well-known botanist Jim McAdam, who specialises in the flora of the Falkland Islands. He had brought along some books about the islands' wildlife for me to swot up on during the flight via Ascension Island.

Reaching the islands for the first time was a magical experience, from watching upland geese and meadowlarks to admiring the huge expanses of white grass on the bus ride into Stanley. I shall always remember my first walk along Stanley sea front with the faint smell of peat smoke in the air, and the first penguin I saw swimming just offshore.

Since that first tour in 1994 I have led groups around the islands for Libby on seven other occasions and have managed to visit a large part of the archipelago. Every trip brings something new, whether birds, flowers or seeing familiar places at different times of year. There is tremendous pleasure in taking people around the Falkland Islands and watching their reactions to the sights and sounds. I have been lucky in that some people have visited the islands with me more than once and are therefore able to share my memories of what we have seen and the events of particular trips. The welcome in each of the places we stay makes it so much easier to settle in and enjoy what that area has to offer.

There have been changes in the time I have known the Falkland Islands. Stanley, in particular, has become a thriving town, although the smell of burning peat does not linger in the air the way it used to, as many people have switched over to oil-fired central heating. The pace of life on the islands is more relaxed than in the UK; people still have time to stop and chat in a way that is reminiscent of the Isles of Scilly but on a larger scale. Away from

Stanley the drop in wool prices has led to a steady increase in the numbers of islanders leaving the camp and moving to work in Stanley. Tourism has been a welcome boost to the outer islands; this fledgling industry has been carefully thought out so as to let the visitor experience the spectacular wildlife without destroying its environment.

Standing on the hilltops gives one a feeling of being on top of the world as the islands are laid out at one's feet. The amazing clarity of light in these islands never ceases to amaze me. The wildlife delights in being tame and very photogenic. I hesitate to think how many photos I have taken of penguins, elephant seals and various other creatures over the years. The Falkland Islands are one of those magical places in the world that capture the imagination, and although the weather is not always clement, the overriding memory is of blue sea, blue sky, teeming wildlife and 'smoko' as soon as you get back indoors.

Will Wagstaff
St Mary's, Isles of Scilly, 2001

FEEDBACK REQUEST

You, the readers, can make an incalculable difference to further editions of this guide by writing to me about your trip. If, upon your return home, you can fine time to send a postcard or longer note with any updates or corrections to the information I have provided, it would be greatly appreciated. The more detail the better, but even the smallest snippet will be of use. Such a snippet might make all the difference to a visitor to the islands in the future.

Happy travels.

Bradt Travel Guides,
19 High Street, Chalfont St Peter, Bucks SL9 9QE, England
Tel: 01753 893444; fax: 01753 892333;
email: info@bradt-travelguides.com;
web: www.bradt-travelguides.com

Part One

General Information

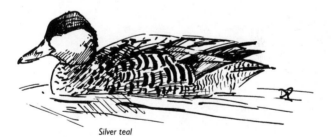

Silver teal

FALKLAND ISLANDS AT A GLANCE

Location Between latitude 51° and 53° south and longitude 57° and 62° west in the South Atlantic

Area 4,700 square miles

Capital Port Stanley

Population 2,200 (plus around 2,000 military personnel and contractors)

Status Dependent territory of the United Kingdom

Executive authority Her Majesty the Queen, represented by the Governor

Flag Blue, with Union Jack in the top left-hand corner and a white shield containing the coat of arms in the centre of the distal half

National anthem 'God Save the Queen'

Language English

Religion Predominantly Christian

Main industries Fishing, wool production, tourism

Currency Falkland Islands pound (equivalent to and interchangeable with GB pound)

Time 3 hours behind GMT in summer, 4 hours in winter. Daylight saving dates in April and September vary from one year to another and should be checked before travelling

International dialling code 00 500

Electricity supply 240V using 3-pin UK type plugs

Background Information

The Falkland Islands are situated between latitude 51° and 53° south and longitude 57° and 62° west in the South Atlantic, some 300 miles to the west of southern Argentina. There are two large islands, East and West Falkland, and over 400 islands, which combine to create a total land area of 4,700 square miles (12,173km²). Three quarters of the islands' population of over 2,000 now live in Stanley, the islands' capital. The remaining quarter is spread over East and West Falkland and 12 of the smaller islands.

Port Stanley and New Island are at opposing extremes, east and west, 148 miles (238km) apart. The coastline is highly indented with many rocky headlands and sandy beaches. Large inland bodies of water are absent but there are many small lakes and pools. Mount Usborne at 2,312ft (705m) in the Wickham Heights range on East Falkland is the highest point on the islands. Natural woodland is not a feature of the islands, the only trees having been introduced around the settlements. Low grasses, ferns and shrubs provide the most typical ground cover, with a fringe of tussac grass around the coast away from any grazing animals.

Although the archipelago is only approximately 300 miles from the nearest landmass, strong winds have maintained a relative degree of isolation from South America, even though the flora and fauna are very similar to that found in Chile and Argentina. Geography and geology combine to exert a major influence on the ability of the flora and fauna to survive on these windswept islands.

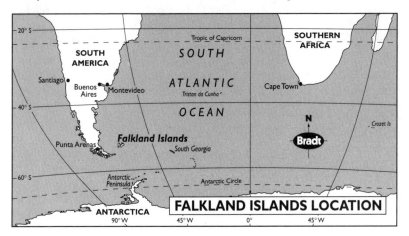

FALKLAND ISLANDS LOCATION

Geographical isolation has limited the numbers of animals that have reached the islands by their own means and has restricted the birdlife to long-distance migrants and strong flyers. The flora of the islands is equally restricted, although isolation has created a number of endemic species and subspecies. Five species of penguin breed around the coasts, making this one of the best places in the world to observe this family. The prospect of seeing elephant seals, killer whales and penguins attracts many visitors to the islands. The Falklands, although not as rich in species of flora and fauna as nearby South America, offer an abundance of spectacular wildlife to gratify man's continuing fascination with nature.

The islands hit the international headlines when Argentina invaded in April 1982, and the subsequent recapture by the British Forces raised the islands' profile in the world at large. A fledgling tourist industry took advantage of this post-war interest to offer holidays to these wild and beautiful places. Income generated by the advent of the fishing industry has increased the standard of living on the islands. Despite the fact that the Falkland Islands are 8,000 miles from the UK there is a very strong British influence. The friendly population and its relaxed attitude to life make an important contribution to any holiday in this unique place.

GEOLOGY AND GEOGRAPHY

The islands were created by folding layers of rock which were uplifted as a result of tectonic plate movements during the Palaeozoic and Mesozoic eras. The most obvious results are the three principal mountain ranges, all in the northern half of the islands. On East Falkland, Wickham Heights run from east to west culminating in the highest point in the islands, Mount Usborne (2,312ft, 705m). This range is very rugged; many peaks are tipped with jagged outcrops and many stone runs occur along the slopes. On West Falkland the other two ranges are more rounded, stone runs being comparatively rare. Byron Heights run from east to west, whilst the Hornby Range runs almost north-south parallel to Falkland Sound, the channel between East and West Falkland. Mount Adam, the second highest point on the islands, reaches 2,297ft (700m) in the Hornby Range. The greatest part of the islands is composed of Palaeozoic sedimentary rocks incorporating quartzite, sandstone and shale. Lafonia, the southern part of East Falkland, is composed of Mesozoic sandstone and shale. These younger rocks have created a landscape that is the most low-lying in the islands, as its greatest elevation is only 196ft (60m). Some of the rocks contain large numbers of fossils indicating that shallow warm seas must have covered the area at some point in its past. *Trilobites, brachiopods* and *crinoids* are amongst the many species of fossil that have been found.

Higher mountains show some signs of localised glaciation in certain areas over 2,000ft (600m). When flying over these areas it is possible to see small corries containing lakes, which probably indicate glacial action. The formation of stone runs has been linked to some form of periglacial activity. The actual mechanism by which these grey rivers of stone were formed is poorly understood. They can run for several miles downhill from the jagged peaks. Some of those on the lowest slopes are steadily disappearing under the encroaching undergrowth, whereas those on higher ground stand out against the local vegetation. It is generally agreed that mud created by the breakdown of the softer rocks carried these hard quartzite boulders down the hill from their point of origin by a process called solifluction, the gradual movement of mud/soil down a slope. It is also thought that freeze-thaw action had some impact upon this process. Suffice to say that there are still several proposed theories for the formation of stone runs.

There are many small ponds and lakes on the islands. Away from the coast they tend to be shallow, peaty pools, formed by localised subsidence in the peat or by erosion hollows filling with water, some of which are connected to the sea via small streams. There are three major rivers on the Falkland Islands: the San Carlos River on East Falkland, and the Warrah and Chartres Rivers on West Falkland. Some bodies of water have been created by sand having been blown across the mouth of a river or inlet thus forming a lagoon or lake. The islands' jagged coastline favours the formation of these features. Rocky headlands protect the many sheltered harbours around the archipelago, often with long sandy beaches on the innermost part of these inlets.

The coastline varies from the low-lying shores of Lafonia and Port Salvador on East Falkland to the high cliffs and rocky bluffs that typify the outer reaches of West Falkland and West Point Island, where the cliffs can rise to 700ft (213m).

Away from the Port Stanley area it is possible to travel for many miles without seeing any houses or other man-made structures apart from fences and tracks. The rolling landscape with its relatively uniform flora creates a unique habitat.

CLIMATE

The paramount climatic feature of the Falkland Islands is wind. The islands are usually described as having an oceanic climate dominated by the prevailing westerlies. Television images of the events of April, May and June 1982, showing the military in action in snow and ice, have resulted in a public perception that the islands are snow-covered throughout the year, as though comparable with the Antarctic. In fact the islands have a rather narrow temperature range from 19°C in January to 2°C in July, with an average annual mean temperature of 6°C. Very warm days are rare during a Falkland summer, although the islands enjoy more sunshine hours than the south of Britain. The recent holes in the ozone layer mean that increased vigilance is necessary to avoid sunburn. The general lack of pollution and dust in the atmosphere also increases the penetration of ultra violet rays, so a high factor suncream is an essential part of the visitor's travel pack.

The islands lie just to the north of the main belt of depressions, which pass through the Drake Passage between the Antarctic and the tip of South America. These continually moving air masses cause frequent changes in the islands' weather. Forecasting is very difficult on the Falkland Islands as the proximity of the South American continent modifies the effect of each weather system locally. The Falklands' saying of, 'if you don't like the weather, wait 15 minutes', can often hold true. The visitor to the islands always has to be prepared for sudden changes in weather and local variations. It is possible to be in sunshine on one island and for it to be wet and windy only a few miles away.

The predominantly westerly winds have created a noticeable difference between the western and eastern side of the islands. Those islands out to the west tend to be dryer and have more sunshine hours than those to the east. Port Stanley and Port Howard are two of the wettest places on the islands, having in the region of 25 inches (630mm) of rain per year, whereas West Point Island on the western side of the islands has an annual rainfall of 17 inches (431mm). This rainfall affects the flora of the islands in that tussac grass and ferns do not grow as well in the west as they do in the wetter east. There is a fairly even level of precipitation throughout the year. In summer months the wind dries the ground, whereas the slightly calmer conditions in the winter result in water lying on the ground for longer periods of time. The average wind speed for the year is 16 knots. Calm days are rare in the summer months and are infrequent in wintertime. Fog is therefore quite uncommon in the islands.

Falkland winters are comparable with those in southern Britain in terms of average temperature, and although snowfall occurs most years, it does not often lie on the ground for any length of time. The one factor that differs from southern Britain is that the winters are longer and the summers shorter. There are records of snow in all months of the year but any such snowfall is usually brief and generally localised, often falling on the peaks over 2,000ft. Visitors to the islands must be prepared for everything and anything as far as the Falkland Islands' weather is concerned!

HISTORY
Discovery and exploration
Quite when the Falkland Islands were first discovered is rather unclear. A group of islands roughly in the area now occupied by the Falklands were drawn on maps from the early 16th century. It is possible that Amerigo Vespucci may well have seen them in 1502, or that one of the ships' companies participating in Fernando de Magellan's expedition, on board the *San Antonio,* may well have seen the islands after deserting. They are thought to have given the islands the name Sanson, from an abbreviation of the ship's name. The islands were included on maps of South America from 1507, although their number and their exact location varied greatly from map to map. The Turkish admiral Piri Reis drew one of these early maps in circa 1520. In the next few years the position of the islands indicated on many Spanish and Italian charts varied between latitude 49° south and 51° south. The name most commonly used by cartographers during the mid-1500s was the Sanson Islands, although it would appear that very few ships actually saw the islands during this period.

The first British claim to the discovery of the islands was on August 14 1592 by Captain John Davis of the *Desire*, which was part of Thomas Cavendish's second expedition. Two years later Sir Richard Hawkins thought he had found the islands and named them Hawkins Maydenlande after himself and Queen Elizabeth I of England. Yet another name for the islands came about after the sighting of the islands in 1598 by the Dutch Captain Sebald de Weert, who promptly called the islands the Sebaldines. This probably accounts for the name Sibbel de Wards, given to the islands by William Dampier who reached Falkland in 1684 with John Cook and Ambrose Cowley. Dampier gave remarkably accurate bearings for the islands. Ambrose Cowley's version was somewhat different and invented the legend of Pepys Island, named after the famous English 17th-century diarist and secretary to the Admiralty. Generations of mariners sought this archipelago in vain, handicapped by the inaccurate descriptions and bearings supplied by hopeful explorers.

Early sovereignty disputes

It has been suggested that man had reached the islands long before the arrival of the first Europeans. The discovery of the presence of large fox-like animals, now known as the *warrah*, by John Strong in West Falkland in1690 raises some unanswered questions. These creatures, now extinct, were closely related to the Fuegian fox of South America. It is possible that the Yaghan Indians might have brought a domesticated fox to the islands for hunting purposes. The presence of the *warrah* on Falkland remains a mystery but could well be a clue as to who first discovered the islands.

Captain John Strong of the sloop *Welfare* made the first landing on the Falkland Islands in 1690. He landed at Port Howard on West Falkland in an archipelago known as Hawkins Maiden Land. His claim to fame was naming Falkland Sound, the strait between East and West Falkland, in honour of Viscount Falkland, the Treasurer of the English Navy. This landing is regarded as crucial by the Falkland Island Government in the long-running dispute over sovereignty. Other ships reached the islands at the end of the 17th and the beginning of the 18th century. William Dampier circumnavigated the islands in 1696, and in 1701 Captain Beauchene discovered the island which now bears his name. The name Falkland being applied to the whole archipelago was first noted in Captain Woods Rogers' account of his exploration of the islands during 1708. Other expeditions that reached the Falklands included one by Lord Anson in 1740, when he suggested using the islands as a base for further exploration of the Pacific Ocean. He then drew up a plan to explore Falkland and its surrounding seas in the hope of locating Pepys Island. It appears that the Spanish rejected this plan when it was put before them, as it could have caused instability in the region. The Spanish claim to the area came as a result of the decision by the Spanish Pope Alexander VI in 1494 to draw a line north to south down the Atlantic, one hundred leagues west of the Azores. He was responding to the question of ownership of the recently discovered New World. He decided that everything to the west of this imaginary line, which included the Falklands, would belong to Spain; everything to the East would be Portuguese. Britain disagreed with this edict, which was arguably the motive for the subsequent voyages of the English explorers Drake, Raleigh and Cavendish.

Another major event in the islands' history was the arrival of the French navigator Louis-Antoine de Bougainville in East Falkland on April 5 1764. He had left his base at St Malo in northern France in 1763 with the aim of establishing a colony at Port Louis. His name for the islands, 'Isles Malouines, derived from the name St Malo, as does the Argentinian name 'Islas Malvinas'.

A further English expedition, under the command of Commodore John Byron, set off to search for the mythical Pepys Island and to explore the Falkland Islands, reaching the archipelago in mid-January 1765. They made their base at Port Egmont on Saunders Island in the northwest of the islands before starting to survey the coastline, leaving Captain John McBride to create a proper settlement there on January 8 1766. In the interim Spain offered to purchase the settlement from the French in an attempt to avoid giving the British the wrong impression regarding sovereignty. Bougainville, having returned to Europe to negotiate terms with the Spanish Court, agreed to transfer ownership to the Spanish in return for £25,000. Meanwhile, on December 4 1766, the British ascertained the French presence at Port Louis and informed the French that they had had a colony at Port Egmont since 1765. The transfer of the settlement at Port Louis from Bougainville to a Spanish Governor, Don Felipe Ruiz Puente took place on April 1 1767. Two years later English and Spanish ships met whilst undertaking surveying work. Each regarded the other as being there unlawfully; letters to this effect were exchanged between the two vessels.

In 1770 a Spanish force, commanded by Don Juan Ignacio de Madariaga, arrived at Port Egmont and occasioned another exchange of letters. The officer in charge of the garrison on Saunders Island, Captain Hunt, stated categorically that the Falkland Islands belonged to Britain. The British forces were removed from Port Egmont when the Spanish returned with a much larger force on July 14 1770. It took the threat of war – after lengthy negotiations – to get an agreement on January 22 1771, whereby the Spanish gave Port Egmont back to the British. The surrender took place at Port Egmont on September 15 1771 with Captain Scott, the commander of the frigate *Juno*, representing the British. The British withdrew from the islands for economic reasons in 1774, leaving behind a flag and a plaque representing their claim to ownership. Argentina claimed subsequently that the British withdrawal was the consequence of a secret deal within the treaty of 1771. The Spanish evacuation of the islands took place in two stages as Spain progressively lost control of its colonies. Spanish troops remained at Port Louis, known then as Port Soledad, until 1806 when the governor Juan Crisostomo Martinez departed, leaving behind a plaque claiming sovereignty for Spain. The United Provinces of the Rio de la Plata, which later became Argentina, withdrew the remaining Spanish settlers in 1811.

In the early part of the 19th century ships of many nationalities called in at the Falkland Islands. Some, mainly whalers and sealers, used the islands as their base. Argentina, having gained its independence from Spain in 1816, claimed sovereignty over the Falkland Islands in 1820 and dispatched David Jewett, commander of the *Heroina*, to assert their ownership. The first Argentinian appointee as governor was Don Pablo Aregusti in 1823. He soon granted a concession of land on East Falkland to Louis Vernet and Don Jorge Pacheco. Their first attempt at colonisation lasted less than a year but Vernet was determined to be more successful with his second expedition in 1826. By 1828 he had been given permission to form a colony and had been granted all of East Falkland together with comprehensive fishing and sealing rights. A garrison and settlers for unskilled labour were well established at Port Louis by the time Vernet became governor in 1829. His appointment caused Britain to protest to Argentina over what was viewed as an Argentinan position of authority on British Crown land. Vernet ordered the arrest of three American schooners for supposed illegal sealing in 1829.

The discovery of these ships' arrest only reached the United States when one of the boats, the *Breakwater*, escaped and carried the news back home. Another of the ships, the *Superior*, was released but the captain of the third ship, the *Harriet*, was taken for trial in Buenos Aires. The US consul in Buenos Aires arranged for the dispatch of the corvette *USS Lexington* under Commander Silas Duncan, which arrived on December 28 1831, destroying the settlement at Port Soledad and declaring the islands to be free of any government. The man left in charge by Vernet, Matthew Brisbane, was arrested and taken to Montevideo. Mutineers murdered the new governor, Don Juan Esteban Mestivier, sent to the islands by Argentina in 1832, shortly after he took up his appointment. The officer in charge of the Argentinian warship *Sarandi*, Don Jose Maria Pinedo, was then in command of the settlement until the arrival of the British in 1832. On December 20 the British reached Port Egmont and posted a notice of possession, then moved on to Port Soledad to take control of the islands on January 2 1833. The British commander, Captain Onslow, gave Pinedo written notice that he was exercising British sovereign rights and would be raising the British flag next day and that Pinedo was expected to lower the Argentinian flag and leave immediately. Pinedo refused to comply with these demands. Nonetheless the Argentinian flag was removed next day and presented to him by the British before he left the islands with all his troops. By the time Matthew Brisbane returned to the islands in April 1833, the settlement had been left in the hands of William Dickson who had been Vernet's bookkeeper. Brisbane and Dickson were murdered during a mutiny by a group of *gauchos* (gauchos were the South American cowboys brought to the islands to manage the cattle imported to the islands from South America) in August 1833. The surviving settlers managed to escape from the settlement and live on some of the small islands offshore until their rescue by the sealer *Hopeful* in October 1833, under the command of Lieutenant Rea, and by *HMS Challenger* in January 1834. The *gauchos* were arrested and taken for trial in England but were released and returned to

Montevideo. Lieutenant Henry Smith, the first officer of *Challenger*, and a ship's crew were left in charge of Port Louis.

British colonisation

The decision of The Colonial Land and Emigration Commissioners that the Falkland Islands were suitable for colonisation in 1840 heralded the arrival of the first settlers from Britain. The first British Governor, Richard Moody, initially used Port Louis as his base. In 1842 he was instructed by Lord Stanley, the British Secretary of State, to investigate the potential of the Port William area as a location for a new town on the islands. The survey work was done from the *Erebus* and the *Terror*, two ships taking part in the Ross Antarctic Expedition. Captain Ross advised that Port William would make a good deep-water anchorage for naval vessels and that the shores of Port Jackson would be ideally suited for the new settlement. It had everything they needed: shelter, fresh water, a natural harbour and a plentiful supply of peat. The work of creating the new town was completed in just under a year on July 18 1845. The capital of the islands was named Port Stanley in honour of the current Secretary of State. Not everyone was in favour of this site; one well-known inhabitant, J W Whitington, is quoted as saying, 'of all the miserable bog holes, I believe that Mr Moody has selected one of the worst for the site for his town'. Despite this opposition the population increased rapidly to the extent that some two hundred residents were present in 1849.

The Falkland Islands, and Port Stanley in particular, saw a dramatic increase in the numbers of ships calling into the islands from the mid-1850s at the time of the Californian gold rush. These ships had been trying to round Cape Horn but were forced to retreat to the islands for repair after being battered by the severe weather around the Cape. The original settlers were soon making a good living as shipwrights or in supplying provisions for these stricken vessels. Many of these boats were condemned on the islands and ended their days as floating warehouses in Stanley Harbour, which became one of the busiest ports in the world during the latter half of the 19th century. This boom lasted until the increasingly reliable steamships began to take over in the late 1890s, the final blow being the completion of the Panama Canal in the early 1900s, which drastically reduced the number of boats needing to call into the islands for repair. The population of the Falkland Islands numbered 1,800 by 1885.

Economic exploitation

Changes were also occurring on the land at this time, although not at such a great rate as in Port Stanley. The first attempt at sheep farming was made on East Falkland in about 1840. The only other stock were large numbers of cattle roaming wild. A merchant from Montevideo, Samuel Lafone, signed a contract with the Falkland Island Government in 1846 to take charge of all the wild cattle in East Falkland. He also bought up all the land south of Darwin that is now called Lafonia, a derivation of his name. The Falkland Island

Company, which had been set up by Royal Charter in 1851, bought out Lafone and set up a trading company, which was soon to become the largest owner of livestock on the islands. West Falkland was opened to settlers in 1867 and, only one year later, all available land was taken up for sheep farming. The larger, outer islands were the next to be taken over by the sheep farmers. The Falkland Island Company continued to expand so that by 1880 the company had 100,000 sheep and several thousand cattle on East Falkland alone. The Company continues to exist although it sold the majority of its land to the Falkland Island Government in 1991. The latter set up Falkland Landholdings Limited to run its farms.

In the latter years of the 19th and the early 20th centuries attempts were made to export frozen sheep carcasses. Prior to this time sheep had been exported live and surplus stock was converted into fat for the soap, candle and lubricant industries. At first the frozen mutton was deemed to be of insufficient standard for the European market, but in 1910 two meat canneries were set up on East Falkland. The good British market stimulated trade during World War I and finance was offered to set up a freezer in the islands at Ajax Bay on East Falkland. This building operated for just two seasons before closing down. Wool still remains the main farm export from the islands. High wool prices led to a demand for Falkland Islands' fleeces, which were brought in from the outlying farms before being shipped to the northern hemisphere.

Whale oil is recorded as having been shipped back from the islands from as early as the late 1700s. Whalers sailing from North America were based in the West Falklands when this area became the principal region to hunt southern right whale and sperm whale. It is thought that oil was taken from elephant seals, fur seals and southern sea lions when there was an insufficiency of whales. It is not thought that many whales were caught in these waters at that time, but the islands provided the ideal base to obtain provisions. Penguin and albatross eggs and the abundance of geese, along with a plentiful supply of fresh water, were all within easy reach of sheltered harbours. Livestock was kept on some islands, thus creating a valuable food source that could be drawn upon between expeditions. There was massive hunting of fur seals for their skins by 1784 when one vessel was reported to be carrying 13,000 pelts. This trade tailed off later in the century, probably as a result of excessive hunting, although it was not completely banned until 1921. Elephant seals were culled for their oil from the late 1700s until the early 1800s, but had become virtually extinct on the islands by the late 19th century, only starting to breed again in the early 1900s. By the late 1850s the elephant seal and the fur seal populations had been almost eliminated and attention was switched to the much more common southern sea lions. These animals were skinned and rendered for their oil until the population became so diminished that the operation became uneconomical. There were three further attempts at commercial sealing on the islands during the 20th century but all failed due to the scarcity of seals.

The dearth of seals gave rise to the penguin oil industry in the early 1860s. Rockhopper penguins and occasionally gentoo penguins were the species taken.

This activity reached a peak in 1864, when no fewer than seven vessels were registered locally to catch penguins. The actual number of birds taken is not recorded but between 1864 and 1866 some 63,000 gallons of penguin oil was shipped out of Port Stanley. At the time it was reckoned that eight rockhopper penguins yielded one gallon of oil. Gentoo penguins being slightly larger would have yielded a little more. It has been estimated that more than half a million birds were killed in that period. The industry began to decline, although there was a slight recovery in the later 1870s, until its final demise in circa 1880.

Fifty years later the southern oceans witnessed the swift expansion of the whaling industry. New Island, to the south of the archipelago, became the centre of operations during its brief life span on the islands. The whaling boats operating out of New Island doubled up as mail and passenger boats in the initial phases of the industry before being replaced by a purpose bought ship. The greater profits being realised further south in the Antarctic saw the closing and removal of the whaling station to South Georgia only just over ten years after it opened.

The activities of these whalers and the export of wool from Port Stanley brought about an escalation in shipping activity around the islands, as imports and exports increased.

British military presence

Throughout the history of the islands there has been a strong connection between the British military and the Falklands. The first British governor of the islands, Richard Moody, was a Royal Engineer and his expeditionary force was composed of men from the Royal Sappers and Miners Regiment. The British government proposed that a local force be set up using civilians; Governor Moody thus created an Infantry Group and a Mounted Corps together with an artillery section. Once the Sappers and Miners had completed their tour of duty on the islands in 1849, a new force was needed to protect the islands. A group of 30 married Chelsea Pensioners were sent out to become settlers and to act as the local police force the next year. Some of the houses they brought with them are still standing in Port Stanley. A Military Guard and Volunteers were set up in 1855 only to be disbanded two years later and replaced with civilian constables. In 1858 a group of 35 Marines, to be called the Falkland Islands Garrison Company, arrived to take over from the pensioners. These in turn were replaced in 1863 by a new detachment of Marines. The governor of the day in 1892, Governor Callaghan, proposed that the military force was no longer needed. The local Falkland Island Volunteer Force was re-established in 1892 followed by a mounted infantry corps in 1900. These volunteers saw active service during the Battle of the Falklands in World War I before being reconstituted as the Falkland Islands Defence Force in 1919, which exists to this day.

World Wars I and II

The strategic value of the islands in the South Atlantic became apparent during World War I. Shortly after the declaration of war in the autumn of 1914 the

British Rear Admiral, Sir Christopher Cradock, visited Port Stanley with his squadron of ships, after having chased three German cruisers, *Leipzig, Dresden* and *Nürnberg*, near the Magellan Straits. On November 1 1914 the German cruisers were sighted off the Chilean coast along with the *Gneisenau, Enden* and *Scharnhorst*. The two squadrons then engaged in battle. Cradock's flagship *HMS Good Hope* and *HMS Monmouth* were sunk with all hands and the rest of the fleet driven off. Prior to this event Vice Admiral Frederick Sturdee had set sail from England on *HMS Invincible* with a fleet of cruisers and instructions to defeat the German squadron under Vice Admiral Graf Von Spee. Sturdee's fleet reached Falkland waters on November 12 1914. On December 8 1914 two of Von Spee's ships, the *Gneisenau* and the *Nürnberg*, were sighted near Port Stanley where Sturdee's ships lay at anchor. Some of the British Fleet opened fire but the range was too great. The two German ships rejoined the rest of their squadron and headed east away from the islands. The British fleet set sail and caught up with the rearguard of the Germans by early afternoon. A ferocious fight ensued, the outcome of which was that almost all of the German squadron, apart from the *Dresden*, was sunk with the loss of 2,000 lives. This victory gave Britain control of the ocean routes around Cape Horn and December 8 lives on as a public holiday in the islands.

Argentina, in common with so many other countries, experienced the growth of nationalist movements between the two world wars. The nationalists envisaged the Falkland Islands as belonging to Argentina. Nationalist pride was superseded by events and this issue was of little significance until after 1945.

The most famous incident during World War II near the islands was the Battle of the River Plate. At the start of the war *HMS Ajax* and *HMS Exeter* were patrolling Falkland waters. With *HMS Achilles*, under the command of Rear Admiral Harwood, they made for the River Plate estuary in December 1939. The British ships were outgunned by the German pocket battleship *Graf Spee* during the Battle of the River Plate, but still managed to trap it in the neutral port of Montevideo where it was later scuttled. The British fleet, including the badly damaged *HMS Exeter*, returned to Port Stanley. The South Atlantic routes remained in British control. Throughout World War II, the Falkland Islands Defence Force manned shore batteries and observation posts around the islands. A battalion of the 11th West Yorkshire Regiment supplemented these men in 1942 and were succeeded by a detachment of Royal Scots, who were the garrison force until the end of the war. The Royal Navy presence in the islands was maintained by *HMS Poursuivant*, which acted as the Naval Office in Port Stanley.

Further sovereignty disputes

Discussions about the islands' sovereignty continued through the 1960s. The islands were discussed by a United Nations committee on de-colonisation in 1964. The Argentinian claim was based on the papal bulls of the 15th century, whilst the British position rested on having the first recorded landing on the Falkland Islands in 1690 and the 'open, continuous effective possession, occupation and administration' of the islands since 1833. Britain was resolved that it would grant the Falkland Islanders self-determination as recognised in the United Nations Charter. Britain claimed that Argentinian control would create a colony rather than remove one. A year later the United Nations general assembly agreed a resolution inviting Britain and Argentina to hold discussions aimed at a peaceful solution to the dispute. These talks continued until just a few months before the Argentinian invasion. This high level of international diplomatic activity led to a series of incidents on the islands. The first of these, on September 8 1964, saw a light aircraft circle Port Stanley before landing on the racecourse. The pilot jumped out of his plane, planted an Argentinian flag, handed a letter stating Argentinian sovereignty over the islands to one of the islanders before hopping back in his plane and flying off again.

More dramatic was the hijacking of a DC4 on an internal flight in Argentina by twenty nationalists calling themselves the Condors. The plane flew up Stanley Harbour before landing on the racecourse, missing the grandstand but hitting some telegraph poles and then sinking into the mud. The nationalists took four hostages before being surrounded by the local defence force accompanied by the only six marines on the islands. They vowed never to surrender but 32 hours later, after a cold night, they gave themselves up to the local priest and were moved to the local church. The heavy swell off Mengeary Point prevented their embarkation onto an Argentinian naval ship in the first instance, but they were eventually taken back to Argentina where nominal prison sentences awaited them. It later turned out that this had been the first of three planes planning to land on the islands. The other planes, with reinforcements and press, were grounded when the president of Argentina was informed of the scheme and temporarily banned all civilian flights.

Later that year one other landing took place, which was to remain a secret for many years. A small detachment of Argentinian marines landed via submarine near Port Stanley for a few hours over a period of nights. Their remit was to explore potential landing beaches near the capital. The second officer on board, Juan Jose Lombardo, rose through the ranks to become Chief of Naval Operations and as such was the man responsible for planning the 1982 invasion by Argentina. The Argentinian press sponsored a plane to reach the islands in November 1968, but the scheme ended in a crash-landing on the road to Eliza Cove, south of Port Stanley. The three Argentinians on board wanted to attract publicity for their cause during the visit to the islands of Lord Chalfont, the Minister of State at the Foreign and Commonwealth Office. As the plane flew over he was talking at a public meeting, called to allay islanders' fears after news had leaked that Britain was negotiating sovereignty with Argentina.

Matters were a little quieter until 1976, when a British research ship, the *Shackleton,* was fired upon by an Argentinian gunboat near Port Stanley, and an illegal military base was set up on Southern Thule, a dependency of the Falkland Islands situated to the south of South Georgia. Despite these incidents, trade with Argentina continued to expand. The only way to reach the islands by air was via South America, departing from Comodoro Rivadava in Argentina. It was possible to reach the islands by cargo ship from Britain but this took several weeks of sailing through what could be very rough seas.

The Falklands War 1982

As far as the general public was aware, the first incident of the 1982 war was the landing on South Georgia of an Argentine scrap metal merchant accompanied by some military personnel on March 18. It was revealed later that concerns about a possible invasion had been raised in the weeks prior to this event. Britain called for the removal of the military men with little response from Argentina. On March 26 the head of the military junta in Argentina, General Galtieri, decided to invade the islands. The first land forces reached the islands on April 2 and took control of Port Stanley after a short battle with the Royal Marines garrisoned on the islands. These soldiers and the governor were taken off the islands and flown to Montevideo. Over the next few days, Argentinian troops consolidated their positions on the islands, also landing on South Georgia and the South Sandwich Islands. The United Nations passed Resolution 502 calling for the cessation of all hostilities, the withdrawal of Argentinian troops from the islands and the resumption of talks between Argentina and Britain. In London, the House of Commons was convened at an emergency session on April 3 and informed that a task force would be sent to liberate the islands. The first British Navy ships left the following week for the South Atlantic, and Britain declared a 200 mile exclusion zone around the Falklands. The American Secretary of State, Alexander Haig, began shuttle mediation between the two countries and Argentina landed over 10,000 troops on the islands. In Europe, the European Economic Community supported Britain by approving trade sanctions against Argentina on April 10. The main task force, under the command of Rear Admiral Sandy Woodward, departed from Ascension Island. Wideawake Airfield on Ascension was the busiest airport in the world on April 16. Alexander Haig's efforts in mediation eventually failed on April 17, and five days later the British government advised all British nationals to leave Argentina. In late April many more ships headed towards the South Atlantic carrying troops and the first action took place involving British forces. After several exploratory landings, the Royal Marines and the SAS retook South Georgia on April 25. At the end of April, President Ronald Reagan of the United States declared his country's support for the British and enforced trade sanctions against Argentina.

Hostilities increased on May 1 when men of the SAS and SBS landed reconnaissance forces on the Falkland Islands for the first time and Port Stanley airfield was bombed by a Vulcan bomber based on Ascension Island. This was followed by a naval bombardment and Sea Harrier attack on Argentinian installations at Stanley and Goose Green. The first aerial combats took place that day when two Argentinian planes were shot down and two others damaged without any British losses. These events were to be overshadowed a few days later when the Argentinian warship, *General Belgrano*, was sunk by torpedoes fired from the submarine *HMS Conqueror* on May 2 and an Exocet missile hit the British Warship *HMS Sheffield* on May 4. Naval bombardment and air battles began to occur more regularly as the British forces neared the islands. 'Active Service', full-time service in the forces, was declared on May 14. That night Pebble Island was raided by the SAS, which successfully destroyed 11 Argentinian aircraft on the ground. Political activity continued until May 19 when the United Nations peace initiative foundered, and on the same day the British Cabinet gave approval for the task force to land.

The night of May 21–22 witnessed the landing of the British task force, under the command of Major General Jeremy Moore, on the western side of East Falkland at San Carlos Water. Several of the British warships were damaged or, in the case of the *Ardent*, sunk, but the land forces were able to get ashore relatively unscathed. Over the next two days attacks continued on the warships in Falkland Sound and San Carlos Water whilst the bridgehead was consolidated. Five thousand men were entrenched on East Falkland by dawn on May 24. The second parachute regiment began their advance on Goose Green on May 26 eventually attacking that settlement and Darwin on May 28. Despite being outnumbered two to one, the soldiers of the Parachute Regiment were victorious at a critical stage of the war. It was during this fighting that Lieutenant Colonel 'H' Jones was killed. Colonel 'H' Jones was the commanding officer of the second parachute regiment which was in the forefront of the battle of Goose Green. His forces were pinned down at the bottom of a slight valley by gunfire from the Argentinian dug-in at the crest of the next hill. Under covering fire, with very little in the way of shelter, he attacked the Argentinian forces. His extreme bravery and that of his men saw the overrunning of the Argentinian forces occupying Goose Green. He was posthumously awarded the Victoria Cross in recognition of his bravery. During this period the British task force was being regularly attacked at sea, losses including *HMS Coventry* and *MV Atlantic Conveyor*. The last few days in May saw the British troops advancing over East Falkland towards Port Stanley. Special forces had taken over Mount Kent so that by May 31 Port Stanley was surrounded.

In early June the British government vetoed the Panamanian-Spanish cease-fire resolution at the United Nations Security Council and gave Argentina one last chance to withdraw from the Falklands. Some of the most dramatic images of the war came from the British landings at Bluff Cove. The attacks made by the Argentinian aircraft on the *Sir Galahad* and the *Sir Tristram* created scenes resembling Dante's inferno. Fifty men were killed on June 8. The battles were fought closer to Port Stanley on June 11, when fighting commenced on Mount Longdon, Mount Harriet, and the Two Sisters. *HMS Glamorgan* was hit by an Exocet missile while withdrawing to sea, after having supported these attacks with her heavy guns. The fighting reached Wireless Ridge and Mount Tumbledown on June 13. The capitulation of the forces of General Menendez, the Argentinian commander, meant that these were the last battles of the war. British forces were welcomed with open arms in Port Stanley later that day. Over the next few days some 10,254 Argentinian prisoners were brought into Stanley. The British forces established a headquarters at Government House and began the consolidation of the Port

Stanley area. General Galtieri was removed as head of the military junta in Argentina on June 17, to be replaced by General Bignone on June 21, who announced that the cease-fire would be observed by all Argentinian forces. Britain formally declared an end to hostilities as soon as the South Sandwich Islands had been re-occupied on June 20 1982.

Post-war to present day

The aftermath of the war saw many changes on the islands, the greatest of which was the construction of Mount Pleasant Airport (MPA), later to become the main base for the British forces on the Falkland Islands. Port Stanley was very busy during the post-war years and the population quadrupled immediately after the cease-fire as most of the British troops came into town. The accommodation problem was initially eased by billeting troops on ships anchored in the harbour. Thereafter, three floating 'coastels' were imported to house all the forces involved in building the air base at Mount Pleasant and generally stationed on the islands. These coastels were anchored to the east of Port Stanley and remained in use until MPA came into service in May 1985, only 14 months after construction had begun. Previously aircraft had had to use the temporarily extended runway at Stanley Airport, from which it was possible to fly to Ascension Island on Hercules transport planes and then on to the UK. The need for a deep water dock in Port Stanley was solved by the building of the Floating Interim Port and Storage System (FIPASS) in 1983–84, which still serves as the main quay for Port Stanley. The Royal Navy constructed its own dock at Mare Harbour in the vicinity of the main military base at Mount Pleasant.

The garrison on the islands numbers 2,000 servicemen. This population explosion has created several changes within the local infrastructure, the most obvious of which being the road linking MPA with Port Stanley and the King Edward VII Memorial Hospital in Stanley – a joint civilian and military venture.

Wool production was the economic mainstay of the islands from the middle of the 1800s until the last years of the 20th century when man-made fibres made it difficult to get a good price for Falklands' wool. In 1987 the introduction of the Falkland Islands Interim Conservation and Management Zone (FICZ) on February 1, to protect stocks against overfishing, was to have a major effect on the islands' economy. Vessels that wish to fish inside this zone, which extends for 200 nautical miles around the islands, have to obtain licences from Port Stanley. Squid accounts for 75% of the catch. The revenue from these licences raises many millions of pounds each year, which has been used to support the islands' health, education and welfare systems as well as improving transport links around the islands.

Travel on the islands was revolutionised in 1948 when the first planes were introduced for travel around the islands. The de Havilland Beaver Seaplanes ran until they were gradually phased out by the Brittain-Norman Islander aircraft that are used today by the Falkland Island Government Air Service (FIGAS) for passengers, mail or freight. The name Beaver Pond can still be found on many islands and refers to planes not animals.

At the end of the 20th century the islands have become self-supporting except in matters of defence. Roads have been built between most of the major settlements, dramatically cutting travel times between farms. A telecommunication network was installed in 1989, linking all the islands, and there are now international satellite communications. Port Stanley has grown considerably since the war and a new school has been completed using the monies created by the fishing licences scheme.

Mineral exploration has had a great impact on the islands. Early seismic surveys by the British Geological Survey indicated the location of substantial reserves near the islands, although none have been found as yet. Investigation of the potential for extracting gold and diamonds from the islands could herald other exciting prospects for the islands' economy.

The last 20 years have seen significant changes in the islands' way of life. The future is rosier for those growing up on the islands today.

POLITICS

The Falkland Islands are a dependant territory of the United Kingdom, the executive authority being vested in Her Majesty the Queen, who is represented by the Governor. The present Falkland Island constitution came into force in 1985, under the terms of which eight councillors are elected from Stanley and four from the 'camp' every four years. (The word 'camp' comes from the Spanish word '*compo*' meaning the countryside.) There are no political parties; all councillors are elected as independents. The Legislative Council, made up of ten members, is chaired by the Governor and sits when called, usually about four times a year. The Chief Executive and the Financial Secretary also attend meetings. This Council holds its meeting in public and is responsible for passing laws for the Government of the islands subject to approval of Her Majesty the Queen through the Secretary of State for Foreign Affairs. Three of the legislative councillors are annually elected by their peers to serve on the Executive Council presided over by the Governor. This Executive Council, which advises the Governor, also includes the two ex-officio members, the Chief Executive and the Financial Secretary. These meetings are held monthly and may also be attended by the Commander of the British forces in the Falkland Islands and the Attorney General, who also attend the meeting of the Legislative Council. The defence of the Falkland Islands and foreign affairs relating to the islands are the responsibility of the British Government.

The flag of the Falkland Islands is blue with the Union Jack in the top left-hand corner and a white shield containing the coat of arms in the centre of the distal half of the flag. The coat of arms contains a white ram above the sailing ship *Desire* with the scroll at the bottom bearing the motto 'Desire The Right'; sheep and wool production being the mainstay of the islands' economy for many years, the *Desire* being the ship of John Davis, who sighted the islands in 1592.

ECONOMY

The economy of the islands has changed more in the last 20 years than at any time in their history. For the last 150 years the export of wool has been the main base for the economy until the introduction of the fishery zone in 1987. At various periods during the 18th, 19th and 20th centuries, seals, whales and penguins have been exploited until their numbers dropped below an economically viable level.

Agriculture

Farming on the Falkland Islands is a monoculture of which the product is wool, which is generally exported to the United Kingdom. Farms on the islands were large; using ranch-style methods they carried approximately 700,000 sheep. Lord Shackleton's report on the islands' economy recommended subdividing the 36 large farms. Accordingly there are now 90 owner-managed farms with an average farm size of 33,216 acres, although sizes do of course vary considerably. The Falkland Island Government, by means of grants and loans made available to individual farmers, has aided this subdivision. Falkland Landholdings Limited was created in 1991 with the purchase of the four remaining farms owned by the Falkland Islands Company. These farms make up about 25% of the farmland on the islands. Further developments included the purchase of a national stud flock of sheep from Australia, with the aim of improving the quality of the islands' wool. The worldwide slump in wool prices has resulted in poor prices being achieved in the wool market.

The Department of Agriculture is involved in projects whose aim is to improve the quality of grasslands and livestock. The United Kingdom Falkland Island Trust is a British registered charity, which is working with the Department of Agriculture in various programmes of research in order to promote the sustainable growth of the islands' agricultural industry. At present four projects are in progress: tree planting, using kelp as a fertiliser, marketing and an educational programme in local schools. The planting of trees on a large scale is not considered a feasible proposition on the islands but a need to shelter livestock, crops and gardens has been identified. Kelp has long been used as a fertiliser in other parts of the world, so it is a logical step to consider the effects of kelp on grasslands and tussac grass, as there are huge reserves of it growing around the islands. The Trust's consultants have assisted in the marketing of various agricultural projects and the Trust has contributed to various, educational, civic and cultural projects on the islands in recent years.

A large percentage of the goods for sale on the islands have been imported from Britain or Chile. The islands are self-sufficient in dairy products and many of the vegetables are grown locally. The hydroponics plant on the outskirts of Port Stanley supplies the town and some of the visiting cruise ships with fresh vegetables.

Fishing

In the years following the 1982 war the islands' infrastructure has undergone considerable expansion, especially after the introduction of the Falkland Islands Interim Conservation and Management Zone (FICZ) to protect fish stocks around the islands. This extends 200 nautical miles from the islands.

Any vessel wishing to fish inside this zone now requires a licence from the Falkland Islands Government. Some 75% of the catch is squid. The annual revenue far exceeds any other income to the islands. This money has been used to support the islands' welfare and educational projects, and has also helped to pay for the recent road-building scheme, which has resulted in most of the major settlements on the islands being linked by a hard-surface road.

Philately

Philately has been a successful source of income over the years, and first day covers were especially popular after the war in 1982. Although stamps have been issued on the islands since 1878, it was another 100 years before sufficient demand justified the establishment of the Falkland Islands Philatelic Bureau. Prior to 1978 the Post Office staff dealt with the running of the philatelic department as part of the day-to-day running of the Post Office. The Bureau is also responsible for the production and sale of stamps for the Government of South Georgia and South Sandwich Islands and is the sales agent for the British Antarctic Territory. The only period that stamps were not issued was during the occupation by Argentinian troops in 1982. Stamps from the Falklands and the aforementioned regions are very popular amongst collectors, so the revenue from the sales of stamps remains a vital part of the islands' economy.

Tourism

Tourists to the islands were few and far between before the events of 1982. Since the construction of the airport at MPA and the regular flights from Britain and Chile, there has been a steady increase in the number of tourists making use of the growing variety of accommodation on the islands. The greatest increase in tourist numbers has been in the cruise ship market, with over twenty thousand visitors reaching the Falkland Islands this way in the summer of 1999/2000. So many visitors landing on the islands imply obvious benefits for the economy, although Falkland Conservation has expressed concern over the negative effect of such a huge influx of visitors on wildlife and the environment.

PEOPLE

The majority of the people who live on the Falkland Islands are of British descent, originating from the sheep farmers and other settlers who came to the islands of their own volition, and from seafarers who arrived and simply never left. The islanders are very friendly and approachable. Until the arrival of modern technology bringing video and television to the islands, radio and telephone were the only means of communication. The result of this was that each settlement was isolated and developed its own community life. Of the total population of over 2,200, some 1,600 live in Port Stanley – the remainder live in *camp*. This figure does not include the military personnel and contractors at MPA, which would add about another 2,000 to the number of residents. The percentage of 'Kelpers', as the Falkland Islanders are called, living in Port Stanley has increased in the last decade as the economic base moves from wool production to servicing the fishing industry.

Living in the *camp* was never easy; the islanders had to be very self-sufficient and able to turn their hand to almost anything. The only fuel for many years was peat, which had to be dug in the summer to dry out on the peat stack before it could be used. Each settlement had its own store and, if large enough, a small school. Living off the land in tune with the seasons was an important part of *camp* life. November was the time of year when 'egging' took place, the gathering of penguin and albatross eggs to supplement the locals' diet. Later in the summer edible berries were collected for making into preserves and pastries. The men were expected to look after the sheep and their dogs, to dig peat and to undertake all the maintenance, whilst the women did the cooking and managed the house and family.

In recent years there has been a steady influx of workers from St Helena to join the British, and a small number of Chileans reside on the island. There is no native language on the islands but there is an identifiable accent that has its origins in the West Country of England. Some words are pronounced differently to their English counterparts. Parts of horses' tack are still called by the names they were given by the gauchos from South America who lived on the islands in the 18th century. This also applies to some of the place names on the islands and to fixtures such as cattle grids, which are sometimes known as *pasa libre*.

RELIGION

The population of the Falkland Islands is predominantly Christian, with several denominations being represented (see *Places of worship*, page 64).

CULTURE

There are a variety of clubs and societies on the islands including a wide range of sports activities, as well as drama and other arts. The majority of islanders keep in contact with what is happening on the islands by reading the weekly newspaper, the *Penguin News*, and listening to the local radio. The increasing number of homes with television has meant a change in lifestyle for many. The Falkland Islands are a very social place, and stopping for a chat is a way of life. The self-sufficient existence has meant that some have turned their craftsmanship into arts and crafts which can be seen displayed around the shops in Stanley.

Previous page Macaroni penguin, Pebble Island (ww)

Above left King penguin, Volunteer Point (ww)

Above right Gentoo and chick (HB)

Below left Albino Magellanic penguin (HB)

Bottom right Rockhopper penguin (ww)

Natural History

The Falkland Islands have been described as one of the last wildernesses in the world. Whether it is the spectacular scenery, the war-scarred history, the throngs of penguins or the impressive elephant seals, there is much for the visitor to do and see.

FLORA
Habitats
The main influence on the environment is the almost barren soil covering the main islands, which is acidic and peaty, and is generally described as cold. This peat can be hard and dry when it is thinly spread over the underlying rock, or thicker and water-retentive in low-lying areas. These two types of habitat are described as hard and soft *camp*. The word *camp* is derived from the Spanish word *campo* meaning countryside. The habitat of the islands can be classified into five major types, with several plant species occurring in more than one formation. Feldmark is most often found at higher elevations where the soil is thin and the vegetation is often eroded to expose areas of clay and thin shaly soil. The typical plants of this habitat are the cushion plants such as balsam bog, *azorella* and both species of *blechnum* fern. This low-growing vegetation is often more coloured than the uniform hues of the lower slopes; the combination of the light and dark greens with the orange and browns of the ferns gives the higher elevations a distinctive appearance. Areas above 2,000ft (600m) show the best examples of feldmark formation, such as those found in the Wickham Heights and on many of the higher peaks in West Falkland. It is also found on some of the higher cliffs and rock stacks in the southwest and northwest of the islands.

Oceanic heath formation covers most of the Falkland Islands below the feldmark zone. There are two distinct types within this formation. Diddle-dee, a stumpy heather-like shrub, dominates the higher, well drained slopes forming a dwarf shrub heath, where the peat is firmer over the rocky ridges or more fertile soil. Other species that grow in association with the diddle-dee include the Christmas bush, mountain berry, balsam bog and almond flower, along with several others. White grass forms the grass heaths that cover almost half of the islands and is the commonest plant on the Falkland Islands. In well-drained areas the white grass forms clumps of vegetation, whilst on wetter ground it forms a flat, lush surface that can be very difficult to traverse in a vehicle. Pigvine and *pratia* are two of the more easily located species growing in the white grass. A variety of other grasses, rushes and sedges are found in the damper habitats. The stone runs interrupt this oceanic heath formation, particularly in East Falkland, thus creating another type of habitat. Plants found in this unique environment include the endemic snake plant, vanilla daisy and the native strawberry.

Where the water table is on or very near the surface, the bog formation predominates. Large regions of East and West Falkland come into this vegetation category. This soft *camp* is home to many of the plant species found on the islands. White grass is still a common plant but there are many wet marshy areas comprising of short rushes and dense carpets of *astelia*. The peat below the vegetative horizon is deep and saturated with water. Sundew is one of the more unusual plants in this habitat, along with several species of short rushes. Close to the many small streams that are typical of this habitat it is also possible to find buttercups, blinks and pimpernel. It is very easy when walking across this soft *camp* to get a boot full of water; it is best to avoid the streams and other such obviously saturated areas.

There are numerous small ponds on the islands that along with the larger lakes and streams support the fresh-water formation. Species seen in this habitat vary from the taller rushes to the low growing arrow-leaved marigold, water milfoil and starwort.

Maritime tussock formation is confined to coastal areas below 650ft (200m) and is dominated by the tall tussac grass. A healthy specimen of tussac grass, growing in favourable conditions, can reach over 13ft (4m) tall and thrives in dense clumps around the coastline. Other species that can be found here include wild celery, cinnamon grass and native woodrush. This habitat was formerly much more extensive around the islands than it is today; overgrazing and fire have probably been the major causes in the decline of this habitat, although pests and disease are also thought to have had some effect. When grazing ceases, it has been shown to recover in some areas but the associated erosion that often follows the removal of tussac grass means this is not always the case. It has been found to be a remarkably difficult plant to reintroduce, although some success is now being achieved. This habitat is one of the most important on the islands, in particular when the numbers of breeding birds that are dependent on tussac grass are considered.

There is one other class of vegetation that can be found on the Falkland Islands, and that is shrubs and bushes. The only two native species are *fachine* and native boxwood, both thought to have been much more widespread prior to the introduction of grazing. They are thought to be able to grow in more than one habitat but are now reduced to surviving away from stock. *Fachine* usually prefers the wetter valleys where it can become the dominant plant, but has also been recorded from sand dunes close to beaches. This and the boxwood are two of the very few plants that can reach over 6ft (1.80m) in height. The boxwood is thought to be native to West Falkland and to have been introduced to East Falklands, being found, for example, growing in gardens around Port Stanley. In the wild it occurs on coastal cliffs and sandy slopes away from the attentions of grazing sheep. It is a popular plant used in hedging around the settlements. The two other most commonly found hedges are gorse, first brought in by the early settlers, and several species of pine tree, of which *macrocarpa* is the most apparent. A wide variety of other species have been tried in recent years although woodland is not a term often used on Falkland. The only real exception to this is the 'forest' at Hill Cove on East Falkland.

Over 160 plants have so far been identified as being native to the islands. Of these 13 are regarded as endemic and therefore not found anywhere else in the world. The native flora is much more diverse than that of any other of the South Atlantic islands. This is almost certainly due to the islands' proximity to South America, as the majority of the plants found on Falkland are also found in Tierra del Fuego. To date over 100 introduced species have been recorded, most originating from Europe. They tend to be concentrated around settlements with an estimated 16% now naturalised. Many of these are usually considered as the common weeds of the northern hemisphere.

The flora of the islands can look rather uniform at times but has a great many attractive flowers hidden away out of the wind; some of the more noteworthy plants of the Falkland Islands are described below.

Tall bushes
Of the three tall bushes found on the Falkland Islands, the prickly leaves of the **gorse** with its yellow flowers, commonly seen forming hedges around many of the older settlements, is the easiest to identify. **Native boxwood**, now a common windbreak in Port Stanley, has a heavily gnarled trunk and when in bloom the white flowers appear in dense crowds towards the tip of each branch. *Fachine* takes a little more searching to find, as it does not grow well in heavily grazed land. Its daisy-like flowers blooming across the upper part of the bush, and the fact that the undersides of the pointed green leaves and the twigs are covered with thin white hairs, give it a distinctive appearance. Probably the best location to see this plant in recent years has been on Saunders Islands, especially near Port Egmont.

Tussac grass
Tussac grass is the most easily identified plant on the islands. Although not as common as once was the case, there are many areas where this plant can be found. A visit to a tussac island such as Kidney Island at the entrance of Berkeley Sound gives a much better appreciation of how the coast of the Falkland Islands must have appeared before the arrival of man in the 16th century. Each plant sends out new leaves every year, the old leaves forming a robust pedestal strong enough to bear the weight of a sleeping sea lion. In the absence of any rodents many of the islands' smaller seabirds can be found nesting in or under the tussac pedestals. This very fragile environment is very easily destroyed in a few careless moments.

Berried plants
Several of the berried plants of the islands produce edible fruit. By late summer the shiny red berries of the very common **diddle-dee** show up as

coloured swathes across the drier landscape. The berry crop varies from year to year; in a good year many species of bird can be seen feeding on this tiny red fruit with a distinctive, tart flavour. Local residents often pick these berries and turn them into jams, jellies and pies. This plant was popular with the early settlers, as its resinous wood was easy to set alight even on the wettest of days. **Tea berries** are less common, occurring as a low creeper in areas with a deep base of peat. The insignificant four-petalled white flowers of spring are transformed into dull pink berries in the late summer, which are thought of as a delicacy on the islands, despite the difficulties involved in picking them. Its leaves were dried and used to make a type of tea by early settlers, hence its name. Late summer and early autumn are the best time to go looking for the **native strawberry** in its favoured drier habitat. Resembling a small shiny raspberry, this distinctive fruit can be hard to find as the berries lie close to the ground and are partially obscured by leaves, but its sweet taste is well worth the effort. Sometimes confused with the native strawberry, the fruit of **pig vine** is not edible by man but is a favoured food of upland geese. This very common plant can be found in most wet areas on the islands, particularly on the banks of streams. Flowering in November is followed by the formation of bright red berries growing on short stems that are just visible under the small rhubarb-like leaves. One of the prettiest flowers on the islands belongs to the **mountain berry**. Despite the name, this plant is widespread, its tiny white flowers hanging underneath wax-red sepals above small dark green leaves, making a most distinctive plant. The fruit is comparatively large and is a dull pink to almost purple. *Nertera depressa* does not have a local name although it is not unusual on the islands, especially in the wetter areas where it can form mats of vegetation. In autumn the dull, round, orange/red berry can be found showing up against a background of small succulent-like leaves. The most striking feature of the **almond flower** is the bloom not the berry. This cup-shaped white flower almost appears to grow straight from the earth as the stem and leaves are relatively inconspicuous. After flowering in mid-summer, a deep purple berry is formed, often around the bases of balsam bogs along with the mountain berry.

Cushion plants

Some of the most unusual looking plants on the islands are the cushion plants. The largest and most intriguing is the **balsam bog**. Densely packed rosettes of flowers form irregular mounds which can reach over five feet (1.5m) in height and have a circumference in the region of ten feet (3m). These mounds are extremely hard and vary in colour from light to dark green, depending on their exposure to sunshine. A faint smell, hence the name balsam bog, exudes from the small globules of white gum that are secreted between the rosettes and eventually harden into small, brown lumps. This plant is usually found in dry rocky ground from low coastal cliffs right up into the feldmark formation. **Coastal nassauvia** is one of the most attractive of the bog plants, forming low cushions or dense carpets of green on low rocks, or in the shrub heath close to the coast, occasionally well above sea level. Tiny, cream-white flowers can be seen throughout the summer and, when found in profusion, produce a sweet smell of nectar, which can be detected even on the windiest of days. This bog, along with **Moore's plantain** and **Falkland false plantain**, are three of the endemic flowers of the islands, and coastal nassauvia is probably the most common of these endemic species. Two other bogs can easily be found on the islands. *Astelia* forms carpets of hard green leaves over very waterlogged peat, and it is the plant most often associated with the term 'soft *camp*' as it is widespread over the islands. The other bog family are the *Azorella* species, of which four are found in the Falklands. They form flat mats, hugging the ground or forming proper cushions, and are most often found in shrub heath on drier ground.

Flowers

A wide range of brightly coloured flowers can be found on the Falkland Islands, many of which are small or are only in bloom for a short time each summer. Some of the most attractive flowers belong to the orchid family of which four are found on the islands. The easiest to find, although this is by no means guaranteed, is the **dog orchid**. Its three white petals, often showing some purple tinges, are best looked for in the oceanic heath formation when in flower in November and December. Many of the endemic flowers escape detection, let alone identification by the casual botanist, while others are much more obvious. The **snake plant**, one of the *nassauvia* family, is one of the strangest plants on the islands. Long straggling stems reaching up to the light around the boulders in the stone runs is how this plant is typically found. Tough, almost scaly, leaves cover the stems that end in club-like heads of densely packed white flowers creating a most unmistakable plant. Two of the brightest coloured of the endemic flowers are the two species of ragwort. **Smooth ragwort** and **woolly ragwort** both have many bright yellow flowers sprouting from green stems and are found in heathlands intermixed with diddle-dee and grasslands around the coasts and inland up to 1,000ft (305m). Distinguishing between these two species is not as easy as their names would suggest, but careful examination of the structure as well as the appearance of the plant will result in correct identification. **Pale maiden**, although now not thought to be an endemic species, is one of the most flamboyant flowers of the Falkland spring. The Falkland pale maiden is now considered to be a larger flowered, wider petalled form of a very widely distributed *sisyrinchium* in South America. Many grasslands and heathlands are still covered with the delicate, white, bell-shaped flowers in the early part of the summer, with some plants still in bloom in February, although they do not flourish in heavily grazed pasture. **Falkland lavender** is one of the most attractive plants on the islands, but is only distantly related to the lavenders renowned for their aromatic oils. A low-growing shrub, which is not particularly noticeable for most of the year, it comes into its own when it blooms in mid-summer and is covered with large, white, lilac or pale blue, daisy-like flowers. It is quite common around the islands, rarely found far from the sea on drier ground, and can appear to form a carpet of colour in certain areas. Another plant that grows on coastal slopes with rather poor soil is the **lady's slipper**. This beautiful red and yellow flower, supposed to look like a ladies slipper, emerges from the centre of a rosette of some very hairy leaves in mid-summer. It is often found in small colonies but is not thought to be common on the islands. The unusually named **Christmas bush** gets its name from the fact that it is covered with off-white flowers from the end of December until January. The islanders used to pick the flowers for decorative purposes. This common plant on the islands is able to tolerate wet or dry ground and a wide range of soil types.

Very few of the plants on the Falkland Islands have been used medicinally, the main exception being **scurvy grass**. This member of the *oxalis* family has a singular appearance with large pearl-white flowers, which are sometimes tinged with pink, resting upon thin, silvery grey leaves that radiate out from a central stem. The early sailors used this plant as a means of avoiding the disease, scurvy. The early settlers on the islands made scurvy grass jam from this plant. Its name has continued to this day, even though in modern times only the plant stalks are used to make a drink. It is most often found near the coast and in the dwarf shrub heath. The other plant used for its anti-scorbutic properties was the **sea cabbage**. This very common plant occurs inland of the tide line on almost every sandy beach on the islands. Its thick, fleshy leaves, silvery grey in colour, form a pale line behind the flotsam and jetsam at the top of the beach. After Christmas, bright yellow flowers appear in bunches, making this one of the most memorable flowers in Falkland.

Of the plants that creep along the ground, one that stands out is the *pratia*, which catches the eye on account of the arrangement of its five petals. They are neatly arranged so as to leave a gap, as if something has eaten one side of each blossom. These flowers are usually white in colour but a pale lilac form is also found. This plant occurs in thick mats on wet peaty ground on many islands. The daisy family is well represented, although one of the first that the visitor finds is usually the introduced **European daisy**. Three other species are native, one of which – the **hairy daisy** – is endemic to the Falkland Islands. **Marsh daisy**, as the name suggests, likes the damper regions whilst the **vanilla daisy** is one of the largest flowing plants of the heathlands, reaching up to 12 inches (30cm) tall. Almost as tall is the only wild representative of the *primula* family, **Dusty Miller**. This plant flowers in the spring, although some occasionally still in bloom in early January, in the dry open dwarf shrub heathland which extends from sea level to the highest mountain ranges on the islands. A thin round stalk supports a round head of pure-white, tubular flowers that each have a yellow centre. At a distance they can appear to look like a patch of small golf balls. Another plant that sends up a ball of flowers is **thrift**. This species is much taller and has deeper pink-coloured flowers than the species found around European coasts. The thrift adorns the rocks and sand around many of the shores through the summer months. Dotted around the wet sand, a little way inland from the beach, are small patches of **pimpernel**. This low growing plant forms small, pink, star-shaped flowers during January before setting seed and disappearing for another year.

One of the few plants used as food in the islands is **wild celery**, a close relative of the cultivated variety, which has the same familiar smell and the same white umbrellas of flower. It is usually found in close association with tussac grass.

Wetlands on the islands tend to be dominated by grasses and rushes. One of the few exceptions to this is the **arrow-leaved marigold**, which can be found in many wet habitats beside salt or freshwater. Its shiny, green, arrow-shaped leaves are mostly prostrate, but in some circumstances will form a more erect flower. Its off-white flowers appear in the centre of each stem in November and December.

The flora of the islands has yet to be fully investigated. Falkland Conservation has a long-running project encouraging visitors with an interest in the flora to inform the charity of any species they find, especially obscure plants, complete with details of when, and most importantly where, they saw the plant in question.

MARINE ALGAE

Kelp beds surrounding the islands are one of the features of the Falklands, damping down the waves even on the windiest of days. Various species of marine algae extend from the intertidal zone out to a depth of 100ft (30.5m), forming bands that can extend up to a mile (1.6km) offshore on all but the most exposed shores. Giant kelp can reach up to 200ft (61m) long, held up to the sun by many small air bladders, and constitutes the bulk of the kelp beds around the Falklands. Many other species occupy separate niches between the giant kelp and the top of the tidal zone, including the bright green leaves of the *ulva* family that are a major food source for kelp geese. A great many species rely on the kelp beds for food and shelter, thus making them one of the most important habitats on the islands.

ANIMALS
Land mammals

Endemic land mammals became extinct on the Falkland Islands when the last **warrah**, or Falkland fox, was shot in 1876. This relative of the Fuegian fox from South America was described by some of the first explorers to reach the islands towards the end of the 17th century. Different races existed on East and West Falkland, although the warrah was probably never very common. Like the fox, its bold, inquisitive behaviour meant that it was perceived as a threat by the escalating sheep-farming industry. A government bounty for each dead animal was the death knell for this species.

It is possible to see ten species of land mammal on the islands today, all introduced by man. Some hitched a ride and have been present ever since man reached the islands, whereas others have been deliberately introduced. Rabbits, hares and cottontail rabbits have been found on the islands in recent times. **Cottontail rabbits** are found only on New Island to the west of the archipelago, whilst **hares** are restricted to East Falkland, in particular the Port Louis area. The rabbit is more widespread, although not common. All three were introduced to supplement the diet of the original settlers.

Three other mammals have reached Falkland without man's intentional help. **Brown rats**, **black rats** and the **house mouse** have been recorded in many locations around the islands and are thought to be responsible for the lack of breeding seabirds in some otherwise suitable habitats. The most destructive of the introduced species on the islands has been the **domestic cat**. Wherever this species is present a dramatic decline in small birds has been noted. In contrast, on Carcass Island, which has remained cat-free, small birds are abundant.

A visit to the southwest of the islands is necessary to see two of the other land mammals. **Guanacos** had been introduced in various locations over the years from South America but can only be seen on Staats Island today. This member of the llama family lives in small herds, which appear to have no predators, so that food supply is the only limit on population numbers. The **Patagonian fox** was present on six islands in the southwest, although work is in progress to eradicate them. Where foxes are present, there are correspondingly low numbers of ground-nesting birds, including geese and other wildfowl.

The most intriguing of the introduced mammals is the **sea otter**, also known as the Fuegian marine otter. This animal, originally introduced to the islands in the 1930s, has managed to stay so well hidden that its present status on the islands is unknown. There is so much suitable habitat for this South American species that only brief sightings have been possible in the intervening years, usually in the southwest or southeast of the islands.

Marine mammals

Watching some of the marine mammals that frequent the islands is one of the most memorable experiences on the Falkland Islands. Fur seal, southern sea lion and southern elephant seal, the only true seal, all breed on the islands. Hunting for **fur seals** in the 18th and 19th century drastically reduced the numbers of this animal, so much so that it almost became extinct on the islands before the first protective legislation was passed by the Falkland Island Government in 1881, although poaching continued for a good many years until this species was totally safeguarded in 1921. At sea identification can be difficult, as the pointed snout and heavy neck are not very visible when the fur seals are porpoising through the water. Males are larger and darker brown than the females with a much heavier neck and head. They reach about 6ft (1.9m) in length and can weigh up to 350lb (158kg). Rocky cliffs with accessible ledges near the water are the preferred breeding site, most of which are found to the northwest and southwest of the islands. Breeding commences in early November when the bulls come ashore to claim their territories, followed by the females a few weeks later just before the pups are born. Colonies are rarely deserted during the year after the pups have departed, as different age groups and sexes are constantly present. The main prey consists of lobster krill, squid and some fish. New Island has the colonies most visited by tourists as elsewhere the seals keep to isolated rocky outcrops.

Southern sea lions also suffered heavily at the hands of the sealers. Formerly occurring in huge numbers, the southern sea lion population appears to have suffered a steady decline despite the cessation of sealing after

World War II. An adult male is an impressive animal weighing up to 700lb (320kg) and reaching a length of about 8ft (2.6m). The name 'lion' stems from the heavy neck of the male that, when dry, looks similar to a lion's mane. They do not have the majestic appearance of the lion as they have a flat forehead and rather small eyes, giving them a rather mean look. The females are smaller, sleeker and are often a lighter brown in colour. Generally they are shy animals who retreat when man approaches, but this cannot be guaranteed as they can move very rapidly and have a fearsome array of teeth. When hauled out on land, they can be seen resting upright with their head tilted slightly backwards; to all intents and purposes they seem to be fast asleep. Appearances are deceptive, as they are very aware of any nearby movement and react very quickly. If the visitor comes across a sea lion whilst on foot it is a good idea to take an alternative route! Southern sea lions breed later in the summer than the fur seal, the bulls setting up their territories in December and the females coming ashore to pup between the middle of December and the end of January. The colonies are at their most active during this time. Towards the end of the summer the males leave to feed up after fasting while protecting their harems, and after a few weeks the females and young also depart. Non-breeders can be seen at the fringes of the colonies during the summer and will come ashore after the males have gone back to sea. Away from the 60 or so colonies on the islands, small groups and lone seals can be encountered almost anywhere, even in Port Stanley. Octopus, squid, lobster krill and fish make up a large proportion of their diet although lone bulls can sometimes be seen hunting penguins near a rookery. This can involve a chase over the land for the more agile seal or a stealthy approach through the shallows to surprise the prey. Sea lions have also been known to take elephant seal young.

Seeing a **bull elephant seal** for the first time is a memorable experience. Initially, members of a group sprawled out on the sand seem to be doing very little except waiting for their old skin to moult and their new skin to grow. Appearances are deceptive as they puff and blow, squabble over who lies where or just argue for the sake of it. Males are immense creatures reaching 18ft (5.5m) in length and attaining weights in the region of four tons (4.06 tonnes). The females are roughly half the size and only weigh a quarter of the males' weight. An inflatable proboscis is the reason for this species' name, although it must be said that it does not greatly resemble an elephant. The proboscis is inflated during territorial displays in the spring when the elephant seals come ashore to lay claim to their preferred sites. It is quite usual to see large scars on the necks of the older males after many years of fighting over the best section of beach. By early October all the females will have arrived and are gathered into harems by the dominant males. Pups can be born from mid-September onwards, the highest concentrations being noted in the first half of October. Just over three weeks later the single pup is weaned, during which period the female is mated, before both leave. The breeding bulls depart by mid-November leaving the beaches for the non-breeding animals to come ashore to moult. Towards the end of the summer, once they have recovered their strength, it is the females' turn to come ashore, to be followed by the males in the early months of the winter. Most elephant seals stay at sea during the winter months, although on favoured beaches, such as those on Sea Lion Island, it is possible to find the occasional animal slumped on the sand. On land they are not the most elegant creatures, but they are sleek swimming machines in the water, well adapted for diving to great depths in search of squid and fish. Early settlers found that a bull elephant seal could yield over ninety gallons of oil and was therefore a valuable export commodity. Within a hundred years of the first records of elephant seals on the islands they were almost extinct. At the beginning of the 20th century small breeding colonies were recorded. Over the years these colonies have consistently increased in number and size, despite a short period of hunting after World War II, until the last decade, when there was an estimated annual production of 5,000 pups. Sea Lion Island is the premier site for this species in Falkland. Moulting elephant seals can be encountered on Saunders Island and on Carcass Island.

Other species of seal that have been recorded on the islands include the **Leopard Seal**, most often seen in the winter months, but which can be seen at any time of year. Its large head, with an enormous mouth full of sharp teeth, make this an easy species to identify. Formerly more common on the islands, there are records of small groups coming ashore on sandy beaches, but only single animals have been noted in recent years.

Apart from man, these seals only have one major predator on the islands: the **killer whale** or orca. These elusive creatures can be an unforgettable sight. Small groups of shags, gulls and terns hovering over the surface on the outer reaches of the kelp are often the first clue given to the presence of killer whales, which appear in small groups or 'pods'. These birds are waiting to feed on any titbits left over after the orca has finished with its prey. The huge, triangular, dorsal fin of the male shows up well when the whale is swimming parallel to the beach, but can be surprisingly difficult to discern as the whale moves towards or away from the observer. Females are not so easy to see, as their dorsal fin is much smaller. Pods normally comprise at least one adult male with a small number of females. The black and white patterning on the under body and flanks is only apparent if it rolls or, more rarely, leaps in the air. The small pale patch behind the dorsal fin is seldom visible. Killer whales are not common on the islands but are regularly sighted in certain areas, possibly in step with the breeding cycle of their main prey, the seals. On Sea Lion Island, one of the best locations to look for this species, they are repeatedly sighted when the elephant pups go out to sea for the first time, and also when the sea lion pups leave the breeding grounds. They can be seen at other times of year but November and February are the preferred months.

Many species of whale and dolphin have been recorded on the islands over the centuries. Nowadays the larger whales are few and far between courtesy of the whaling industry. However, in recent years **southern right whales** have begun to be seen more regularly in some of the deeper waters around the outlying islands, in particular near New Island and at the mouth of Berkeley Sound. **Long-finned pilot whales** can be seen in small groups throughout the summer months, and strandings of this species are not uncommon around the islands, as, for example, on Pebble Island in the early 1980s. Many other species of whale have been seen from the cruise ships that pass through Falkland waters, including the very rare **blue whale**.

Two of the smaller cetaceans are frequently observed in the islands; **Commerson's dolphins** and Peale's dolphins can be seen on most visits. The former is smaller, about 6ft (1.8m) long, and prefers sheltered waters, often playing in the bow wave of boats entering harbour. Port Howard has been an excellent place to see and photograph these attractive black and white dolphins as they speed alongside the boat. The origin of the local name 'puffing pig' can be heard as they gasp for air before diving back into the clear blue water. As soon as they see or hear an engine they make a beeline for the boat, their rounded dorsal fin hardly visible as they zoom through the water. **Peale's dolphins** are larger, up to 8ft (2.5m) long, and are generally much more lethargic swimmers, although they experience moments of frenzied activity, leaping out of the water and splashing around in the shallows. The taller dorsal fin, with its more pronounced curve towards the rear, is quite distinctive, as is the reduced amount of white visible on the upper parts when compared to Commerson's dolphins. They are habitually found moving along the edges of the kelp beds that surround the islands, appearing to have favourite haunts to which they regularly return.

BIRDS

The visitor's general impression after a trip to the Falkland Islands is that it is full of birds of all shapes and sizes, and yet there are large areas with hardly any breeding birds. Those species that are able to live and breed on the islands have found their niches and have exploited them to the full, with little competition, and therefore seem to occur in disproportionately large numbers at certain locations. Predation by rats and cats has reduced the numbers of some land birds and smaller seabirds in many areas, but by visiting islands – such as Carcass Island and Sea Lion Island – where such animals have not been introduced, it is possible to see most of the breeding birds of the Falkland Islands in one trip. Of the 59 species that habitually breed on the islands, most are water birds making use of the pools and lakes as well as the ample shoreline and good feeding offshore.

Penguins

The penguin family are well represented on the island, with five species nesting annually, plus the occasional vagrant from the Antarctic or subantarctic islands. A visit to the **king penguin** colony at Volunteer Point on East Falkland is the highlight of many a trip to the islands. By far the largest breeding penguins on the islands, they can turn up on almost any island, sometimes mingling with gentoo penguins when they come ashore to moult. Small breeding groups are found on some of the other islands but the sheer numbers of birds at Volunteer Point make it a truly memorable wildlife spectacle.

Gentoo penguins are much more widespread. Their preference for nesting on low ground means that their colonies are much more accessible than some of the other species of seabirds. Some colonies do not conform to this rule by choosing hill-sites a long walk from the beach. The Falkland Islands shelter a large percentage of this species' global population, and the gentoo is one of the few penguins that stays around the islands in large numbers during the winter months. These are the most comical of the penguins, waddling to and from their rookeries, always using the same route. A tall elegant penguin with a distinctive white blaze above and behind the eye and, as is the case with most of this family, a rather guttural call. Throughout the breeding season there is always some activity, whether it is the adult bird robbing bits of nesting material from its neighbour's nest in the early part of their season, or the young racing around the colony later in the summer, chasing their parents to persuade them to give up the meal that they have just caught out at sea. As they usually lay two eggs, there are often two juveniles begging for food by January.

The **rockhoppers** are the smallest of the islands' breeding penguins, yet they locate their rookeries on some of the most inhospitable coastline. Their climbing ability is second to none for a seabird, as they make their way up some of the steepest slopes to their cliff-top nesting-site using only the sharp claws on their powerful feet to cling to the rock face. The colonies are noisy, smelly and marvellously photogenic. The vivid yellow tufts above each red eye contrast with their otherwise shining black and white plumage. Rockhopper penguins, unlike the other species of penguin breeding on the Falklands, can often be found in mixed colonies with other seabirds. King shags and black-browed albatrosses are the most frequent cohabitants, along with the occasional **macaroni penguin**. The latter is at the northern limit of its range and breeds in very small numbers, usually just a handful of pairs mixing in with the larger rockhopper penguin rookeries. It is a stockier, taller bird with fiery crests meeting on the forehead. Greater numbers of predators tend to be found on the perimeter of these mixed colonies. Turkey vultures, skuas and gulls are the most numerous, with snowy sheathbills appearing in large numbers around some of the more isolated colonies. Rockhopper penguins are the most pelagic of the penguins breeding on the islands; satellite tracking has found that they cover vast distances when out at sea, regularly reaching the South American coast.

Magellanic penguins are the first species of penguin encountered by most visitors to the islands. Their habit of breeding in burrows dug into the peaty soil results in rather more diffuse colonies than is true of other penguins. They are found on almost every coast with suitable nesting grounds and access to the sea, always avoiding cliffs and settlements. As with all the smaller local penguins, two eggs are laid at the start of the summer. By January the young are large enough to be exploring the environs of their burrows, dashing back for cover at the first sign of danger.

Grebe
Two species of grebe breed on the islands' freshwater pools, although they can occasionally be seen on freshwater streams near the sea and can spend some time on coastal waters during the winter. The white-tufted grebe is slightly

more widespread than the silvery grebe, although they can often be found on the same stretches of water. Slightly smaller than white-tufted grebe, the **silvery grebe** is a delicate, paler-looking bird with a distinct black nape patch and attractive fan-shaped plumes on the ear coverts during the summer months. The **white-tufted grebe** in breeding plumage has an almost all black head and neck, with a white patch on the rear of the face fanning out from behind the eye. In winter time the throat is a pale off-white colour, while the neck and crown are dull brown. Grebes are very active birds and are constantly diving, so their presence on a particular pool is not always immediately obvious, especially as they like to nest in pools with a healthy growth of aquatic vegetation, on which they build their nests.

Albatross

The only species of albatross to nest on the islands is the black-browed albatross but other species have been seen from the islands at certain times of year. Late summer and early autumn are good periods to look for **royal albatross** from headlands such as Cape Pembroke on East Falkland or Tamar Head on Pebble Island. These huge birds can only be seen properly with a telescope, despite their enormous wingspan. A visit to a **black-browed albatross** colony is an unforgettable experience, situated as they are along the tops of cliffs on some of the westernmost islands. Looking offshore from almost any vantage point on the Falklands one can see black-browed albatrosses, but to see them at their best a visit to a colony is a must. West Point Island and New Island are home to two of the best-known colonies, as these two islands are included in the itineraries of most of the cruise ships that call into the islands during an austral summer. For the land-based visitor Saunders Island is the most accessible. These graceful birds return each year to their mud-pot nests situated high on the cliffs. One egg is laid in early October and the young are ready to leave in March and April. Once fledged these young will wander the southern oceans until they are ready to start breeding in their fifth season, having come to inspect prospective breeding sites for a few weeks in the previous two years. Recent concerns about the declining populations of this species, in the Falklands and elsewhere, have led to a campaign to raise awareness of the large numbers of these birds that are accidentally killed by the long-lining fishing industries in the South Atlantic.

Petrels

Effortless, gliding flight is a characteristic shared with the **southern giant petrels**, which breed on the islands. These long-winged birds have a wingspan of about 80 inches (203cm) and a stocky, heavily built body. A heavy bill creates the impression of a massive head. The scavenging habits of this species gave rise to its local name of stinker, and this close association with humans can give the impression that there are more of these petrels around the islands than is actually the case. Older birds tend to show a pale head and fore-body, while younger birds are more uniformly dark brown. Birds with almost white plumage, apart from a few single black feathers, are thought to originate from further south and are seen most years but do not join the breeding colonies. A single egg is laid on flat ground close to the shore, often near a slope to give them sufficient updraft to assist takeoff. These birds are very shy when nesting, so it is absolutely necessary to give them a wide berth in order to avoid disturbing the colony. Maybe albatrosses are more elegant in flight, but giant petrels are nonetheless fantastic birds to watch gliding low over the water with the merest twitch of a feather sending them in another direction.

Various other members of the petrel family can be seen from, or nest on, the islands. The **prions** are sometimes visible like grey and white spectres flitting between waves. They are best observed at sea around the west of the islands or from some of the exposed headlands in a strong gale. Nowadays they only nest on some of the outlying islands, but do so in large numbers. Coming ashore at night, they are most often seen from ships around the islands. **Southern fulmars** and **pintado petrels** pass the islands during the spring and the autumn en route to and from their breeding grounds further south. These are probably the most common non-breeding species of petrel that can be seen from the shore.

Other nocturnally breeding seabirds include white-chinned petrels, sooty shearwaters and great shearwaters. All three fly low over the sea with outstretched wings shearing the surface of the water. **Sooty shearwaters** breed in large numbers on Kidney Island at the southern entrance to Berkeley Sound, and therefore big flocks can be seen in the vicinity of this island. This tussac island is also prime habitat for white-chinned petrels and great shearwaters, although they are found in much lower numbers. **White-chinned petrels** and sooty shearwaters are an even, dark brown colour, with the exception of the silvery underwing of the sooty shearwaters. The latter are smaller birds flying in a very dynamic manner, unlike the more relaxed albatross-style flight of the white-chinned petrels. **Great shearwaters** have the same colouring on the upper parts, apart from a dark cap and white bands over the nape and rump. The underbody is white apart from a dusky patch on the belly and a dark bar along the underwing. All three can be seen at sea around the islands but the entrance to Berkeley Sound is the most likely locality to see them.

Three species of **storm petrels** breed on the islands but the best way to see them, other than a lucky sighting at sea, is to visit a tussac island at night. Consequently, few visitors see black-bellied storm petrels, grey-backed storm petrels or Wilson's storm petrels, as these tiny seabirds are so elusive. Another very small seabird is the **Falkland diving petrel**, which again breeds in some of the more inaccessible islands in the archipelago. This minute black and white seabird has rarely been reported in large groups. It is only found on those very unusual, flat, calm days when something as small as these birds can been seen.

Shags

A walk along almost any shore on the islands will bring the visitor within binocular range of **rock shags**. Their cousins, the **king shags**, are not quite as numerous but can be found without too much difficulty. Both species are typical cormorants, with long thin necks often the only visible part of the bird when sitting on the sea. On land they can sometimes be seen roosting together on rocky outcrops, but tend to have differing requirements for choice of breeding site. Rock shags are found building nests on cliff sides or on other steep slopes, whereas the king shags prefer to nest on flat open ledges at the top of the cliffs, often in association with rockhopper penguins.

Herons

A widespread resident on the islands, the **black-crowned night heron** can be found feeding in fresh and salt water. When feeding, these herons are a solitary species, but they can be found roosting communally on old wrecks, jetties and on low rocky cliffs. Generally described as crepuscular, they can sometimes be seen by day feeding along the more isolated waterways. As with all herons they are very patient fishermen, standing still for what seems an eternity before striking with lightning speed. Colonies of black-crowned night herons are most often found in reed beds, tussac grass and trees, or on low cliffs close to their feeding grounds. This normally silent bird lets out a harsh squawk when disturbed, hence its local name 'quark'. The name 'quark pond' often indicates the presence of this species. At the nest the young make such a wide range of hisses and guttural noises that it can sound as though several species are present. The dapper adults are in stark contrast to the brown, streaky plumage of the rather demonic-looking immature birds. The race of black-crowned night heron found on Falkland is endemic to the islands.

Waterfowl
Swans

Usually only one species of swan, the **black-necked swan**, breeds on the islands. The coscoroba swan, although best regarded as a vagrant from South America, bred successfully on the island in the 2000/2001 season. Black-necked swans are the largest breeding bird on the islands but tend only to frequent a few favoured locations. Some of the largest counts have been obtained on Pebble Island, but the Hawk's Nest Ponds area on West Falkland and the Goose Green region on East Falkland are also good places to look for this shy species. The well-documented, shy behaviour of black-necked swans usually results in distant views of this elegant species. The rare good views reveal the red bill and the bump in front of the eye. When their cygnets are small, they sometimes get a free ride on their parent's back, so that all that can be seen is a tiny white head peeping out from beneath the adult's wings. Once the young are able to fly, all the birds leave the lakes and ponds to spend the winter months on tidal streams and estuaries, where they undergo their annual moult during the early autumn.

Geese

Three breeding species of wild geese are represented on the islands. The term ubiquitous definitely applies to the **upland goose** on the Falkland Islands. They have been recorded breeding on almost every acre in the islands. The white head, neck and breast of the male make them one of the first birds the visitor identifies on arrival, whereas the browner, more camouflaged plumage of the female and the young cause them to be less detectable. In the early 20th century the government classed them as a pest and introduced a bounty payment for goose beaks, as they were perceived to be in competition with the sheep for pastureland. Subsequently it was found that the only problems occurred on greens and re-seeded grasslands near freshwater. Upland geese have been a welcome addition to the local diet since the time of the early settlers, and their feathers have been used as brushes for sweeping and painting. Their presence on the islands has been better tolerated in recent years. It is possible to see them grazing beside the road in Port Stanley, often on Victory Green, easily visible from the Upland Goose Hotel.

The other white goose on the islands is the male **kelp goose**. As the name suggests, this is a much more maritime species spending most of its time eating many of the algae that grow in the intertidal zone along the shore. Rarely seen more than a few yards from the coast, they will eat short grass a little way inland and in autumn will go in search of ripe diddle-dee berries, but otherwise only come above the beach to bathe and drink in fresh water. The white plumage of the male contrasts with the female's barred underparts and glossy black back, which renders her almost invisible on the beach. They remain in pairs throughout the year, usually staying on their territory, although small flocks are sometimes seen at the beginning and end of the breeding season.

The third species of wild goose, the **ruddy-headed goose**, is almost as numerous as the upland goose. Both male and female initially look rather like a female upland goose but are smaller birds that have much finer barring along the flanks, paler flight feathers and dull orange, not yellow, legs. Ruddy-headed geese have a much more upright gait and are generally noisier, especially when taking off. They do not range as far inland as upland geese, preferring to stay close to the coast. The numbers of ruddy-headed geese that breed on Falkland have become internationally important as a result of the species' population crash in South America. Since 1985 this species has been removed from the list of pest species that are legally hunted on the islands as a result of their increased global importance.

The larger **ashy-headed goose**, although superficially similar to the ruddy-headed goose, is the complete opposite in that it is a very rare bird on the Falkland Islands but is still common in South America. **Feral domestic geese** are included on any checklist of the birds of the Falkland Islands as they are considered to be wild birds. Since their introduction in the late 1700s they have maintained populations in settlements in East and West Falkland and some other outlying islands.

Ducks

Nine species of annually breeding duck can be seen on the islands. Almost every bay or inlet on the islands has a pair or small group of **Falkland flightless steamer duck** cruising around the shallows. This endemic species is one of two very similar species of steamer ducks that breed on the islands. It has been remarked that the only safe way to distinguish between the two is to wait until one takes off! Flying steamer ducks prefer large bodies of freshwater and are not commonly noted on the sea. Their longer wings, lighter body structure, especially around the head and bill give them a much sleeker appearance than the stocky big-billed Falkland flightless steamer duck. Adults of the latter species are often found in pairs or family groups spread over extensive kelp beds or spaced out along the shore, as they are extremely territorial. In late summer flocks of up to 200 immature birds may gather together in favoured feeding areas. The name steamer originates from the 'steaming' action they use when escaping predators or chasing away other birds from their territory, as they race over the surface of the water with wings and feet sending up sheets of water. In windy conditions younger, and therefore lighter, birds are just about capable of flight, but only over short distances. A large percentage of their day is spent on the water diving for crabs and shellfish they pick up from the seabed. **Flying steamer ducks** are equally aggressive to their own kind, so it is unusual to see more than one pair on a particular lake, unless it has sufficient food supplies and is large enough to accommodate two pairs. This very shy species does not usually tolerate close approach by man, whereas the Falkland flightless steamer duck will quite often ignore the presence of anything other than another steamer duck. Observed at close range, it is possible to see the spurs on the forewing that the males use for defending their territory. Males of both species have an orange bill and are much paler on the head than the dull green/brown bill and darker head of the females.

Of the remaining species of duck, two, the **cinnamon teal** and the **red shoveler**, are thought to be only sporadic breeders on the islands. The **speckled teal**, also sometimes known as the yellow-billed teal, is the smallest duck of the region and the most widespread. This neatly marked, brown duck with a bright yellow bill in the male and a dull yellow bill in the female is most often encountered on fresh water, but can occasionally be seen on the sea. Typically this bird is found in small groups, often heard before seen, and may allow close approach unless it accompanies its young.

Frequently confused with the yellow-billed teal, the **yellow-billed pintail** is superficially very similar in that it is a brown duck with a yellow bill. On closer inspection the long neck, more rounded head and longer tail, together with its larger size, should identify this species. It is also found on the region's rivers and lakes and has been reported from the sea in the winter months. It is the least common of the annually breeding ducks on the islands but it is not confined to any particular site, having been regularly reported from East Falkland (especially Lafonia), Pebble Island and a few of the larger lakes.

By taking advantage of both fresh and salt-water habitats, the **crested duck** is one of the most numerous on the islands. At first glance it appears a rather drab bird, but when seen in good light its plumage is an intricate pattern of browns and whites with a chestnut patch in the outstretched wing and a bright red eye. This elegant duck is a vocal species; small groups are constantly quacking and making a range of other noises amongst themselves.

The other two species of wildfowl that a visitor can expect to see on the islands are chiloe wigeon and silver teal, the most attractive of the resident ducks. They have similar habitat requirements; the freshwater pools of Lafonia are the strongholds for both species. With a few exceptions, these two species are not easy to find on any of the islands to the west of Falkland Sound, although the Hawk's Nest Ponds on West Falkland and some of the pools on Pebble Island have been reliable locations in recent years. Chiloe wigeon can sometimes be found on the sea but are more easily seen on the freshwater lakes along with the silver teal. Neither species is very tolerant of man and will soon move out to the centre of any lake. The head pattern on a **silver teal** is very distinctive: black crown, white cheek and blue bill, which has a splash of orange near the base. The rest of the body is neatly barred with black, brown and white. **Chiloe wigeon** has an equally characteristic head pattern with a white crescent-shaped mark in front of the eye and a white patch behind the eye on an otherwise dark head. The orange flanks and white-edged black mantle feathers can be difficult to see at a distance. This is one of the larger species of duck on the freshwater pools, appearing to float higher on the water than most other ducks. On calm days the clear whistling calls of these charming ducks echo across the water.

Birds of prey

The only vulture to be found on the islands, the **turkey vulture**, can be seen around the whole archipelago, soaring high in the sky on calm days or hugging the contours in a howling gale. Their incredible mastery of the air is very different to their ungainly hop and waddle on the ground. The wrinkled head and all black plumage, along with its scavenging habits, do not make this one of the most popular birds on the islands. For many years they were thought to be killing the sheep they ate, hence the bounty paid for each of their rather ugly heads. Only in recent times have they been seen as scavengers rather than as predators.

Shrieking calls from oystercatchers are often the first hint that a **peregrine** is about to strike. **Cassin's falcon** is the local name for the race of peregrine falcon that breeds on the Falkland Islands. Waders such as oystercatchers and dotterel are amongst a wide range of prey taken by this sleek killing machine. The breeding range of the peregrine on Falkland is concentrated at the north and south of the islands, although wandering birds can turn up almost anywhere, as they sometimes have to travel for many miles to find food. Prions, caught several miles out to sea then brought back to a convenient sea cliff to be plucked, are a welcome supplement to their diet in the summer months.

Red-backed hawks are easy birds to see on the Falkland Islands, whether sat on a roadside telegraph pole or observed in the distance quartering the ground. This member of the buzzard family occurs in light and dark colour phases, the under parts ranging from a deep russet brown to white. The colour of the mantle is the best way to distinguish the sexes; the males have slate grey feathers and the female's mantle is a bright, reddish, brown. Red-backed hawks soon indicate if the visitor is too close to the nest by circling above the site and calling. Occasionally they have been known to try to dive bomb those who get too close. Introduced rats and mice have been a welcome addition to their diet, along with the usual prey of small birds, including the chicks of almost all the local waterfowl. They are very determined predators, seeming able to shrug off the mobbing of a gull colony as they single out one chick before plucking it from the ground and carrying it off to eat in peace and quiet.

The only member of the bird of prey family to be represented by two species breeding on the islands is the caracara. The globally threatened striated caracara still maintains a foothold on the islands, as does the more widespread crested caracara. The Johnny Rook as the **striated caracara** is known is the rogue of the bird world. These long-legged birds are very inquisitive, always the first to investigate anything new that just might be a source of food. Their habit of capturing interesting objects for a better look has resulted in many lost hats, gloves, lens caps, cameras etc. This tameness, allied to a bloodthirsty attitude to anything smaller or less healthy than themselves, put them into conflict with the early sheep farmers. The outcome of this was a bounty paid for every beak, resulting in many hundreds of birds being killed until the act was annulled in 1920. The present-day population is concentrated around some of the outlying islands, with very few breeding records in close proximity to any settlement on East or West Falkland. This species has undergone a steady reduction of numbers in South America, so that the small Falkland Island population of probably less than 1,000 pairs (*Atlas of the Breeding Birds of the Falkland Islands* Woods 1997) is important for the survival of this species. The **crested caracara**, or *carancho*, has a wider distribution on the islands and in South America. The shy, timid nature of this bird has probably been its saviour as they are very difficult to approach, always managing to detect the presence of any intruder before the intruder sees them. Larger than the striated caracara, with a black crown highlighted by a pale face and large orange beak, it is an attractive species. In flight the broad black wings show a white 'roundel' towards to the wing tip, which aids identification from afar. A bounty, paid upon the production of their beaks too, probably accounts for their timid behaviour.

Waders

Wading birds are found in most habitats on the Falkland Islands. Two species of oystercatchers can be seen around the shores. The startlingly black and white **Magellanic oystercatchers** are the most common; the sooty-black **blackish oystercatchers** are a little more secretive and less obvious. Their preferred breeding and feeding habitats differ, as Magellanic oystercatchers are usually found on open sandy beaches with low, grassy hills and the occasional freshwater pond nearby, whilst the blackish oystercatchers frequent rocky shores with good supplies of their staple food, mussels. These are not absolute requirements, as they can be found away from the typical habitat. They are a typically vocal species of oystercatcher and their high-pitched whistling call carried on the wind is one of the evocative sounds of the islands. The call of the blackish oystercatcher is very reminiscent of that made by the European oystercatcher, even though the Magellanic oystercatcher is closer in appearance. Both species make their nest close to the top of the beach in a small scrape, which they sometimes line with small pieces of shell or lichen, and they are very vigorous in defending their eggs and their young from any marauding predators.

Magellanic snipe can be found in a wide range of habitats from tussac islands to the open, white-grass plains, although their cryptic plumage conceals them well until they spring into the air from their hiding-places. In the early part of the breeding season the 'drumming' noise made by the tail feathers as they perform their display flights can be heard around the islands. Some birds seem oblivious to man and can be watched, probing the ground with their long bills, from only a few feet away.

Soft, piping calls heard whilst walking over diddle-dee heathlands are often the first clue that the visitor is in the territory of a **rufous-chested dotterel**. This attractive bird is widespread throughout the islands on the drier heaths. Its reddish-brown breast, dark, horizontal breast line, and narrow, white eyebrows make this an easy species to identify. As soon as any intruder, man, sheep or cattle, enters the territory of a male dotterel, it starts calling and keeps a very wary eye on the progress of the unwelcome visitor. They have been known to try to drive off any livestock that get too close to the nest. This rather solitary species does gather into small flocks at the end of the breeding season. It is thought that some birds then leave the islands for the winter months before returning in August.

The **two-banded plover** is not quite as prevalent on the islands as the rufous-chested dotterel but can be encountered on most islands. Both species have a similar feeding technique in that they hunt by sight for the small invertebrates that make up a large proportion of their prey. A short run, stop and look, before another short run, can identify these two birds at great distance, as they look like clockwork toys running over the landscape. The male of this delicate plover, with its two black breast bands (the upper one usually incomplete) and its rufous nape and crown, is much easier to find than the duller marked female. Two-banded plovers are a coastal species rarely found far from the shore, preferring sandy beaches to rocky coasts. The nest scrape can be situated anywhere from the top of the beach to the diddle-dee heaths a little way inland.

Several other species of wader have been recorded from the islands, most occurring as vagrants during the spring and autumn. The most numerous of these, and therefore the most likely to be seen on a visit to the islands, are the **white-rumped sandpipers** which breed in arctic North America and winter on the islands, forming large flocks in favoured locations such as around the pools on Pebble Island. These inconspicuous waders are best sought on open sand and mud flats, or short grassy turf. Their most distinctive feature is the white rump that is only visible during flight. White-rumped sandpipers have grey-brown upper parts and white under parts, making them rather drab birds in comparison with the resident waders.

Gulls

The sea hen, as the **Falkland skua** is known, is a summer visitor to the islands that can be found harassing other birds (in particular, shags, gulls and terns) to obtain food. This large, brown, thickset seabird breeds in loose colonies on grassy headlands or hill tops not far from the sea around the coast of the Falkland Islands. They can be very aggressive in defending their nest sites, diving at any intruder and hitting them with their outstretched legs. They deliver painful blows, which are very effective in driving away man and beast. Not all are this ferocious; some well-known birds are so tame that they will allow themselves to be picked up, but discretion is much the better option when coming across a colony of skuas.

Kelp gulls, dolphin gulls and brown-hooded gulls all breed on the islands, the latter being the least populous. The ability of the **kelp gull** to extract food from a variety of sources has resulted in it being the commonest gull on the islands, seen in every possible habitat, as happy to glide over the settlements as to follow fishing boats miles from land. These birds nest in large colonies sometimes mixed in with dolphin gulls. The black and white plumage of the kelp gull is very different to the mid-grey under parts, black mantle and wings of the **dolphin gull**. The latter also has a heavy, red bill and legs of a similar hue, making it one of the most attractive gulls in the world. It is by far the more aggressive of the two, finding food by harrying other birds, scavenging, or taking advantage of the rubbish provided by man. It can also be very vigorous in defending its nest site and yet, where man has trained it, it will take food offered from the hand. **Brown-hooded gulls** are the hardest of the three gulls to find away from the breeding grounds. They can often be found nesting on beaches or shingle bars in lakes in the company of South American terns and kelp gulls, but spend most of their time feeding over the kelp beds or over some of the islands' more active tide races. Small parties of gulls can sometimes be seen hovering low over the surface of the sea. The brown hood is only present when the bird is in breeding condition; some of the older birds develop a pink flush to the under parts in spring and early summer. When feeding over the kelp beds they can look rather similar to the South American tern but have a less fluid wing action and have a white leading edge to the forewing in contrast to the almost uniformly grey-white thinner wing of the tern.

South American terns are absent from the islands during the winter months, re-appearing in late September to breed on shingle and sandy beaches, or on rocky headlands. Some pairs will seek a similar habitat near the larger lakes on the islands. This graceful flier has a well-deserved reputation, similar to the skua's, for protecting its nest site against all comers. The first warning is a harsh cry coming from aloft as the adult bird positions itself above the nest. A swift retracing of footsteps would then be to the advantage of all parties, for continued disturbance can lead terns to desert their eggs, and they have been known to inflict a painful blow to those who ignore the warning cry.

Snowy sheathbills are one of those species whose whiter than white appearance is deceptive. A pure white, pigeon-like bird found around many of the big rockhopper penguin/king shag colonies, it is usually found feeding on anything from regurgitated food to dead chicks and stolen eggs, as befits a well-practised scavenger. Sheathbills can be found here throughout the year, but they are non-breeding, immature birds whose populations increase during the winter.

Owls

Finding either of the two species of owl that breed on the Falkland Islands takes some planning and a great deal of luck. **Barn owls** are very rare on the islands due to their nocturnal behaviour and the lack of suitable breeding habitats. The chances of seeing barn owls are minimal, even though they patrol a very wide territory. **Short-eared owls** are more numerous but are still difficult to find, as they are most common on tussac islands, or in locations where the small bird population has not been decimated by introduced ground predators. The island race of short-eared owl has adapted to the scarcity of land mammals and small birds by becoming mostly nocturnal, snatching storm-petrels, diving petrels and large insects such as camel-crickets, which breed prolifically on these tussac islands.

Passerines

The stretch of sea between mainland South America and the Falkland Islands means that very few small birds reach the islands. Some strong fliers, such as the **barn swallow** and the **Chilean swallow**, can be seen most years, but have not as yet been able to establish a breeding presence on the islands. Nine other immigrant species breed on a regular basis and exhibit characteristics of racial or specific endemism. One other, the **house sparrow**, has been introduced by man and subsists around some of the larger settlements including Port Stanley. The introduction of cats, rats and mice many years ago has brought about a decline in the numbers of the **tussacbird** but this species is still the most numerous of the small birds on the islands. It is now confined to tussac grass islands and to places such as Carcass Island where the aforementioned predators are absent. This species is very tame and incredibly inquisitive, perching on visitors' shoes, investigating camera bags and generally inspecting anything that could conceivably hold a scrap of food. At first glance its dull black plumage, only enlivened by a dull yellow bill, does not make it the most attractive of birds, but its cheeky character soon endears it to all. Tussacbirds spend most of their time not far from the top of the beach, although on some of the smaller islands they can be found almost anywhere.

One species that appears to have benefited from man's arrival is the **dark-faced ground-tyrant**. This close relative of the flycatcher family, although still common around cliffs and other rocky outcrops, has learnt that there is a good supply of flies and other insect life around the settlement buildings. Its habit of perching on a good vantage point, to keep an eye out for prey, is thought to be one of the reasons that the species has not been decimated by the introduced cats and rats, as happened with the tussacbird, which is habitually a ground-dweller. The grey-brown, dark-faced ground-tyrant is present over most of the islands and goes by the local name of 'news bird', as it often approaches any visitors to its territory, calling as if waiting to exchange gossip.

There are two species of wren breeding on the islands, the Falkland grass wren and **Cobb's wren**. The latter is an endemic species closely related to the house wren of South and North America. Formally thought to have existed in large numbers, the presence of cats, rats and mice have restricted its range to those tussac grass islands upon which these predators have not been introduced. As a result the wrens are very common along the upper shore on islands such as Sea Lion Island, Carcass Island and Kidney Island but are absent over much of the archipelago. Initially they can be difficult to see but soon give themselves away with their rattling 'chirr' call as they hop around the boulders at the top of the beach, disappearing under one rock and popping out from under another a few feet away. Cobb's wrens often adopt the typical wren pose of tail in the air when alarmed, and then vanish in the blink of an eye, their warm brown plumage matching the colour of the kelp strewn along the tideline. **Falkland grass wrens** are much more widespread, inhabiting many of the white-grass plains, especially where the grass and reeds form clumps, as well as the bands of tussac grass. However, the difficulty in detecting the presence of this species after they have ceased singing makes any attempt at comparison of numbers with the more evident Cobb's wren unreliable. These streaky brown birds run about between clumps of vegetation like mice, rarely flying unless flushed. Despite being the smallest of the breeding birds on the islands, its song in springtime carries a long way over the grasslands or the reedbeds by some of the larger lakes where they breed.

The **Falkland pipit** is the best of the resident song birds. Called the 'skylark' by early settlers, it sings as it soars, before parachuting to the ground, with its tail held up, emitting a series whirring notes. As is the case with many good songsters, it is a well-camouflaged bird when on the ground, creeping around the grass stems in its preferred white-grass habitat. Visitors travelling across the open grasslands of the islands will regularly disturb Falkland pipits, whereas stopping to look for this secretive species will often prove futile.

The **Falkland thrushes** can be found in a range of habitats from settlement gardens to tussac grass islands. Their loud song is a familiar sound in the Falkland spring as, perched on prominent song posts, they can be heard over the normal sounds of farm life. One of the largest land birds on the islands, they can be seen hopping around lawns or other areas of open grass as well as feeding under the fringes of mature tussac grass. The male shows a slightly darker head than that of the female, but both have rusty brown underparts with darker brown backs and tails. They are strong fliers, seeming to have no trouble in getting from one area to another even on the windiest of days. **Long-tailed meadowlarks**, on the other hand, are not such skilful fliers. The flailing of their wings keeps them airborne as they move from place to place in small flocks, but it is not uncommon to see one blown at great speed through the air on windy days.

The **black-throated finch**, the larger of the two finches on the islands, is the most widespread. Black-chinned siskins are rarely found far from the coast and prefer to nest in the hedges and bushes of many settlements. Black-throated finches have the appearance of a northern hemisphere bunting in that they are big-headed, long-tailed birds that feed by hopping along the ground with the body held in a horizontal posture. Found in a wide range of grassland and shrub habitats, including the perimeter of dense banks of tussac grass, the male and female black-throated finches were once thought to be two species as their appearance is so dissimilar. Males with their powder-blue/grey head, black eye and chin edged with white, with green in the wings, tail and belly, are a very different bird to the brown-streaked female. It is thought that this species was more common on the Falkland Islands before the introduction of cats, and the burning of white-grass in spring, which, whilst encouraging new grass growth for the sheep, destroys nesting habitats. The island race of black-throated finches has assumed increasing importance for the conservation of this species due to the decline in the southern South American race. The monotonous little ditty that is the song of the black-throated finches is one of the sounds of spring. Less frequently heard is the jangling song of the **black-chinned siskin** coming from the branches of a pine tree or echoing from deep within the tussac grass. The thin, piping call of the siskin is often the first clue that they are nearby, as they can be rather inconspicuous at times, despite the yellow and brown plumage of the male with his neat little black cap and chin. The female is a duller version of the male without any black on the head or chin.

House sparrows seem to fit in with the very 'Englishness' of Port Stanley and the larger settlements, where they have settled since their initial arrival from Montevideo in 1919. It appears that they hitched a ride on four different boats and only took a few years to spread around the major settlements of the islands. They seem to be able to cope with the windy weather on the Falkland Islands, but did decrease in number after the cold winter of 1995.

Migrants

Various other species of bird have been noted as reaching the islands since records began. Some, such as **sanderlings** and **cattle egrets** are reported most years, but a great many others are only recorded as very rare vagrants. Broadly speaking, these vagrants can be put into three main categories; firstly there are an increasing number of records of long-range North American migrants, which have 'overshot' the southern limit of their normal wintering range. The second group consists of species which are undertaking short-range migrations in South America and are then blown off course at a crucial moment during their flight. The third group includes the species, mostly seabirds, which breed well to the south of the islands but which come back into the Falkland waters at the onset of winter before returning south during the austral Spring. **Pectoral sandpiper** and **Baird's sandpiper** are good examples of the first group; **white-crested elaenia** and **fire-eyed duicon** correspond to the second category, whilst **southern fulmar**, **pintado petrel** and **grey-headed albatross** fulfil the criteria of the third category.

INSECTS

Insects are probably the least studied class of animal on the islands; many of those species that have been identified on the islands are beyond the scope of this guide. Some insects are easily found and are identifiable by the layman whilst others, more elusive, call for closer scrutiny. The **green spider** is one such species, which despite its wide distribution throughout the islands can often be hard to find. A search along a sheltered hedge or in a stand of *blechnum* fern in the lee of a rocky outcrop can usually bring to light a large-bodied spider with a bright green abdomen that has a pale, white, central stripe. Some may not be as brightly marked as others but inspection of other webs will often yield a better-coloured specimen. One of the largest insects on the Falkland Islands, and prey for several species of bird, is the **camel cricket**. In common with many insects that have adapted to survive in windy environments, these are wingless and reach up to one inch (2.5cm) long with legs and antennae that are almost double the body length.

Moths and butterflies are by far the most common insects encountered by the visitor to the Falkland Islands. Many species of moth, some of which have become flightless, are rather small and therefore difficult to find, but some of the larger species are strong fliers, fluttering around lights at night or dwelling in the vegetation. Careful examination of each specimen is needed to confirm its identity. Butterflies are scarcer and, until recently, only three species had been recorded on the islands. One of these, a pale blue butterfly, has been observed on several occasions over the years but never conclusively identified. The only species thought to breed on the islands is the **queen of Falklands fritillary**, which is a medium-sized, dull-orange butterfly with many small black marks forming a pattern towards the outer edge of each wing. This fast-flying butterfly is very difficult to approach or photograph, thus making it difficult to identify. In good years it is widely reported but in wet, cold years very few are recorded. Westerly winds between mid-summer and early autumn provide the right conditions for the arrival of the **southern painted lady**. Larger and more brightly marked than the fritillary, this fast-flying species is equally difficult to photograph. A fourth species has recently been added to the list of butterflies seen on the Falkland Islands; this is the **Brazilian painted lady**, which was first reported in the summer 1999–2000. This species is very similar to the southern painted lady and could possibly have been overlooked in the past as the more extensive black and white markings in the fore wing and the size of the two 'eyes' on the upper surface of the hind wing are not easy to see on this very mobile insect. When perched, it can be seen that the under wing has a much more defined pattern with two large 'eyes' and a blue subterminal line, both features absent from the southern painted lady.

SEASHELLS AND CRUSTACEA

A walk along the tideline will find a range of seashells thrown up by the last gale. The rough seas mean that many are broken up as they lie on the beach, but a careful search should find some complete shells. The best-represented family are the familiar limpet shells, of which the most numerous is the **common limpet** that can be found clinging to rocks in the intertidal zone or washed up on the strand line. Limpets are a favourite food of the blackish oystercatcher, which can often be found chiselling them off the rocks, either eating them on the spot or running the gauntlet of the marauding gulls to take them back to the nest for their young. One of the most attractive of the limpets is the rather delicately painted **keyhole limpet**, which is easily identified by the hole in the top of the shell and the reddish-orange lines that radiate to the edge. In sheltered waters where the sand is relatively undisturbed, **clams** may be found. These rather thick shells are found below the surface protecting the animal's body, which is a rarely exploited food source on the islands. Another species of bivalve that has been eaten by man are mussels, the largest of which, the **blue mussels**, can reach up to seven inches long (17cm), growing on kelp strands or piers and jetties. This species is washed ashore in large numbers to form piles of bleached shells at the top of the beach. By searching through the piles of shells left at the top of some of the beaches, the presence of a gastropod can be detected even if the shell is not present. The **rough thorn drupe** is a whelk which can grow to 2½ inches (6cm) long and which preys on many species of bivalves. If a fresh shell is found, the spike on the lower edge of the shell may still be present. It uses this spike to force open the shells of bivalves such as clams and mussels; its other method is to use its radula, a rough 'tongue', to rasp a hole in its prey's shell. Any shell presenting a small round hole has been the prey of the drupe. The complete shell of a **lobster krill** is rarely seen on the beach, and yet they leave their mark like no other creature. This ten-legged shrimp has the appearance of a small, red lobster and two of its 'legs' are tipped with pincers, the largest reaching some 2½ inches (6cm) long. These crustaceans are very common around the islands, feeding on the nutrients brought by the northward flowing Falkland Current. In turn they are the food for many of the birds and some of the animals that breed on the islands, especially towards summer's end, when they form vast swarms which sometimes tinge the sea with red. This red pigment takes quite some time to break down and can cause pink-coloured patches on the sand or stains in the droppings of seals and penguins.

CONSERVATION

The wildlife of the Falkland Islands attracts many tourists to the islands. The teeming seabird colonies and huge sea mammals that are found in magnificent scenery make the Falkland Islands an outstanding location. However, this special place is in need of special protection. The first law designed to protect the wildlife was the Wild Animals and Birds Protection Ordinance, which became law in 1913 and only applied to a few species. The complete banning of hunting of any fur seals followed this in 1921. Very little changed over the next 40 years until 1964 when the Bird Protection Ordinance was revised and nature reserves were established. The Nature Reserves Ordinance made it possible for the flora and fauna of certain habitats to be preserved. Wildlife reserves are sites with total protection where no farming is allowed, whilst the wildlife sanctuaries are on private land where wildlife is protected and farming allowed to continue. Probably the best-known wildlife reserves are Jason Islands, New Island and Kidney Island. The steady acquisition of small islands resulted in a total of over 50 wildlife reserves, some owned by the government, some owned by private individuals.

In 1980 a new conservation body, the Falkland Island Foundation, was formed. It has since merged with the Falkland Islands Trust to form Falkland Conservation. The late Sir Peter Scott conceived the idea of a conservation charity after a visit he and other conservationists made to the islands in 1979. Falkland Conservation is a charitable organisation concerned with protecting the unique wildlife of the Falkland Islands. It belongs to the global organisation BirdLife International, which is working to protect birds and their habitats, and to the World Conservation Union (IUCN). Research projects on seabirds, including penguins, are in progress to learn more about ecological factors and distribution, and also to monitor any threats to their populations. Based on its findings, Falkland Conservation advises the Falkland Islands Government on a wide range of issues affecting wildlife. This includes environmental assessments and how to protect any wildlife from potentially harmful developments. It is also involved in direct action such as organising beach cleans, rescuing oiled seabirds, planting tussac grass and rat-eradication programmes. Members of Falklands Conservation receive regular newsletters and a biannual journal, *The Warrah*. There is a youth section, which is part of the 'Wildlife Watch' run by the Wildlife Trusts in the United Kingdom, and which issues the newsletter, *Rocky's News*. The 1964 ordinances were replaced in 1999 by the Conservation of Wildlife and Nature Bill, which sought to ensure that the Falkland Islands Government met its international obligations under the Bonn, Ramsar or Biodiversity Conventions.

New Island, one of the best-known wildlife refuges on the islands, is divided into two: New Island North and New Island South. The northern part of the island is run as a private nature reserve whilst the southern part is recognised as a wildlife sanctuary and as such is no longer stocked. This is now the base of the New Island South Conservation Trust, a registered charity that aims to conserve the unique habitat on New Island and to encourage research into wildlife on the island by providing facilities for long-term field studies.

Black-crowned night heron

50

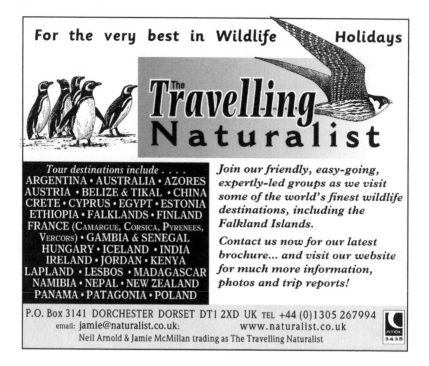

Practical Information

WHEN TO GO

To see the islands at their best it is advisable to plan a visit during the austral summer, October to April, when the tourist industry is geared up to ensure that visitors truly appreciate the archipelago, its wildlife and its way of life. The long summer evenings of December and January offer a welcome respite from winter in the northern hemisphere. It is possible to visit the islands at any time of year, however some of the accommodation closes out of season.

The reproductive cycles of the wild animals and birds may dictate when a visit to the Falklands is scheduled. Penguins are a major attraction and they, in common with many other breeding seabirds, are at their most vocal when displaying in the early months of the summer. Chicks abound in mid-summer. Southern elephant seals and southern sea lions can be seen throughout the tourist season, as can the scarce fur seal. The greatest concentrations of these impressive beasts are to be found during the pupping seasons in spring and mid-summer. Killer whales, although far from common, are best observed when the pups start leaving the beaches.

As is to be expected, the flora is much more impressive in springtime when the majority of plants are in bloom, however there are always some late spring and summer flowers, and several species produce attractive berries in the early autumn.

It is possible to come to the islands to fish for sea trout from September 1 to April 30, although September/October and mid-February to mid-April are thought to be the optimal times for this species. Falkland mullet are not so seasonably variable and can be caught throughout the fishing season.

HIGHLIGHTS/SUGGESTED ITINERARIES

Any visit to the Falklands would not be complete without going to some of the premier wildlife sites. It is not possible to do justice to the islands in a short stay. A minimum of two weeks is recommended in order to experience the authentic way of life on the archipelago. It is possible to see something of the islands in a brief visit, but that would only provide a frustratingly superficial glimpse of what the islands have to offer.

The wide range of accommodation available in **Port Stanley** makes this the ideal place to begin and end a visit to the Falkland Islands. There are now other places to stay within easy reach of the main airport at Mount Pleasant, such as Darwin, but the islands' tourist industry makes Port Stanley the focal point of any tour. Port Stanley has a far greater range of activities and entertainments than elsewhere, although there is much to be said in favour of the peace and quiet found in smaller settlements. Visiting groups tend to use Port Stanley as their base and visit three other islands later in their stay. Sea Lion Island Lodge, Pebble Island Hotel and Port Howard Lodge (East Falkland) are roughly similar in size and should be booked in advance to avoid the disappointment of missing any of these wonderful islands.

Any itinerary for a visit to the Falkland Islands should include a few days in Port Stanley. Exploring the town, its environs and the Falklands Islands Museum will require two or three days. Recommended day trips from Port Stanley include Gypsy Cove for a first glimpse of penguins and Volunteer Point for the majestic king penguins colony.

Sea Lion Island Lodge has some of the most spectacular wildlife right outside the door. Magellanic penguins can be heard calling to each other in the quiet of the night. A short walk in any direction from the lodge will bring the visitor in contact with elephant seals, sea lions, penguins and a range of other seabirds. It is possible to walk the whole island in a day, but a more leisurely approach would reveal so much more. As an introduction or a conclusion to a tour of the Falklands, Sea Lion Island is always enthralling.

A short flight away is **Port Howard Lodge** where it is possible to discover what living in *camp* is all about, whilst enjoying the hospitality of one of the best lodges on the islands. This working farm is set in some magnificent scenery and constitutes the ideal base to explore the wide expanses of West Falkland. The small museum next to the lodge gives another dimension to this settlement. The lodge is well known as one of the best centres for fishing on the Falkland Islands. Vast areas of West Falkland are now accessible from Port Howard thanks to the new road, and it is possible to be based here for several days whilst exploring the region. Recommended excursions include a boat trip to Narrows Island accompanied by the playful Commerson's dolphins, an outing to Fox Bay through some spectacular scenery to the wool mill and the penguin colonies, and a trip to the northwest of the island past Hill Cove and back through Turkey Rocks. Port Howard is a rather underestimated location as far as viewing the wildlife is concerned. Local trips will yield many breeding birds, including penguins at Fox Bay, as well as a typical selection of grassland and heathland flora, especially on Narrows Island.

Another short flight to the northwest brings the visitor to **Pebble Island**, where the various habitats shelter many of the bird species that breed on the Falkland Islands. The large pools on the eastern side are home to huge concentrations of waterfowl and the penguin rookeries are amongst the largest colonies seen on the islands. In recent years the presence of two rare species of penguin, the erect-crested penguin and the macaroni penguin, has meant that it has become one of the very few places in the world where six species of penguin can be observed in one day. It is possible to spend a minimum of three days on Pebble Island without returning to any of the wildlife sites, but a week would be preferable. This abundance of wildlife set in spectacular scenery, all within a short drive from a very relaxing hotel, makes this island a desirably integral part of any tour of the Falkland Islands.

These three locations combined with those that can be reached from Port Stanley make up the bare minimum of a trip to the islands. Other suggestions for the island-based visitor include at least two days on the fabulous **Carcass Island**, with its throngs of small birds, and **Saunders Island**, home to the magnificent black-browed albatross colony. Saunders Island can be visited as a day trip from Pebble Island if the idea of self-catering on Saunders Island does not appeal.

For passengers aboard one of the cruise ships which frequent the islands, any itinerary that includes Port Stanley, West Point Island and New Island is going to provide an excellent introduction to the Falkland Islands.

TOUR OPERATORS
Local tour operators
Four travel agents are based on the Falkland Islands. They will be happy to create a costed itinerary for a visit to the islands, including airport transfers, accommodation, local transport and excursions.

Falkland Islands Company Travel Services West Store, Stanley; tel: 27600; fax: 27603; email:fic@horizon.co.fk; web: www.the-falkland-islands-co.com.
International Tours & Travel Beauchene Shopping Centre, Stanley; tel: 22041; fax: 22042; email: int.travel@horizon.co.fk; web: www.tourism.org.fk/pages/int-tours-travel.htm; (Jennie Forrest).
Stanley Services Travel PO Box 117, Port Stanley; tel: 22622; fax: 22623; email: office@stanley-services.co.fk; web: www.tourism.org.fk/pages/stanley-services.htm; (Carole Bedford).
Sulivan Shipping Services Ltd PO Box 159, Stanley; tel: 22626/22627; fax: 22625; email:sulivan@horizon.co.fk; (John Pollard).

International tour operators
Many tour operators advertise trips to the Falkland Islands, of which the majority visit most of the wildlife sites. Some companies have a great deal more Falklands experience than others, which should be borne in mind when making enquiries.

UK
Wildlife tour companies
Animal Watch Granville House, London Rd, Sevenoaks, Kent TN13 1DL; tel: +44 (0)1732 741612; fax: +44 (0)1732 740736; (Sarah Gillem).
Avian Adventures 49 Sandy Rd, Norton, Stourbridge, West Midlands DY8 3AJ; tel: +44 (0)1384 372013; fax: +44 (0)1384 441340; email: aviantours@argonet.co.uk; web: avianadventures.co.uk; (Gerry Griffiths).
Birdquest Two Jays, Kemple End, Birdy Brow, Stonyhurst BB7 9QY; tel: +44 (0)1254 826317; fax: +44 (0)1254 826780; email: birders@birdquest.co.uk; web: www.birdquest.co.uk; (Mark Beaman).

Blue Planet Tours PO Box 40, BPT House, Rue du Closel, Vale, Guernsey GY1 3BD; tel: +44 (0)1481 266562; fax: +44 (0)7781 366562; email: info@bp-tours.com; web: www.bp-tours.com; (Tim Earl).

Field Studies Council Montford Bridge, Shrewsbury, Shropshire SY4 1HW; tel: +44 (0) 1743 850164; fax: +44 (0) 1743 850178; email: fscheadoffice@ukonline.co.uk; web: www.field-studies-council.org; (Anne Stephens).

Go Fishing Falklands/Windows on the Wild 2 Oxford House, 24 Oxford Rd North, London W4 4DH; tel: +44 (0)208 7421556; fax: +44 (0)208 747 4331; web: www.tourism.org.fk/windows-on-the-wild.com; (Maggi Smit).

Hosking Tours Pages Green House, Wetheringsett, Stowmarket, Suffolk IP14 5QA; tel: +44 (0)1728 861113; fax: +44 (0)1728 860222; (Davis Hosking).

Island Holidays Drummond St, Comrie, Perthshire PH6 2DS; tel: +44 (0)1764 670107; fax: +44 (0)1764 670958; email: enquiries@islandholidays.net; web: www.islandholidays.net; (Libby Weir-Breen).

Limosa Holidays Suffield House, Northrepps, Norfolk NR27 0LZ; tel: +44 (0)1263 578143; fax: +44 (0)1263 579251; email: limosaholidays@compuserve.com; (Chris Kightly).

Naturetrek Cheriton Mill, Cheriton, Alresford, Hampshire SO24 0NG; tel: +44 (0)1962 733051; fax: +44 (0)1962 736426; email: info@naturetrek.co.uk; web: www.naturetrek.co.uk; (David Mills).

Ornitholidays 29 Straight Mile, Romsey, Hampshire SO51 9BB; tel: +44 (0)1794 519445; fax: +44 (0)1794 523544; email: ornitholidays@compuserve.com; web: www.ornitholidays.co.uk; (Nigel Jones).

Photo Travellers PO Box 58, Godalming, Surrey GU7 2SE; tel: + 44 (0)1483 425448; fax: +44 (0)1483 419270; (Liz Ballard).

The Travelling Naturalist PO Box 3141, Dorchester, Dorset DT1 2XD; tel: +44 (0)1305 267994; fax: +44 (0)1305 265506; email: jamie@naturalist.co.uk; web: www.naturalist.co.uk; (Jamie McMillan).

Wildlife Adventures Sandpiper Rd, Whitstable, Kent CT5 4DP; tel: +44 (0)1227 275936; (Melyvn Crow).

Wildlife Worldwide 170 Selsdon Rd, South Croydon, Surrey CR2 6JP; tel: +44 (0)20 8667 9158; fax: +44 (0)20 8667 1960; email: sales@wildlifeworldwide.com; web: www.wildlifeworldwide.com; (Chris Breen).

Wildwings International House, Bank Rd, Kingswood, Bristol BS15 8LX; tel: 0117 965 8333; fax: 0117 937 5681; email: wildinfo@wildwings.co.uk; web: www.wildwings.co.uk.

Other tour companies
Falklands Experience 29 Queen's Rd, Weston-Super-Mare, Somerset BS23 2LH; tel: +44 (0)1934 622025; fax: +44 (0)1934 622025; email: MajorRonnie@aol.com; web: www.tourism.org.fk/feh.htm; (Major Ronnie Spafford).

Holt's Battlefield Tours Golden Key Building, 15 Market St, Sandwich, Kent CT13 9DA; tel: +44 (0)1304 612248; fax: +44 (0)1304 614930; (David Storrie).

European tour companies
All the following companies offer wildlife tours, except where stated.

Above and left Elephant seals,
Sea Lion Island (ww)

Below Sea lions (ww)

Above Black-browed albatross and tussac grass, West Point Island (ww)

Right King shag, New Island (ww)

Below Shags and penguins on New Island (ww)

Belgium

Discovery Expeditions I Herethoutseweg 142, PO Box 206, Herentals; tel: +32 14 22 49 01; fax: +32 14 22 63 24; email: discovery.expeditions@glo.be; (Geert Henau).

Denmark

Ibis Excursions Ganløseparken 46, Ganløse, 3660 Stenløse; tel: +45 48195940; fax: +45 48195945; email: jeffprice@ibis-excursions.dk; web: www.ibis-excursions.dk; (Jeff Price).

France

Chasse et Pêche 12 rue de Saussere, 75017 Paris; tel: +33 1 47 64 47 47; fax: +33 1 47 64 47 48; (Guy Geffroy). A fishing tour.

Natur'ailes 36 rue Lavoisier, 69120 Vaulx-La-Cote; tel: +33 72 04 43 22; fax: +33 72 04 09 01; (Yves Thonnereux).

Objectif Nature Chateau de Gillevoison, 91510 Janville sur Juine; tel: +33 1 60 82 22 29; fax: +33 1 39 31 01 19; (Alain Endewelt).

Grandnord-Voyage Nature 15 rue Cardinal Lemoine, 75005 Paris; tel: +33 1 40 46 05 14; fax: +33 1 40 26 73 20; (Dominique).

Germany

Duma Naturreisen Neckerstaden 4, 69117 Heidelberg; tel: +49 06 22 1 163020; fax: +49 06 22 1 166880; (Friedrich Neumann).

Windrose PO Box 110349, Berlin, Germany; tel: +49 30 20 17 21 0; fax: +49 30 20 17 21 17; (Michaela Wenig).

Natur-Studienreisen Untere Dorfstrasse 12, 37154 Northeim; tel: +49 05 55 1 99470; fax: +49 05 55 1 9944720; (Kerstin Sander).

Italy

Patagonia Trekking Via Le Chiuise 64, 10144 Turin; tel: +39 11 43 77 200; fax: +39 11 43 77 190; web: www.mistral.it/patagoniaworld; (Mauro Olivero).

Netherlands

Beluga Expeditions Martin Luther Kinglaan 282, 1111 LP Diemen; tel: +31 020 416 6230; fax: +31 020 698 2448; email: beluga.adventures@wxs.nl; (Jonneke Van Eijsden).

Thika Travel Kerkplein 6, Postbus 34, 2638 ZN, Kockengen; tel: +31 246 242526; fax: +31 346 242525; email: thika@knoware.nl; web: www.thika.nl; (Hilde Sanders).

Sweden

Aventyrsresor Flemington 68, Box 12168, S-102 24 Stockholm; tel: +46 8 654 11 55; fax: +46 8 650 41 53; (Thomas Bergenfeldt).

Switzerland

P & J Reisen Vorderstöckli 1, CH-6391 Engelberg; tel: +41 41 637 2402; fax: +41 41 637 3733; (Peter Pluss).

Arcatour, Bahnhofstrasse 23, Ch-6301 Zug; tel: +41 42 21 97 79; fax: +41 42 22 34 06; (Ruedi Bles).

American tour companies

Ladatco Tours 2220 Coral Way, Miami, FL 33145; tel: + 1 305 854 8422; fax: +1 305 285 9504; email: mds@ladatco.com; web: ladatco.com. Ladatco is the authorised US reservations office for the Falkland Islands.

Tread Lightly Travel Box 329, Juniper Meadow Rd, Washington Depot, CT 06794; tel: +1 860 868 1710; fax: +1 860 868 1718; email: patread@aol.com

Joe McDonald Wildlife Photography Inc 73 Loht Rd, McLure, PA 17841-9340; tel: +1 717 543 6423; fax: +1 717 543 6423; email: hoothollow@acsworld.net; web: www.hoothhollow.com.

Joseph Van Os Photo Safaris Joseph Van Os PhotoSafaris, PO Box 655, Vashon Island, WA 98070; tel: +1 206 463 5383; fax: +1 206 463 5484; email: info@photosafaris.com; web: www.photosafaris.com. Photo safaris.

Travel Wild Expeditions, Joseph Van Os PhotoSafaris, PO Box 655, Vashon Island, WA 98070; tel: +1 206 463 5383; fax: +1 206 463 5484; email: info@travelwild.com; web: www.travelwild.com. Natural history tours.

Cruise ships

An increasing number of visitors are reaching the islands on board the cruise ships that call in on their way to South Georgia and to the Antarctic. Cruises calling at the Falklands can be arranged through the following tour operators:

Abercrombie & Kent International Inc *USA* 1520 Kensington Rd, Oak Brook, Illinois 60523 2141; freephone +1 800 323 7308; tel: +1 630 954 2944; fax: +1 630 954 3324; email: info@abercrombie.com; web: www.abercrombie.com.
UK Sloane Square House, Holbein Place, London SW1W 8NS; tel: 0845 0700601; fax: 0845 0700607; email: info@abercrombiekent.co.uk; web: www.abercrombie.co.uk

Carriage Travel Services 722 Lima Rd, Fort Wayne, Indiana 46818, USA; tel: +1 219 489 3299; email: info@carriage-travel.com; web: www.carriage-travel.com.

Wildwings 577–579 Fishponds Rd, Fishponds, Bristol BS16 3AF, UK; tel: +44 (0)117 9658333; email: wildinfo@wildwings.co.uk; web: www.wildwings.co.uk.

Zegrahm Expeditions 192 Nickerson St #200, Seattle, WA 98109, USA; tel: +1 206 285 4000; fax: +1 206 285 5037; email: zoe@zeco.com; web: zeco.com.

RED TAPE

The Falkland Islands are relatively free of red tape apart from the usual entry formalities. All travellers arriving on the islands should have a valid passport, and visa if required, and return air tickets or evidence of prepaid onwards travel arrangements. The visa requirements are broadly the same as those for the UK. Visitors must also have sufficient funds to cover their stay on the islands and have pre-booked accommodation. Before the baggage is collected every passenger is gathered in the baggage-retrieval lounge to listen to a briefing on the current minefield situation. This includes displaying some of the mines that were used during the 1982 war and the general whereabouts of the minefields.

A Falkland Islands Departure Tax will be levied on the islands for those visitors who have not paid this in advance through their tour operator. At present the tax is £10.

One further restriction that the visitor should be aware of is that, as all the land on the Falkland Islands is privately owned, permission should be granted from the owner before crossing land for whatever reason.

Embassies

The Falkland Islands' status as an overseas territory belonging to Britain means that all diplomatic business is dealt with in London and as such the islands have no overseas embassies.

GETTING THERE AND AWAY
By air

There are two air routes to the Falkland Islands, from RAF Brize Norton in Oxfordshire, England or via commercial airlines to Santiago, Chile, then connecting with the LanChile flights via Punta Arenas to Stanley. The LanChile flights operate every Saturday. The Royal Air Force flights leave the UK six times during a four-week period. Typically this means leaving the UK on Sundays, Tuesdays and Thursdays and returning on the corresponding Tuesdays, Saturdays and Thursdays. This schedule may change during bank holiday periods. The RAF baggage allowance is 60lb, with any excess regarded as freight, only carried if there is space, and charged at £13.40/kg. The RAF flight takes 18 hours including a stopover of about two hours on Ascension Island, during which time the plane is refuelled and stocks of food are replenished. Four meals are provided during the flight, two in each leg of the journey. Travellers using the RAF flight are advised that, as this is not a commercial flight, it can be delayed or diverted. An overnight bag should be taken as hand luggage and any onward travel should take possible delays into consideration. On disembarking at Ascension Island all passengers are directed to a NAAFI lounge/compound where toilet facilities can be found and drinks are available from a small duty-free shop. No access is permitted to the plane until the call for boarding is relayed over the public-address system. During this brief stop on Ascension there is usually an announcement to the effect that those passengers wishing to make a donation to a charity box may get a rather impressive stamp in their passports. Travellers wishing to get such a stamp should remember to take their passports with them when they leave the plane.

If planning to travel independently on the RAF flight the visitor must deal directly with the travel co-ordinator at the Falkland Islands Government office in London. Full information and a travel form can be obtained from this office: Travel Co-ordinator, Falkland Islands Government Office, 14 Broadway, London SW1H OBH; tel: +44 (0)20 7222 2542; fax: +44 (0)20 7222 2375. Tourists from outside the UK can board the LanChile flight in Santiago, via Puerto Montt and Punta Arenas to the Falkland Islands. The monthly link via Argentina calls at Rio Gallegos on its way to the islands, returning one week later. Connecting with the LanChile service is a FIGAS flight from Mount Pleasant to Port Howard on West Falkland, and on to Pebble Island. This flight is designed to give short-stay visitors the maximum time with the wildlife, and must be pre-booked with FIGAS or with one of the local tour operators.

By sea

It is also possible to book passage on the islands' freight vessel the *Tamar*. They offer a limited passenger service on their scheduled trips to and from Punta Arenas in Chile. Contact Lewis Clifton at Byron Marine Limited, No 3 'H' Jones Road, Byron House, Stanley, Falkland Islands; tel: 22245; fax: 22246; email: byron@horizon.co.fk.

HEALTH

No inoculations are required when planning a visit to the islands. However, those passengers travelling on the RAF flights are recommended by the Ministry of Defence to be inoculated against yellow fever in case the flight has to be diverted to a yellow fever risk area. Visitors travelling to the islands via South America should consult their doctor as to which inoculations they may require. It also makes good sense to be up to date with a tetanus jab (ten yearly). The hospital in Stanley has qualified doctors, dentists and other medical staff to cope with any contingencies. The islands' water supply is safe to drink.

SAFETY

The Falkland Islands must be one of the safest places for the single traveller to visit. Crime is relatively unknown; muggings and pickpockets belong to another world. The friendly islanders will often go out of their way to assist the visitor. The one question often asked about the islands concerns minefields and any other military activity. Apart from a few vehicles in Stanley, occasional planes and helicopters, the military presence is more or less confined to the area around Mount Pleasant. Life on the islands carries on pretty much as it always has done. The image of the Falkland Islands and minefields is unfortunately engraved on public consciousness outside the islands. The total mined area is a minuscule part of the islands, only affecting patches around Stanley and smaller fields at Goose Green, Fitzroy, Fox Bay and Port Howard. All minefields are clearly marked and fenced off. Islanders quite rightly point out that no civilian has yet been injured by mines or any unexploded device since the minefields were laid by Argentinian troops in 1982.

Driving on the islands is a unique experience whether it is over the *camp* or along the modern road network. There have been accidents along the road between MPA and Stanley, mostly due to excessive speed on a loose surface. Driving along this road, with its deep roadside ditches, in windy conditions demands a great deal of concentration. The well-concealed boggy areas have trapped many a vehicle passing over the *camp*, and local knowledge can save a lot of hard digging.

WHAT TO TAKE

To experience what the Falkland Islands have to offer means spending a lot of time outdoors. The weather changes rapidly, making a waterproof coat, a hat or hood, and several layers of clothing essential. The wind dominates during the summer, which must be borne in mind when preparing clothes for the trip. A good pair of shoes or walking boots is very necessary, as the ground can be uneven and slippery in some locations. A lightweight pair of waterproof trousers is a useful inclusion. Away from Stanley it is customary to have a light pair of shoes to wear indoors, leaving the outdoor shoes by the door. The strong sunshine on the islands can very quickly burn unprotected skin, so a high factor suncream and lipsalve should be packed. All personal medical supplies and toiletries should be brought with the visitor, as supplies may well be limited on the islands. Camera films and batteries can sometimes be difficult to obtain, especially after a cruise ship has called in, so the visitor is advised to bring all they require. Most of the wildlife is very tame, but although binoculars are almost redundant at times, they do make a tremendous difference in getting the best views. Many of the hotels and lodges have a limited supply of reading material.

MONEY

The Falkland Islands pound is equivalent to one pound sterling. The notes and coins are similar to those used in the UK but each has its own design. It is possible to use British money on the islands, as the two currencies are interchangeable. Exchange facilities are available at the only bank on the islands, The Chartered Bank on Ross Road, Stanley. Travellers' cheques are accepted here and at many other commercial outlets. Mastercard and Visa can be used at an increasing number of outlets on the islands. It is important to bear in mind that there is no cash machine, although the bank will give cash against credit cards with proof of identification. Some other credit cards such as Amex, Eurocard and Diners cards can be used at selected outlets. UK cheques, with guarantee cards, can be used on the islands, although a charge of £2 is made for processing each transaction. Falkland Island currency is not readily exchangeable outside the islands; it is therefore a good idea to make sure you are not still in possession of any when you leave.

GETTING AROUND
By air

Travelling around the islands is much easier than it was prior to the early 1980s. The quickest way to get between the islands and settlements is by air on the Falkland Islands Government Air Service (FIGAS). These planes operate from their base at Stanley Airport and can take up to eight passengers plus pilot, although many airstrips are only capable of accepting planes with a reduced number of passengers. Luggage is limited to 30lb (14kg) per passenger. Schedules are organised on a day-to-day basis depending upon demand. There are usually at least two flight times starting from Stanley, at 08.00 and then again in mid-morning, using the three planes. The flight schedules are announced on the radio on the evening before or can be obtained by using 'faxback' from FIGAS on 27500. Contact FIGAS, Port Stanley Airport, East Falkland, Falkland Islands; tel: 27219; fax: 27309; email: figas.fig@horizon.co.fk.

By sea

It is possible to travel between the islands onboard the *Tamar FI*, the inter-island cargo vessel operated by Byron Marine. This ship has two twin berths, which are much in demand, so early booking is essential. The shipping schedule is usually established a few weeks prior to departure. Contact Lewis Clifton at Byron Marine Limited, No 3 'H' Jones Road, Byron House, Stanley, Falkland Islands; tel: 22245; fax: 22246; email: byron@horizon.co.fk

At present there is only one boat equipped to take the visitor around the islands. The *Golden Fleece* is a 65ft (19.5m) steel ocean-going yacht that can sleep eight. This boat has spent a lot of time with film crews on board in the Falklands and in South Georgia but also does tourist cruises around both archipelagos. The skipper, Jerome Poncet, has had 20 years' experience in these waters.

Contact Jerome Poncet, Southern Latitude Trading Ltd, Beaver Island, Falkland Islands; tel/fax: 42316; email: golden-fleece@horizon.co.fk; web: www.tourism.org.fk/pages/fleece.htm.

By land

The improved road network now links most of the major settlements on the islands; all others can be reached by traditional routes over the *camp*. The visitor to Darwin, Pebble Island, Port Howard and Sea Lion can be transported by the lodges' four-wheel drive vehicles.

Taxis

Taxis can be used around Port Stanley and to Mount Pleasant:

Stanley Cabs tel: 22600
Lowe's Taxis tel: 21381

Transfers between Mount Pleasant and Stanley connecting with the RAF and LanChile flights are available from Falkland Islands Tours and Travel, Stanley, Falkland Islands; tel/fax: 21775; email: astewart@horizon.co.fk.

Car hire

It is possible to hire self-drive four-wheel-drive vehicles from the following companies:

The Falkland Islands Company Ltd Crozier Place, Stanley, East Falkland; tel: 27600; email: fic@horizon.co.fk
Jeff and Tracy Porter tel/fax: 21574; email: tporter@horizon.co.fk.
Ian Bury 63 Davis St, Stanley; tel: 21058; fax: 22643

Drivers with an overseas licence are allowed to drive for up to 12 months.

ACCOMMODATION

The accommodation of the islands varies from hotels, to guesthouses, to self-catering and camping. The rates charged vary according to season, so each establishment should be contacted to confirm charges at the proposed time of travel. The Falkland Islands Tourist Board has divided the accommodation into three groups according to cost: over £60 per night, between £31 and £60 per night, and under £30 per night. These are listed below as expensive, moderate and inexpensive respectively. For accurate up-to-date prices contact the establishments concerned.

Expensive
Upland Goose Hotel 20/22 Ross Rd, Stanley; tel: 21455; fax: 21520; email: fic@horizon.co.fk.
Malvina House Hotel 3 Ross Rd, Stanley; tel: 21355; fax: 21357; email: malvina@horizon.co.fk.
Sea Lion Lodge Sea Lion Island; tel: 32004; fax: 32003; email: sealion_lodge@horizon.co.fk.

Moderate
Dolphins Guest House 46 John St, Stanley; tel/fax: 22950; email: fprintz@horizon.co.fk.
Emma's Guesthouse 36 Ross Rd, Stanley; tel: 21056; fax: 21573; email: emmas@horizon.co.fk.
Sparrowhawk Guesthouse 7 Drury St, Stanley; tel: 21979; fax: 21980.
Darwin House Darwin, East Falkland; tel: 32255; fax: 32253.
Port Howard Lodge Port Howard; tel/fax: 42187; Guest phone: 25125; email: rlee@horizon.co.uk.
Pebble Island Hotel Pebble Island; tel: 41093; Guest pay phone: 25127.

Inexpensive
Kay McCallum's 14 Drury St, Stanley; tel: 21071.
Sue Binnie's 3 Brandon Rd, Stanley; tel: 21051.
Scotia House 12 St Mary's Walk; tel: 21191; fax: 22434.
Hilary Pauloni's 63 Fitzroy Rd, Stanley; tel: 21079. Non-smoking.
Tenacres Stanley; tel: 21155; fax: 21950; email: tenacres@horizon.co.fk. Non-smoking.

Accommodation in camp
There is a wide range of accommodation in *camp* in this price band. Serviced accommodation is available on some islands, otherwise accommodation is self-catering. For individual details see relevant chapter.

Carcass Island West Falklands; tel: 41106; fax: 41107.
Weddell Island West Falkland; tel: 42398 ; fax: 42399.
Saunders Island West Falkland; tel: 41298; fax: 42196; email: davidpe@horizon.co.fk.
West Lagoons Farm Hill Cove, West Falkland; tel: 41194. A self-catering caravan is proposed for this location in the 2000–2001 season.

Holiday cottages
East Falkland
Home Farm Douglas Station, East Falkland; tel/fax: 31109.

Smylies Farm Port San Carlos, East Falklands; tel: 41013. Full board accommodation is also available at the farmhouse.
Salvador Lodge Gibraltar Station, East Falkland; tel: 31199; fax: 31194.
The Pod Port San Carlos, East Falkland; tel: 41018; fax: 41019. Two other self-catering options are nearby.
The Garden House Port Louis, East Falkland; tel: 31060; fax: 31061.
North Arm Farm East Falkland; tel: 32080; fax: 32081.

Basic houses are also available for rent at North West Arm, Danson Harbour and Fanny Cove all on North Arm Farm from the same address for £10 per person per night.

West Falkland
Crooked Inlet Farm West Falkland; tel: 41102.

Camping
There are no official campsites on the Falkland Islands. Camping is permitted in certain areas but only with the owner's permission. Some areas of a farm may well be out of bounds during the lambing season. Campers are usually required to be completely self-sufficient. Certain guidelines should be obeyed, and any further requests by the owners.

- No fires should be lit for any reason.
- Cooking should be on a paraffin or gas cooker and never be left unsupervised when lit. Fire can be very destructive in the dry grasslands and can burn for many years in peat.
- Gates are always to be left as they are found.
- Farm animals must never be approached or disturbed in any way.
- All litter must be removed upon leaving the site.
- Vehicles should not leave the track without permission.
- Information on destination and length of trip should be given before departure.

Areas available for camping include:

Salvador Lodge Gibraltar Station, East Falkland; tel: 31199; fax: 31194.
Port Sussex Farm, East Falkland; tel: 32203; fax: 32204; email: psussex@horizon.co.fk.
Estancia Farm East Falkland; tel: 31042.
Rincon Grande Farm East Falkland; tel: 31119; fax: 31149.
Bold Cove Farm Bold Cove, West Falkland; tel: 42178; fax: 42177.
Port Stephens Farm West Falkland; tel: 42307; fax: 42304. For safety reasons arrivals and departures must be announced beforehand to the owners. All visitors must arrive by land or sea. Vehicles are not permitted off-road. Some areas are out of bounds in the lambing season.
Saunders Island West Falkland; tel: 41298; fax: 42196; email: davidpe@horizon.co.fk.
Spring Point Farm West Falkland; tel: 42001. There is no road so all arrivals and departures must be by sea or air.

FALKLAND ISLANDS COUNTRYSIDE CODE

1 Always ask permission before entering private land.
2 Keep to paths wherever possible. Leave gates open or shut as you find them.
3 Be aware of the high fire risk throughout the islands. Be extra careful if smoking. Take cigarette butts away with you.
4 * Do not drop litter. Take your rubbish home with you.
5 Do not disfigure rocks or buildings.
6 * Do not touch, handle, injure or kill any wild bird or other animal.
7 Never feed wild animals.
8 Always give animals the right of way. Remember not to block the routes of seabirds and seals coming ashore in their colonies.
9 Try to prevent any undue disturbance to wild animals. Stay on the outside of bird and seal colonies. Remain at least 6m (20ft) away. When taking photographs or filming stay low to the ground. Move slowly and quietly. Do not startle or chase wildlife from resting or breeding areas.
10 * Some plants are protected and should not be picked. Wildflowers are there for all to enjoy and they should be left where they are found.
11 *Whalebones, skulls, eggs or other such items may not be exported from the Falkland Islands. They should be left where they are found.

*Such actions (with few special exceptions) may constitute an offence in the Falkland Islands and could result in fines up to £3,000.

Adopted for the Falkland Islands from guidelines adopted by members of IAATO, South Georgia Management Plan, Galápagos Rules for Preservation and the Code of Conduct for visitors to the Antarctic.

Four farms owned by **Falkland Landholdings Ltd** allow camping. As above, permission must be granted by the manager. These farms are at:

Goose Green Farm Goose Green, East Falkland; tel: 32270; fax: 32271.
North Arm Farm North Arm, East Falkland; tel: 32080; fax: 32081.
Fitzroy Farm Fitzroy, East Falkland; tel: 32384; fax: 32383.
Walker Creek Farm Walker Creek, East Falkland; tel: 32486; fax: 32485.

Further details of the accommodation listed above can be viewed at the **Falkland Islands Tourist Board** website at: www.tourism.org.fk.

EATING AND DRINKING
The food on the islands is very British in character with much use made of the homegrown vegetables, local lamb, mutton, beef and fish. Portions are habitually on the generous side with 'smoko' – home made cakes and biscuits with tea or coffee – being taken in the gaps between meals. Outside of Port

Stanley there is nowhere to eat out other than the lodges and the larger guesthouses, and then only by prior arrangement. The range of places to go out for a meal in Stanley is changing all the time, from à la carte through to fish and chips and bar lunches.

All of the lodges are licensed and stock a good range of beers, wines and spirits. The same can be said for the hotels in Stanley. There are also six pubs in Stanley, which are open between 10.00 and 23.00 on Monday to Thursday, between 10.00 and 23.30 on Friday and Saturday and between 12.00 and 14.00, and again between 18.00 and 22.30, on Sundays. All drink is imported into the islands. Despite the transport costs, drinks are not as expensive as might be expected due to the differing tax levy between the islands and the UK, the main source of the imported drink. Draught beer was brewed on the islands for a short while in the late 1980s but this brewery has since closed down.

PUBLIC HOLIDAYS

Public holidays are on:

January 1		December 8	Battle Day
Good Friday		December 25	Christmas Day
April 21	Queen's Birthday	December 26	Boxing Day
June 14	Liberation Day	December 27	Christmas
August 14	Falkland Day		Sports Day

The other major sports event, West Falkland Sports, takes place around Easter time.

PLACES OF WORSHIP

The Anglican services are held in the Christ Church Cathedral on Ross Road every Sunday. Holy Communion is at 08.00, Family service/Communion and the Sunday School is at 10.00. Evensong is at 19.00. The cathedral is open daily between 08.00 and 17.00.

The Tabernacle of the United Free Church is in Barrack Street; this blue and white church is a short walk up the hill from the western end of the Post Office. Services are held on the first and second Sundays of each month at 10.00, and at 19.00 on the third and fourth Sundays.

St Mary's, the Roman Catholic Church, is the white building with the red roof opposite the Post Office on Ross Road. Weekday services are held at 09.00 and those on Sunday are held at 10.00.

The Kingdom Hall for Jehovah's Witnesses is in Dean Street; for further information call 21267.

For details of meetings of the Baha'i Faith contact M Smallwood, their secretary, on telephone number 21031.

SHOPPING

As would be expected for such a small community, the opportunities for shopping are not as highly developed as in more heavily populated areas. There is however a wide range of goods aimed at the tourist market on sale in Stanley.

They range from the expected postcards, T-shirts, baseball hats and other clothing, through a range of cuddly toys (mainly penguins), to jewellery, paintings, drawings, leatherwork, local handicraft and other mementoes. Not to be forgotten are the knitwear shop (formerly at Port Howard but now in Stanley) and the wool mill and associated shop at Fox Bay. Most of the larger lodges have a range of postcards, T-shirts and other articles for sale. Falkland stamps are a popular item with their associated first-day cover and other philatelic items.

Basic provisions can be bought in the larger food stores in Stanley or in the stores in the larger settlements.

ARTS AND ENTERTAINMENT

Probably the best-known of the artists on the islands is James Peck, who has his studio and gallery on St Mary's Walk in Stanley. A look around the shops will see many other examples of local artwork on display or for sale. An annual craft fair is held in the latter part of the winter, July or August, outside of the usual tourist season. A great deal of locally made craftwork can be found on sale in Stanley. The other annual display is the Horticultural Show, which takes place in Stanley at the end of February or in early March. Entertainment on the islands is typical of that of a small British town with a variety of clubs and organisations covering many aspects of community life. The recent advent of television on the islands does not seem to have reduced the number of islanders listening to the local radio for their entertainment and news. In the absence of a cinema, video rental has been popular for several years.

PHOTOGRAPHY

The light on the Falkland Islands can be a photographer's dream, illuminating the clear blue skies, the deep blue sea and the abundant wildlife. Not every day is like that of course, but there are plenty of photographic opportunities. The most frequently heard comments made by professional photographers visiting the islands indicate that they are glad they brought plenty of film and that avoiding dust was very important on windy days. When taking photographs it is very important to admire the wildlife from a respectful distance. The guidelines suggested by Falkland Conservation are to be obeyed at all times.

Spare batteries can sometimes be bought on the islands but cannot be guaranteed, and the same is true for film, lens caps, filters etc. The ability of the wildlife to change from one photogenic pose to another is legendary and consumes great quantities of film. Long lenses are not really very useful for most of the local wildlife, although they can have their uses for taking close-ups of seabirds. Wide-angle lenses are very useful, as there are many magnificent panoramas that would make superb photographs. A good lens cloth and a dusting brush are essential on the islands. As the visitor is rarely far from the sea, salt spray is another problem to be considered.

Visitors bringing video cameras to the islands will have just as much to film. Much of the wildlife is very lively, whether it be squabbling elephant seals, baby penguins or just the sea crashing on the shore. Wind noise can be a problem with some video cameras.

HINTS ON PHOTOGRAPHY
Nick Garbutt and John Jones

All sorts of photographic opportunities present themselves in the islands, from simple holiday snaps to that one-off encounter with a blue iguana. For the best results, give some thought to the following tips.

As a general rule, if it doesn't look good through the viewfinder, it will never look good as a picture. Don't take photographs for the sake of taking them; be patient and wait until the image looks right.

Photographing **people** is never easy and more often than not it requires a fair share of luck. If you want to take a portrait shot of a stranger, it is always best to ask first. Focus on the eyes of your subject since they are the most powerful ingredient of any portrait, and be prepared for the unexpected.

There is no mystique to good **wildlife** photography. The secret is getting into the right place at the right time and then knowing what to do when you are there. Look for striking poses, aspects of behaviour and distinctive features. Try not only to take pictures of the species itself, but also to illustrate it within the context of its environment. Alternatively, focus in close on a characteristic which can be emphasised.

Photographically, the eyes are the most important part of an animal – focus on these, make sure they are sharp and try to ensure they contain a highlight.

Look at the surroundings – there is nothing worse than a distracting twig or highlighted leaf lurking in the background. Getting this right is often the difference between a mediocre and a memorable image.

A powerful flashgun adds the option of punching in extra light to

MEDIA AND COMMUNICATIONS
Newspapers and broadcasting

There are two weekly newspapers, *Penguin News* and *Teaberry Express*. The Falkland Island Broadcasting Station based in Stanley operates 24 hours a day, and coverage includes world and local news, music, and sports programmes. The daily flight times for the Falkland Island Government Air Service planes are announced twice a day. This radio station runs in conjunction with the British Forces Broadcasting Service (BFPS) and the Services Sound and Vision Corporation (SSVC) on 550kHz AM and 96.5MHz FM. Television reception is now possible in the islands, either by direct satellite or via the military base at Mount Pleasant. Videos are popular and are available for rent in Stanley.

Telephones

The telephone system on the islands is maintained by Cable and Wireless plc, which also provides direct dialling worldwide via satellite linkage. There are no mobile phone networks on the islands at present. The 2m VHF network, which operates in a similar way to CB radio, is still used in *camp* although less transform an otherwise dreary picture. Artificial light is no substitute for natural light, though, so use it judiciously.

Getting close to the subject correspondingly reduces the depth of field. At camera-to-subject distances of less than a metre, apertures between f16 and f32 are necessary to ensure adequate depth of field. This means using flash to provide enough light. If possible, use one or two small flashguns to illuminate the subject from the side.

Landscapes are forever changing, even on a daily basis. Good landscape photography is all about good light and capturing mood. Generally the first and last two hours of daylight are best, or when peculiar climatic conditions add drama or emphasise distinctive features. Never place the horizon in the centre – in your mind's eye divide the frame into thirds and exaggerate either the land or the sky.

Film

If you're using conventional film (as against a digital camera), select the right film for your needs. Film speed (ISO number) indicates the sensitivity of the film to light. The lower the number, the less sensitive the film, but the better quality the final image. For general print film, ISO 100 or 200 fit the bill perfectly. If you are using transparencies for home use or for lectures, then again ISO 100 or 200 film is fine. However, if you want to get your work published, the superior quality of ISO 25 to 100 film is best.

• Try to keep your film cool. Never leave it in direct sunlight.
• Don't allow fast film (ISO 800 and above) to pass through X-ray machines.
• Under weak light conditions use a faster film (ISO 200 or 400).

so in Stanley in recent years. A licence, available from the post office, is required to operate this equipment.

Internet

Email is slowly taking over from fax as a means of sending messages around the islands and to the outside world. The majority of the larger businesses and accommodation now use email. An internet café has been set up in Stanley, The Hard Disc Café, where islanders and visitors can send email, have access to the internet and use other services such as photocopying.

BUSINESS

The opportunities to set up a business are limited by the number of residents on the islands (currently just over two thousand), and the lack of premises. Jobs that cannot be filled from local resources by the Falkland Island Government are advertised in the UK. These positions are usually skilled technical or professional posts; the successful applicant is employed on contract terms on a supplemented salary.

CULTURAL DOS AND DON'TS
The islands are very British in character and have no major cultural differences from the UK. Living in a small community means there is a high level of respect for other people and their property. If visitors have a problem, the islanders will do their best to help them.

LOCAL CHARITIES
Most of the charity work on the islands concerns wildlife and environmental conservation. The best known is **Falkland Conservation**, which has offices in London but is based in Port Stanley. The office on Ross Road in Stanley has items for sale, welcomes all callers and is interested in any wildlife sightings of note. Their London Offices are at 1 Princes Avenue London, N3 2DA. By joining the charity the visitor is helping to protect the islands' wildlife and aiding the wide range of research work that is being undertaken by Falklands Conservation. The other charity with a wildlife-based remit is the **New Island South Conservation Trust**. Based on New Island, this organisation seeks to increase awareness of the penguins, albatrosses and many other species of bird that breed locally.

Part Two

The Guide

Long-tailed meadowlark

70

Port Stanley

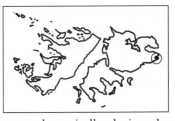

Port Stanley is probably the smallest and most remote capital city in the world. It was situated on a north-facing slope in order to catch the sun throughout the year. The official existence of Port Stanley began in July 1845, when the islands' capital was moved from Port Louis to an area originally called Jackson's Harbour. It grew dramatically during the Californian gold rush in the mid-1800s and this boom lasted until the 1890s. Subsequently Port Stanley has continued to be the commercial centre of the islands and the main port of access. There was heavy fighting in and around Port Stanley during the 1982 war. Since the war the capital city has dramatically increased in size in direct proportion to the revenue derived from the newly established fishing industry. The history of Port Stanley is perhaps best illustrated by the shipwrecks that are dotted along the seafront. A wide range of architectural styles prevails in the city, ranging from the magnificent Christ Church Cathedral, to Jubilee Villas, to the new hospital and school. Upland geese and Falkland flightless steamer ducks frequent the waterfront, whilst turkey vultures and kelp gulls glide over the city. It is also one of the few places on the islands where house sparrows, introduced during the 19th century, have remained plentiful. Port Stanley is where many Falkland holidays start and finish, and therefore it has a good selection of accommodation and tour operators able to cater to visitors' tastes and interests.

HISTORY

Port Stanley originates from the instruction of Lord Stanley, the British Secretary of State, to Governor Moody at Port Louis, to investigate the potential of Port William as the location of a new town. Captain Ross of the Ross Antarctic Expedition made a comprehensive survey of the area and informed Governor Moody that Port William had a good deep-water harbour, which would easily be accessible to the Royal Navy fleet. The sheltered waters of Jackson's Harbour were deemed suitable for the new port. Work was initiated in July 1843 and was finally completed on July 18 1845. At Governor Moody's suggestion, the capital was renamed in honour of the Secretary of State, and so Port Stanley came into being. Local opinion was not completely in favour of this choice, one contemporary quote describing the area as 'the most miserable bog hole' in the islands. By 1849 the population had risen to 200 souls. These residents became increasingly affluent on account of the high prices they could charge for repairing ships that had been damaged on the fierce Cape Horn route. Ships were then forced into the Falklands in search of the nearest port with facilities to repair large vessels. During the California gold rush, and also the ensuing Australian rush, business boomed as many unseaworthy ships were forced to take shelter in the islands. Provisioning of these boats was another facet of the growing prosperity of the port. Among these general merchantmen were Welsh barques that had taken coal to South America and were then returning to Swansea or Cardiff laden with copper ore. Port Stanley was one of the busiest ports in the South Atlantic at this time. By the 1890s the numbers of sailing vessels calling into the harbour began to decrease with the introduction of the more reliable steamships. The completion of the Panama Canal in the early 1900s reduced the amount of traffic that had to round Cape Horn, therefore drastically reducing the numbers that needed to call in for repair. Whaling and sealing activities around the islands and in adjacent seas meant a different type of vessel used the harbour around the turn of the century.

High wool prices in the early 20th century led to a demand for fleeces from the Falkland Islands. These were brought in from the outlying farms before being sent to their final destination from Port Stanley. The port experienced a large number of ship movements during and after the Argentinian invasion in 1982. The floating hotels, known as 'coastels', used by the military to accommodate their forces after the war, prior to the construction of the new base at Mount Pleasant, ensured there was plenty of activity in the port. The introduction of the Falkland Islands Interim Conservation and Management Zone (FICZ) on February 1 1987, which extends for 200 nautical miles around the islands, has resulted in many more ship movements in Port Stanley. Vessels have to visit the islands to collect local fishing licences, to fetch provisions, to visit agents and to land some of their catch. The licensing of survey work investigating hydrocarbon deposits near the islands may well lead to increased shipping activity in Port Stanley.

The capital continued to expand on land in step with the escalation of traffic in the harbour. Population growth entailed the need for more fuel. Peat was cut in progressively greater quantities from the hillside behind the town. A severe winter in 1879 covered the ground with snow between May and August. The citizens awoke around midnight on November 29th to find that thawing snow had flooded the peatbogs, causing a moving mass of peat, 4ft (1.2m) in depth, to gush through the town. The avalanche of peat swept away everything in its path from its genesis to the east of the town down to the sea. Miraculously, nobody was killed. All communications between east and west Stanley were severed. The only means of contact was by boat. It took a week to dig a trench at the back of the hill in order to drain the water from the peat workings. Water retention in this area remained a problem for some years. On June 2 1886 a second landslide occurred. As with the first slip, a large mass of saturated peat broke off from ridge above the town and made its uncontrollable descent, demolishing all buildings or filling them with turf before pouring into the harbour. Remarkably, despite the fact that this second slip was also at night, only two lives were lost. The most notable building to be washed away was the Exchange Building, which had been used as a school and a church. Christ Church Cathedral, consecrated in 1892 and completed in 1903, now occupies the site of that building.

GETTING THERE

Port Stanley can be reached by land, sea or air. The majority of visitors who reach the capital do so via the cruise ships that call in at the islands. They anchor in the harbour or out in Port William. Visitors are then ferried ashore to land at the Public Jetty midway along the seafront. It is also possible to arrive from Chile on board the ship *Tamar*, run by Byron Marine. Although there are various overland routes to Port Stanley, most modern traffic uses the all-weather road, which leaves the town to the south and leads on around the slopes of Sapper Hill. This is the route used to reach the military base and international airport at Mount Pleasant (more usually referred to as MPA) and all other destinations on East Falkland. The drive from Stanley to the airport takes an hour through typical Falkland habitat.

Visitors landing on the islands from overseas airports can only do so at Mount Pleasant. The airport at Port Stanley is used for internal flights by the Falkland Island Government Air Service (FIGAS). This service is used to transport people and goods all over the islands, and is therefore the only practical way for visitors to travel around the islands. The Islander aircraft have a capacity of eight passengers with a luggage limit of 30lb (14kg) per passenger. Stanley Airport has a hard surface but other landing strips may be on grass or on the beach, thus requiring a reduced payload. Consequently, tourists travelling in groups around the islands may well be put in more than one plane and therefore reach Stanley at different times. The airport is a ten-minute drive to the east of the town.

GETTING AROUND

Port Stanley occupies such a small area that it is possible to walk the length and breadth of the town in one day and still have time to explore.

Taxis

Taxis can be ordered for those who do not wish to walk.

Stanley Cabs Tel: 22600.
Lowe's Taxi Service Tel: 21381.

Car hire

It is possible to hire vehicles, mostly Land Rovers, in Stanley but they are usually limited to travel on the made up roads and are not for *camp* driving.

Ian Bury 63 Davis St, Stanley; tel: 21058; fax: 22643.
Falkland Island Company Tel: 27679; fax: 27679; (Stephen Luxton).
Tracy Porter 5 Jeremy Moore Av, Port Stanley; tel/fax: 21574.

LOCAL TOUR OPERATORS
Several tour operators based in Stanley offer motorised guided tours, whether to explore the town or to make excursions around East Falkland.

Discovery Tours Fieldhouse Close, Port Stanley; tel: 21027; fax: 22304; email: discovery@horizon.co.fk; (Tony Smith). General, wildlife, battlefield tours and filming.
Montana Short 4 Dairy Paddock Rd, Port Stanley; tel/fax: 21076. General, wildlife, fishing and photographic tours. Also walking tours.
Ten Acre Tours PO Box 48, Port Stanley; tel: 21155; fax: 21950; email: tenacres@horizon.co.fk; (Sharon Halford). General and wildlife tours.
Hebe Tours Tel/fax: 21561; email: nrowlands@horizon.co.fk; (Neil Rowlands). Fishing and wildlife tours.
South Atlantic Marine Services Ross Rd, Port Stanley; tel: 21145; fax: 22674; email: sams@horizon.co.fk; (Dave and Carol Eynon). Vehicle and boat excursions, wildlife and diving trips.
Seaview Tel: 22669; fax: 22670; email: seaview.sawle@horizon.co.fk. Boat trips around harbour and beyond to Kidney Island, Sparrow Cove and Port Harriet Point.

WHERE TO STAY
Hotels
Of the many places to stay in Port Stanley, the two largest are the Upland Goose Hotel and the Malvina House Hotel. Both are situated on Ross Road, which means that they have uninterrupted views over Stanley Harbour. The older of the two is the Upland Goose Hotel, originally called the Eagle Inn, then Ship Hotel, before assuming its present identity in 1969. It is the best-known hotel in the islands. The Malvina House Hotel, named after Malvina Felton who lived in the original Malvina House in the1890s, opened as a hotel in 1983 and has since been enlarged and upgraded. Both establishments cater for over 30 guests and welcome non-resident patrons. Major credit cards are accepted.

Upland Goose Hotel 20/22 Ross Rd, Stanley; tel: 21455; fax: 21520; email: fic@horizon.co.fk.
Malvina House Hotel 3 Ross Rd, Stanley; tel: 21355; fax: 21357; email: malvina@horizon.co.fk.

Guesthouses
There are three guesthouses in Port Stanley. **Emma's Guest House**, situated near the public jetty on Ross Road, can sleep up to 16 guests. Contact Mrs Emma Steen, 36 Ross Road, Stanley; tel: 21056; fax: 21573; email: emmas@horizon.co.fk. The other two are a few minutes walk inland. **Sparrowhawk Guest House** on Drury Street sleeps 11. Contact Mr M

Jackson, 7 Drury Street, Stanley; tel: 21979; fax: 5+00 21980. The third guesthouse, **Dolphins**, is larger, sleeping up to 21 guests. Contact June and Norman Clarke at 46 St John Street, Stanley; tel: 22950; email: fprintz@horizon.co.fk. This establishment operates as a bed and breakfast guesthouse with evening meals and packed lunches available on request at extra cost.

Other accommodation

There are five additional bed and breakfast places to stay in Port Stanley. **Kay McCallum's** (14 Drury Street; tel: 21071) sleeps four. If fully booked, backpackers are permitted to erect their tents in the back garden. Evening meals and hot lunches are also available to non-residents. **Scotia House** (12 St Mary's Walk; tel: 21191; fax: 22434) has two family rooms sleeping three in each. Wildlife and battlefield tours can be arranged on request. There is one double room at **Sue Binnie's** (3 Brandon Road). Spanish and English are spoken. **Hilary Pauloni's** (63 Fitzroy Road; tel: 21079) has one twin room. Packed lunches and evening meals are available on request. **Tenacres** on the outskirts of the town sleeps four; half board can be arranged. Contact Sharon Halford, Tenacres, Stanley; tel: 21155; fax: 21950; email: tenacres@horizon.co.fk. The latter two establishments are non-smoking.

WHERE TO EAT

There is a range of places to eat in Stanley to suit every pocket. Bar lunches are available from the five public houses in town. **The Conservatory Restaurant** at the Malvina House Hotel serves à la carte menus at lunch and dinner. **The Beagle Bar** in the same establishment serves light lunches. **The Upland Goose** has a restaurant (closed on Sundays) and bar meals in the Lounge Bar. The **Falklands Brasserie** at 3 Philomel Place is open all day for hot drinks and serves late lunches and evening meals. **The Woodbine Café** on Fitzroy Road acts as a café and take-away, serving fish and chips etc. It is open Tuesday to Saturday from 10.00 to 14.00 and Wednesday and Friday from 19.00 to 21.00. **Shorty's Diner** at West Hillside is open six days a week (closed on Wednesdays) from noon until late, serving a variety of meals. A little further out of town is the **Lighthouse Seamen's Centre** on FIPASS road, which serves hot and cold drinks with cooked meals available on Friday and Saturday evenings.

SHOPPING

When shopping for food and provisions in Port Stanley it usually means visiting the two supermarkets, the West Store and the Beauchane Centre. There are other smaller stores specialising in one product or another. There are several gift shops, which sell souvenirs along with other goods, scattered around the town. They stock a range of postcards, clothing, jewellery and other gifts popular with visitors. Some items can be in short supply after a visit from some of the larger cruise ships. It is therefore worth checking when such large vessels are due so as to beat the crowds to the shops.

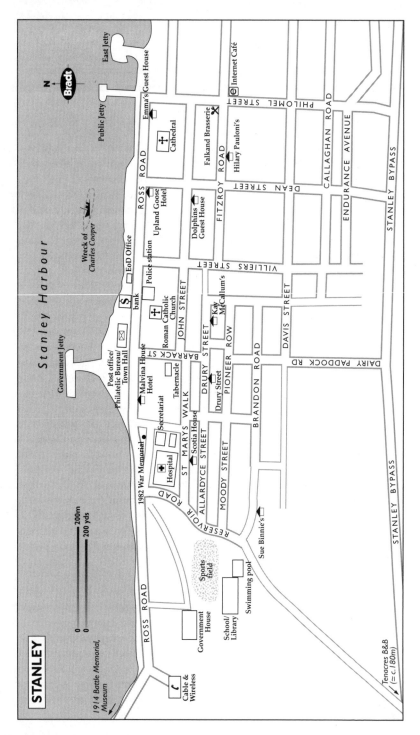

WHAT TO SEE
City walk

The oldest and most interesting part of the city is along the sea front and in the first few streets behind Ross Road, which runs along the water's edge. The wrecks that lie along the waterfront date back many years. A self-guided maritime history trail has been established. Visitors can use the signposts in conjunction with the illustrated booklet available from the Falkland Tourist Board Office and other shops. A stroll along the sea front will give the visitor a snapshot of most of the major events to have occurred on the Falkland Islands.

The **Falkland Islands Museum** constitutes a good starting-point for a history lesson about Port Stanley. By following Ross Road West past the memorials and the wreck of the *Jhelum,* then turning into Holdfast Road, the visitor arrives at the museum on the right. The name Holdfast comes from the instruction 'hold fast' given to the Land Forces here in June 1982 by the commander, Major General Sir Jeremy Moore, until he had obtained the Argentinian surrender. This building was originally built in 1981 for the Argentine Air Force, which was running a twice-weekly service to the mainland at the time. After the war the commanders of the British Forces used it until the new base at Mount Pleasant was finished in 1985. It was opened as a museum in 1989 in order to testify to island life before 1982. It is possible to visit this museum several times before seeing all the exhibits. There is no set route around the building; the visitor is left to investigate whatever catches the eye. The displays cover all aspects of the islands, ranging from Natural History, farm life, ships, shipwrecks and ship repair to the military history of the island, with many items from the 1982 war. Many of the musical instruments are still played upon request. There is something of interest for all visitors to this amazing building.

Lying in the shallow water at the western end of town are the remains of the *Capricorn.* This Welsh barque, built in 1859, was carrying coal from Swansea to the west coast of South America when her cargo caught fire. She was scuttled in shallow water with the aim of extinguishing the fire before her master put in to Falkland to carry out repairs. Having been condemned as unseaworthy, she was then used as a lighter in Stanley Harbour, then for storage, before being scuttled in her present position. During World War II the *Capricorn* was used as the head of a small jetty. Most of her hull was stripped for use as firewood in the late 1940s. The large shed on the waterfront a little further along Ross Road was used by the Beaver Float planes between 1953 and the early 1980s, when they were phased out. It is still known as the **Beaver Shed**.

The wreck of the *Jhelum* is one of the largest hulks still visible in Port Stanley. This ship lies at the end of a very rickety walkway known as Packe's Jetty opposite Sullivan House. This three-masted barque, built in 1849 in Liverpool, spent most of her working life plying between Europe and South America, carrying general cargo out and bringing guano, nitrates or copper back to Europe. She set sail for Europe, laden to the gunwales, on July 13 1870, and just managed to round Cape Horn before reaching the islands in a very poor condition. The crew refused to sail any further. She was surveyed, then condemned and scuttled in her present position.

Walking back towards the town, the road curves up to a low promontory upon which the **1914 Battle Memorial** is situated. This monument commemorates the Battle of the Falklands fought on December 8 1914, in which the British Squadron under the command of Vice Admiral Sturdee destroyed the German Squadron under Vice Admiral Graf Von Spee. A public holiday on the Falklands was declared on this date. Every year there is a parade and a ceremony, which includes a display by the Royal Air Force and the Royal Navy. The memorial was paid for by public subscription and was first unveiled on February 26 1927.

A few crested ducks and Falkland flightless steamer ducks are often found feeding along the tide line on either side of this promontory. The ever present southern giant petrels seem to delight in flying as close to the sea wall as they can, just lifting a wing to drift out to sea before returning whence they came.

Ross Road continues past the satellite dishes that bear witness to Cable and Wireless's operations on the island. The large trees between here and the governor's residence, Government House, are a good place to look for some of the smaller birds such as black-chinned siskins and the occasional swallow blown in from South America.

Government House, originally built in 1845, has been regularly extended, improved or just generally altered over the years. Every Governor and his wife seem to have added their own touch to the building. Each spring, when the gorse hedges are in bloom, this is a very picturesque situation in the lee of the *macrocarpa* trees. The conservatory at the front of the house is home to one of the most prolific grapevines on the islands. The house itself is full of all manner of memorabilia from throughout the ages. Outside the west entrance are a pair of brass guns cast in 1807, and elsewhere there is a harpoon gun that was presented by a South Georgia Whaling Station and a shell that is supposed to have come from the German cruiser *Leipzig*. The bullet holes still visible in the walls mark the most dramatic period in the history of this building, which suffered during the invasion and subsequent recapture of Port Stanley from the Argentinians.

The large building behind the sports field, just beyond Government House, is the new **Community School**, which was opened in August 1992. This impressive structure provides the islanders with a swimming pool, library and a wide range of leisure and sports facilities. The large blue-roofed building is the **King Edward Memorial Hospital**, which is a joint civilian/military hospital. The smaller properties along Thatcher Drive in front of the hospital provide sheltered accommodation.

The newest memorial along the waterfront is the **Liberation Monument** standing in front of the secretariat just before the government dockyard. This monument was paid for by public subscription, erected by volunteers, and officially unveiled on June 14 1984. The military personnel who gave their lives to liberate the islands are remembered on the surrounding wall.

Liberation Day, June 14, is marked in the islands each year by a public holiday. The **Secretariat** houses the islands' administrative offices and treasury buildings. Adjacent to these buildings is **Cable Cottage**, now the Attorney General's Chambers, which housed the Stanley end of the telegraph cable that linked the islands to Montevideo in the early 1900s.

The **Government dockyard**, which also included the department of works, is the oldest part of Port Stanley, begun in 1843. Originally it included storerooms, workshops, a jail, a magazine and a smithy. One building, **Gilbert House**, was originally used as a staging post for newly arrived settlers to the islands. This was their home until permanent accommodation could be found. It then became a small hospital before being partially destroyed by fire in 1984. It now houses the councillors' office and the government archivist. The support to the outer end of the government jetty comes from the remains of the *Margaret*. This vessel, built in 1836, reached Port Stanley in 1850 on her way from Liverpool to Valparaiso. She was leaking, damaged and dangerously overloaded when she reached the islands. She was condemned, although remained in the harbour for some years before being cut down, filled with rubble and used for the base of the end of the jetty.

The Malvina House Hotel is opposite the entrance to this tiny dockyard. One of the buildings along the road houses the offices of **Falkland Conservation**, a non-governmental environmental charity, which is involved with a wide range of research and advisory roles concerning the islands' wildlife. Continuing along Ross Road, the next collection of buildings includes the **Post Office**, which houses the philatelic department, the **Town Hall** and the justice department. At present the Police Station is opposite the Town Hall, but a new **Police Station** is due to be built soon on the outskirts of the town. The colourful building further down the road is the **Catholic Church**, in which services are held at 10.00 on Sundays and at 09.00 on weekdays. This church was built in 1899 whereas the original Church was a much smaller building, built in 1886, and is now the church hall. The only bank on the islands is the Standard Chartered, which has its new offices just beyond the Town Hall. The old offices are now the mineral department on the other side of the road. The **Explosive Ordinance Disposal** (EOD) office is just opposite the police station. The EOD distributes current minefield maps for those visitors who are planning any walking around Stanley and its environs.

The grassy lawn beyond the EOD, opposite the Upland Goose Hotel, is known as **Victory Green**. The mast displayed in the middle of the green is the mizzen-mast of the SS *Great Britain*, which lay for many years in the outer harbour at Sparrow Cove before being transported to Britain in the 1970s. The four old cannons spaced out along the green originated from Port Louis, the original capital of the islands. The other guns are 19th century Hotchkiss guns, which are fired on celebration days and to salute visiting ships. From this vantage point it is possible to look over the water to the northern banks of the harbour and see the names of four ships spelt out in white stones on the dark vegetation. These names are *Beagle, Barracuda, Protector* and *Endurance*. The *Beagle* and the *Barracuda* were naval cruisers on protection duty around the islands at the end of the 1800s. They were also involved in keeping law and order among the whalers and sealers that were based on the islands at the time, and to keep poachers from the islands. *HMS Protector* was an Antarctic ice patrol-ship that patrolled Falkland and Antarctic waters from 1955 until it was replaced by *HMS Endurance* in 1968. *Endurance* entered the world headlines in 1982 when she participated in the retaking of South Georgia by the British forces. Previously, she had been due to be withdrawn from service, but continued after the war until replaced by the new *Endurance* in 1991.

The hulk of the **Charles Cooper** lies a short distance offshore opposite the West Store, the largest shop on the islands. The *Charles Cooper* was an American ship, dated 1856, which arrived in Port Stanley leaking badly on September 25 1866 on passage from Philadelphia to San Francisco with a cargo of coal. The cost of repair proved too great and she was sold on the islands. This is one of the best preserved of the hulks in Stanley Harbour, thanks to its alloy roof, but little of the main deck remains. The carved transom is now in the Stanley museum. In 1968 she was bought by the South Street Seaport Museum in New York, as one of the last examples of a North Atlantic packet ship. It is also popular with the local bird life as rock shags, gulls and turkey vultures favour it as a roosting site. Another wreck lies just inshore of the *Charles Cooper*, the **Actaeon**, or what remains of her. This ship was built in New Brunswick in 1838 and put in to Port Stanley on January 27 1853, on her way from Liverpool to San Francisco with a cargo of coal. She had been beaten back whilst trying to round Cape Horn and had put into the islands for repair but was scuttled after a survey found she was unseaworthy. Very little remains above water, and the outline of the vessel is best seen from the air when flying over the harbour.

Christ Church Cathedral and its whalebone arch must be one of the best-known, most photographed buildings in the islands. It is the southernmost cathedral in the world and for part of its history was the main cathedral for the missionary diocese of South America. Consecrated in 1892 and finished in 1903, it has remained in use to this day. The whalebone arch, situated next to the cathedral and made from the jawbones of two blue whales, was presented to the islanders in 1933 by whalers from South Georgia. The arch and the cathedral were renovated in 1991.

At the head of the public jetty in front of **Jubilee Villas**, amongst the oldest buildings in Port Stanley, is a small plaque commemorating the visit of HRH Prince Alfred, Duke of Edinburgh in 1871, the first royal visit, and the visit of the present Duke of Edinburgh in 1957. The ruins of the **William Shand** are best seen from the public jetty looking towards the East Jetty. This barque, built in Greenock in 1839, visited Port Stanley on the outward journey from Liverpool to Valparaiso in February 1859, and returned to the islands after a severe battering as she tried to round Cape Horn two months later. She was condemned and ended her days in Stanley.

Ross Road ends at the junction with Philomel Street. By following the road around the Falkland Island Company's yard, it is possible to continue along the waterfront along Ross Road East. A backwards look at the East Jetty reveals two more casualties of the rough seas around Cape Horn. The wreck of the

Egeria has been roofed with corrugated metal and used as a storage area for wool and other cargoes. She was a barque from New Brunswick, built in 1859, and reached Port Stanley in 1872 on her way from London to Callao, Peru with a cargo of cement. Like so many ships before, she was thwarted by the Cape Horn weather and put into the islands damaged and leaking. She was condemned and scuttled adjacent to the *William Shand*. The last wreck visible on this walk is the *Fleetwing*, which lies on the foreshore opposite the offices of the Falkland Island Company. Built in South Wales in 1874 she spent most of her life carrying phosphates. She reached the islands in October 1911 with a cargo of coal, destined never to leave.

Port Stanley has expanded rapidly in recent years. In the not so distant past the cemetery was at the eastern end of the town. There are now several new housing estates built to the east of the cemetery. Facing the harbour, in front of the cemetery, is the war memorial. This **Cross of Sacrifice** includes the roll of honour of the 43 Falkland Islanders who died during active service during the two World Wars. The **cemetery** has been in use since the 1840s. The headstones narrate the events of the last 160 years. The oldest headstones are situated towards the western edge of the grounds. Victims of the Battle of the Falklands in 1914 and of the Battle of the River Plate in 1939 are buried here. On the slopes behind the graveyard is the **memorial wood**, which has been created to make a living shrine to those who lost their lives in the events of 1982.

Further afield

For visitors wanting a longer walk from Port Stanley, **Moody Brook** is a good destination at the western end of town. The first part of the walk leads along Ross Road and past the Beaver Shed. The **Golf Course**, situated beyond the last houses, is open daily. Competitions are played regularly, particularly on Sundays. Moody Brook, a short drive from here, is named after Richard Moody, the first governor of the Falkland Islands. There is a plaque on the north bank to commemorate the site where the first and last shots of the Falkland War were fired in 1982. On a clear day it is possible to see the length of Stanley Harbour as far as the wreck of the *Lady Elizabeth* in the east.

Another superb view over Port Stanley can be had from **Sapper Hill**, which overlooks the town from the west. This viewpoint is reached by returning to Stanley past Government House, following Reservoir Road to the Stanley-MPA road and turning on to the track that leads up the hill. By taking the Stanley Bypass and turning left into Dairy Paddock Road the visitor soon reaches one of the most unusual gardens in Stanley. Next to the sign 'say no to whaling' are the impressive skulls of killer whale and sperm whale along with a metal sculpture of a whale.

To the south of Port Stanley, especially behind the Airport Road, are the peat diggings that used to be the source of the peat burnt in the town. Prior to the 1982 war a household would annually use about 120 cubic yards ($92m^3$) for heating and cooking. The convenience of gas, oil and electricity has resulted in a decline in the amount of peat cut, so that many of the peat banks are no longer being used.

Port Stanley must be one of the most colourful capital cities in the world, with its brightly painted wood and metal. There are very few stone or brick built houses. The local stone is not suitable for use in construction and the cost of importing bricks is too high to be used in general building work. Wood and galvanised tin are much cheaper and seem capable of withstanding the Falklands weather. The corrugated iron sheets used in roofing and for walls are known locally as 'wriggly tin'. Many houses were brought down in kit form and assembled on the spot. Some of the best preserved of the older houses are those in **Pioneer Row**, two streets up from the Government Jetty. In 1849, 30 prefabricated cottages were brought out and erected by 30 married pensioners from Chelsea and Greenwich in London. They were to form a garrison and be part of the colonisation of the islands that was being encouraged at that time. Port Stanley has expanded considerably in recent years, most of the houses still being constructed from timber with tin commonly used in cladding.

For those wanting a longer walk out to the sites made famous during 1982, such as Tumbledown, Two Sisters, Wireless Ridge and Mount Longdon, the visitor is advised to take with them a current minefield map, available from EOD, and to make sure that someone knows where you have gone and your expected return time.

There is a lot for the visitor to see and do in the Port Stanley area. The grid-like layout of the town means that it is difficult to get lost for long. The traffic going up and down the hill has priority so care must be taken at any crossroads. It is the ideal place to base a visit to the Falkland Islands.

East Falkland

Once Port Stanley has been explored, there are many sites in East Falkland that can be reached on a day trip from the islands' capital. The recently expanded road network on East Falkland now reaches most of the settlements north of the Goose Green/Darwin area. The majority of the visitor sites are within a three-hour drive of Port Stanley. Some sites require a full day to get there and back, with enough time to look around, while others can be visited in a few hours. It is also possible to use Darwin as a base for exploring the surrounding countryside. The majority of minefields found on the Falkland Islands are concentrated around Port Stanley. These are all fenced, signposted and indicated on the maps that are available from the Explosive Ordinance Disposal (EOD) office on Ross Road in Stanley.

GYPSY COVE, CAPE PEMBROKE AND SURF BAY
Gypsy Cove
Gypsy Cove is within easy reach of Port Stanley, as it is only a 15-minute drive from the hotels or the jetty. It is a popular first stop for many first-time visitors to Falkland, providing for many their introduction to penguins. Gypsy Cove can get very busy during holiday periods and when large cruise ships call into Stanley Harbour. On busy days there may well be a warden on site. The wardens will give visitors information and instructions about the wildlife of the area. All visitors are asked to follow the wardens' advice in order that the wildlife is not disturbed in any way.

Getting there
The road passes the **totem pole** outside the industrial site almost opposite the hydroponics garden about five minutes from Stanley. Many of the vegetables consumed on Falkland are cultivated in these greenhouses. The pole was first erected by the British troops and decorated with signs mentioning the name of their hometown and the intervening distance. This has been added to over the years so that most of the cities of the world are mentioned, plus nearly every locality in the UK.

The road from Port Stanley to the airport becomes more built up every year in step with the city's expansion. The first turn off on the left leads to the

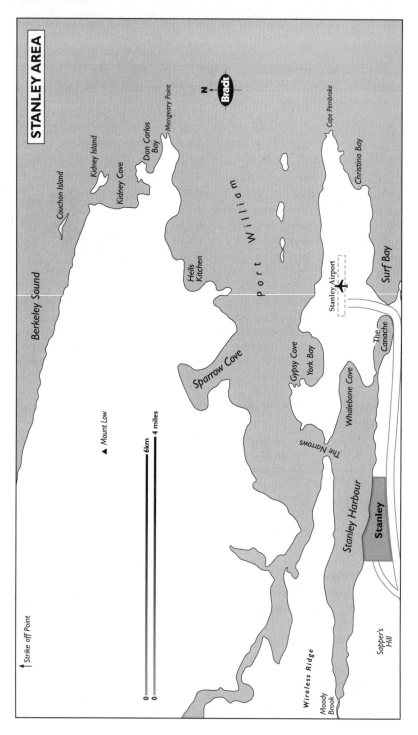

STANLEY AREA

floating dock known as **FIPASS** (the initials stand for Floating Interim Port and Storage System), the unloading point for all the larger cargo vessels that call in. The tarmac road continues towards the airport past the **Canache**, a shallow lagoon where sailing ships used to come for repair and to have their hulls scraped, a process known as careenage. The name Canache is a corruption of careenage. At low tide during the summer white-rumped sandpipers can be found along the shore in the company of the resident two-banded plovers.

It is possible to reach Gypsy Cove via the airport road, bypassing the airport around the western perimeter before joining the main track overlooking **Yorke Bay**. The small pond near the airport can be a good site for wildfowl during the summer months. On fine summer days Yorke Bay used to be a very popular beach for the inhabitants of Port Stanley. Sadly, it is now out of bounds due to the presence of mines and has been fenced off.

The alternative route crosses the narrow bridge at the Port Stanley end of the Canache. The two ships sunk in the mud beside this narrow bridge were originally used for fishing before being converted to carry cargo around the islands. The *Golden Chance* lies well up the beach whilst the *Gentoo* is in deep water. The latter was brought into the islands in 1927 and based at Pebble Island until 1965. It was then used for a variety of cargoes until being moved to the Canache, where it sank during the Argentinian occupation of 1982.

The track continues around the edge of Canopus Hill to **Whalebone Cove**. The most impressive shipwreck still visible on the islands, the *Lady Elizabeth*, known locally as *Lady Liz*, is stranded in the middle of the beach with the steam tug *Samson* on the northern shore. The *Lady Elizabeth* was built of iron in 1879 in Sunderland (UK), was 223ft (68m) long and weighed 1208 tons. She had visited the islands on several occasions before her final trip. On one of these visits she was carrying the bricks and cement for the new cathedral being built in Port Stanley. Her last voyage began in December 1912, carrying wood from Vancouver to Mozambique. She hit severe gales off Cape Horn where deck cargo and four men were washed overboard, before putting into Berkeley Sound to the northeast of Port Stanley on March 12 1913. On entering the sound, she hit Uranie Rock, holing her and losing a section of keel. She was towed into Port Stanley by the tug *Samson,* where her owner's intention was to repair the hull so that she could continue her voyage. This was not to be her destiny, as she was later condemned and sold to the Falkland Island Company for £3,350. The sails were used as covers for calf-pens at Darwin. The hull was used as a floating timber warehouse alongside the East Jetty in Port Stanley for three years before being moved further out into the harbour and used for general storage. She broke free from these moorings on February 17 1936 and drifted ashore to her present position. The masts still standing high in the sky give the impression that she is just waiting for the weather to change before setting out on the high seas again. The **Samson** joined the *Lady Liz* ashore in Whalebone Cove in 1945, after gale force winds caused her moorings to break. She had been built in Hull in 1888 and reached Falkland in 1900. The Falkland Island Company brought her to the islands because a powerful tug was needed in the islands. The *Samson* was involved in saving several vessels, and their crews, which had hit the treacherous Billy Rock at the entrance to Stanley Harbour. She was in use as a lighter from 1924 onwards, until she broke adrift and ended up at her present location. The grasslands at the head of Whalebone Cove are full of pale maiden. This delicate, yellow-centred, white flower blooms can be seen in profusion around here in springtime. From the track, looking out over the *Lady Elizabeth,* it is possible to see along the southern edge of Stanley Harbour, and past Port Stanley out to Mount Tumbledown, the Two Sisters and Mount Harriet.

What to see

Gypsy Cove is on the northeast part of the peninsular, which ends at Cape Pembroke. This area is recognised as a Wild Animal and Bird Sanctuary because of the variety of wildlife seen here. There is a gravel car park from which a track leads down to the cove itself. The higher section of the bank is covered with diddle-dee, which leads on to tussac grass on the steeper slopes and, eventually, sea cabbage growing in the loose sand by the beach. The main attraction here is the small colony of Magellanic penguins that have located their burrows in the sloping banks of the cove. The soft peaty earth is ideal for penguins to burrow in. The reverse of the coin is that it is all too easy to crush the burrows in this fragile ground. These birds are present at this site between October and March, and they lay two eggs during November, hatching them during late December and early January. Those birds not actively engaged at the nest can be seen gathered in small groups on the sand or bathing in the shallows. It is important that these birds do not waste energy moving away from curious visitors, therefore Falkland Conservation guidelines recommend that the visitor maintain a distance of at least 7.5m from the birds, adding the proviso that if they look nervous then the visitor should retreat further. The other guidelines issued by the charity (applicable everywhere on Falkland, not only at this site) are that the visitor should proceed carefully in the vicinity of the burrows and should not obstruct the birds' passage between their burrows and the sea. They also advise not to walk through the tussac grass, an easily damaged habitat where many birds nest. Finally the visitor is warned to move slowly, avoiding sudden movements when near the wildlife. Other birds to be seen here include Falkland flightless steamer ducks that often gather in sizeable flocks on the end of the long sandy beach in Yorke Bay. The rocky outcrops on the outer edge of the Cove are used as a nesting-site by a small group of rock shags and have also been home to nesting black-crowned night herons in the past. The fences delimiting the minefields on Yorke Bay are well marked and should not be crossed at any time. These fences are used as perches by many of the small birds of this area. In springtime black-throated finches and grass wrens can be found singing from these wires. A leaflet about Gypsy Cove can be obtained from Falkland Conservation or the Falkland Island Tourist Board. The view from here out

Above Port Howard (ww)

Left Kelp goose nest and thrift, Narrows Island (ww)

Below Pebble Island (ww)

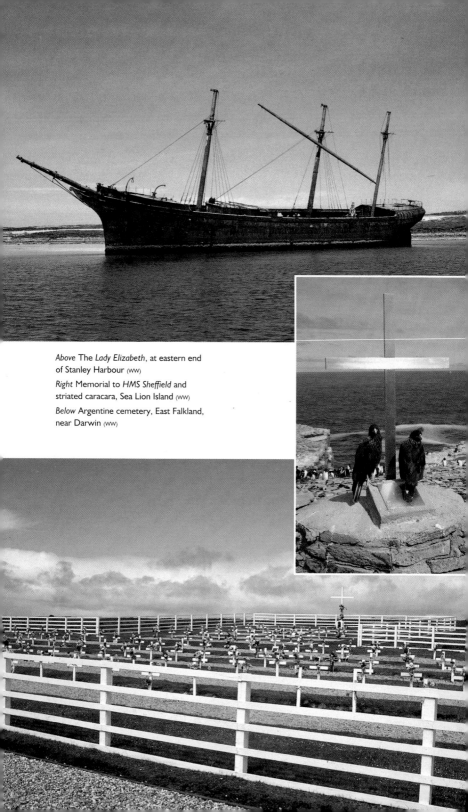

Above The *Lady Elizabeth*, at eastern end of Stanley Harbour (WW)

Right Memorial to *HMS Sheffield* and striated caracara, Sea Lion Island (WW)

Below Argentine cemetery, East Falkland, near Darwin (WW)

across Port William towards Mengeary Head is superb. Almost directly opposite Gypsy Cove is Sparrow Cove, which for many years was the home to the *SS Great Britain* before it was taken back to the UK. On windy days black-browed albatrosses can be seen gliding low over the water along with a scattering of feeding penguins and terns.

Cape Pembroke
Getting there
Cape Pembroke is seven miles from Port Stanley and is the most easterly point of the Falklands. In order to reach the cape itself, it is necessary to go back around the perimeter of the airport, via the main road, then left onto the track that leads toward the lighthouse. Once past the initial section of track, there are many different routes along the headland. Some of these can get very boggy and are therefore very difficult to drive through. Local knowledge is a major advantage in finding the correct route.

What to see
There are some shallow pools in the peat on the southern side of this headland, which usually accommodate an interesting selection of wildfowl. Silver teal have been known to breed on these ponds in the past. Concealed among the more common plants, the visitor can find some of the more unusual, such as dusty miller, pimpernel and dog orchid. The latter flowers before Christmas; consequently the basal leaves are all that is visible for most of the summer. The small rocky beach on the south side, **Christina Bay**, is a good site to look for kelp geese and Magellanic oystercatchers. The banks of kelp that get washed ashore here furnish a comfortable resting place for sea lions. The lighthouse is at a short distance along the track.

The waters surrounding the entrance to Port William, stretching along the coast as far as Port Stanley, are very dangerous, with a strong tidal race, several small islands and rocks, including the infamous **Billy Rock**. The latter has claimed more than its fair share of shipwrecks over the years with many lives lost. The need for some sort of beacon became apparent when Port Stanley was established during the 1840s. The first markers were not lit and were only of use during daylight hours. The first painted marker was replaced by a larger construction in 1849, followed by the erection of the present **lighthouse** in 1855. This was a cast-iron structure brought from London. This 60ft (18m) lighthouse was first lit on December 1 1855, its light visible up to 14 miles away. The light was run on rape oil and was turned by a clockwork motor. The light burnt 1,000 gallons of oil annually. At one point sea lion oil was unsuccessfully tried as an experiment to cut the costs of keeping the lamp alight. The first lighthouse keeper was William Creed who lived with his family in a cottage built at the base of the tower. All the provisions for the keepers and the light had to be landed by boat at a place known as the gulch, instead of being hauled the seven miles from Stanley. Before the advent of telephone and radio, messages in daytime were sent using signalling flags, and at night horses were used to inform the authorities in Port Stanley of any shipping movements and to raise the alarm if any boat was seen in trouble. Horses were kept close to the tower for this purpose. Despite the light, ships in trouble were not a rare occurrence. This system was replaced in 1912 when the wireless station was built in Stanley. The light was modernised during the late 1800s and again in 1906, when it was rebuilt on better foundations. The new paraffin light could reach 16 miles out to sea and continued to function until the Argentine forces landed in Yorke Bay in April 1982. It has remained unlit ever since having been replaced by an automatic solar-powered light and radar reflector situated a few yards away. The foundations of the keepers' houses can still be seen beside the old lighthouse. The light was vandalised after the war but has now been refurbished by the Alistair Cameron Memorial Trust.

Falkland Conservation has recently begun a programme of replanting tussac grass near the end of the point. There are still some stands of the original tussac grass, but these have been over-grazed and eroded over the years. The end of the headland has now been fenced off to stop any straying animals grazing on the new plants. Southern sea lions come to sleep in the more mature stands or can be seen resting on the rocks near the water's edge. In some of the more sheltered hollows it is possible to discover some hardy clumps of thrift and pimpernel. The fast flowing tides bring a lot of food within the reach of the many seabirds that breed nearby. It is not unusual to see mixed flocks of birds feeding a short distance out to sea. Penguins, gulls, terns and shearwaters are regularly observed from here. This exposed headland has proved to be an ideal spot for keen birdwatchers to observe many of the seabirds that breed in the Antarctic, especially during the equinoctial gales.

Surf Bay

There is one further stop of interest on the way back to Port Stanley. Surf Bay is reached by turning eastwards off the main road at the inland end of the Canache. The long beach is a spectacular sight when the waves are crashing on to the sand, the wind picking off their crests as they reach breaking-point. Falkland flightless steamer ducks and scatterings of terns and gulls can be seen feeding on the kelp beds behind these breaking rollers. In some years a small group of elephant seals have come ashore to moult in the small bays to the south of the beach on Hooker's Point. White-rumped sandpipers and two-banded plovers frequent the banks of kelp along the tide line.

KIDNEY ISLAND AND KIDNEY COVE

Kidney Island is a small tussac-covered island lying at the southern entrance of Berkeley Sound. Opposite this island, on East Falkland, is Kidney Cove. Kidney Island is a government-owned reserve that can only be reached by boat. It is not used as pasturage and, consequently, retains its original flora. Regarded as being an important area for breeding seabirds, Kidney Cove is one of the few places on Falkland where four species of penguin breed. It is accessed either by land on the rather long drive from Port Stanley or by boat from Stanley to Sparrow Cove, followed by a short drive to Kidney Cove on the Murrell Farm. Kidney Cove is out of bounds as it was mined during the 1982 war, but the visitor gets an unimpeded view of the local wildlife from behind the fences.

Kidney Island

A visit to Kidney Island gives the visitor a good idea of what much of the coastline of Falkland must have been like before sheep and other grazing animals were imported. The number of visitors to the island is limited and an approved guide must accompany all parties. The island lies about nine miles by boat from Port Stanley but is less than a mile from the Murrell Farm on East Falkland. It is a narrow island of about 79 acres, three quarters of a mile long and half a mile across. Most of the north-facing side of the island is low-lying, but steep cliffs, with one extensive bay, face east between two rocky headlands. The southwestern side of the island is much lower where the tussac grass comes down to the sea, leaving a narrow beach of rock and sand. All landings are made on this sheltered sand. This island has a very dense covering of tussac grass, making it essential for all members of any visiting group to remain within reach of each other and their leader. This dense growth makes walking problematic, especially as burrow-nesting seabirds use the whole island. There are also some boggy areas, so good footwear and waterproof clothing are needed for a visit to this unique island.

Getting there

The trip from Port Stanley usually takes less than an hour and gives the visitor a very good opportunity to get some photos of Port Stanley and the surrounding area from the sea. As the boat passes through the Narrows at the entrance to Stanley Harbour, there is a chance of seeing Peale's dolphins as they regularly play in the bow wave of incoming and outgoing boats. Once in Port William there are more seabirds present, mostly rock shags and king shags with accompanying gulls and terns. This boat trip can also afford the visitor the chance to see a jigger at close range, when their skippers bring them into the sound to renew their licences or to see their agents. These rather strange boats with their long lines of lights running the length of their upper decks show up at great distance at night, as they fish for the squid that come into Falkland waters towards the end of the summer.

Along the northern coastline towards Kidney Island, black-browed albatrosses, gentoo penguins and Magellanic penguins start to appear along with the familiar southern giant petrels. Once round **Mengeary Point**, sooty shearwaters suddenly become the commonest birds, shearing low over the sea on calm days or flashing past the boat in a great display of controlled flight. For the keen birdwatcher there is a possibility of finding great shearwaters mixed in with the masses of sooty shearwaters. The sheltered water channel between Kidney Island and Kidney Cove is a good place to watch gentoo penguins elegantly negotiating their way to the shore. Two beaches, **Don Carlos Bay** and the small strand to the south of Kidney Cove, are worth inspection from the sea because resting southern sea lions often head there. This whole area is

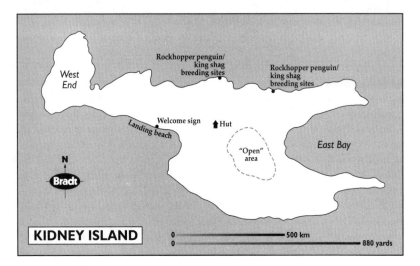

out of bounds, as mines were planted throughout in 1982. Gentoo penguins can be seen landing on the beach, walking up through the minefield to reach their colonies at the back of the beach. Fortunately, they are not heavy enough to detonate the mines.

Landing on Kidney Island involves anchoring in the kelp-beds on the southwestern side of the island before coming ashore in a rubber dingy. A sign at the top of the beach indicates some of the do's and don'ts of the island. The danger of fire is paramount on account of the abundance of flammable tussac grass, so obviously smoking is totally banned here. It is also important that bottles, lenses, and lens filters are not lost on the island as their light-magnifying effects could also start a fire. Trips to Kidney Island are very much governed by the weather and it is not unusual to have to postpone a trip to the island for a day or so. For those determined to explore this island, it is a good idea to allow for an alternative date in the itinerary in case the weather causes a change of plans. As the weather may also curtail the time spent on the island, the crew of the boat will usually provide a ship-to-shore radio so that plans can be changed if the weather worsens.

To arrange the boat trip contact **Seaview Limited**; tel: 21155; fax: 21950; email: seaview.sawle@horizon.co.fk.

What to see

Dolphins sometimes follow the rubber dingy on its way to the shore, often coming very close to the boat. Sometimes a lone sea lion will trail behind the boat, curious to see what is going on. Along the narrow beach, groups of Magellanic penguins and Falkland flightless steamer ducks survey each new arrival with interest. As this island has no rodents, there is nothing to prevent large numbers of small birds from breeding. The most obvious are the tussacbirds, which come out to the anchored ships and then follow visitors around the island, picking off whatever insect life is disturbed by passing feet.

There is no defined path through the tussac grass. It is advisable, when still aboard the ship, to get a bearing on the roof of the small hut visible on the brow of the hill. This is the island's only building and has been used for many years by those studying the breeding birds and other wildlife. Its most famous use was by Oscar and Eleanor Pettingill, who first stayed here in the late 1950s, when they made a film for Disney about Falklands' wildlife. It has been repaired several times over the years but could never be classed as luxury accommodation! Once heading in the right direction the first section is up an incline to the plateau on the top of the island. The highest point of Kidney Island is slightly less than 60ft (18m).

Almost all the island is thick with tussac grass, although there are some slightly more open areas to the east of the hut. It is here that wild celery and the indigenous strawberry can be found. The latter grow best on the top of the dead tussac grass, the white flowers at their most attractive before Christmas, the bright red fruit ripening later in the summer. These are popular with the Falkland thrushes that feed in this area. These thrushes often indicate the presence of a short-eared owl. This predator is rarely active during the day unless flushed or discovered by the thrushes, which then proceed to mob the owl until it leaves their territory. It is difficult to make quiet progress through the tussac grass, and the resident Magellanic penguins are never very impressed by visitors walking past their burrows. The braying call of the 'jackass', as it is locally called, soon becomes a very familiar sound.

The visitor should pause at regular intervals to admire the bird life overhead, which constitutes a perfect foil to the creatures scuttling around at ground level. Turkey vultures make up the majority of the birds wheeling round. These huge birds seem to be able to fly in almost any weather conditions. Crested caracara breed on the island, but being very shy are never easy to find on Kidney Island. Other birds passing overhead include terns and brown hooded gulls, which breed in small numbers on the ends of the rocky promontories on the southeast side of the island. Southern giant petrels do not breed here but seem to enjoy flying low over the island, passing barely above head height on occasions.

By crossing directly to the other side of the island, it is possible to reach the **rockhopper penguin colony** on the typical rocky outcrops. These cliffs are 16ft (5m) high and made up of quartzitic sandstone. Some of the flatter ledges to the northern end of the cliff are home to rock shags and are also used by roosting black-crowned night herons. The main cliffs still have rockhopper penguins breeding on the upper slopes, although they have been fewer in number in recent years. The occasional macaroni penguin joins this colony, especially in springtime. King shags also breed at the top of this outcrop. The most prolific seabird on Kidney Island is the sooty shearwater, which returns to the island during the spring. By mid summer, large numbers gather to the east of the island waiting for darkness to fall. When it is fully dark, these birds fly in over the island before finding their own burrows. Scientists think that their well-developed sense of smell plays a large part in their nocturnal ability to locate their burrows. During the summer the birds take it in turns to supervise the nest, allowing the mate to head out to sea. The reason for this nocturnal behaviour is that they are easy prey on the ground during daytime, so only come ashore after dark to avoid their predators. In calm weather multitudes of shearwaters gather on the sea. Wheeling spectacularly aloft in large groups before landing again, they are constantly in motion in windy weather, rarely settling for long. The only other species of shearwater that breeds on Kidney Island is the great shearwater, which can occasionally be seen in the larger flocks of sooty shearwaters. If the flock has been settled for a while, it is quite usual to see rockhopper penguins and Magellanic penguins passing through on their way to the shore. The other notable seabird breeding on Kidney Island is the white-chinned petrel, known locally as the 'cobbler', because its song supposedly resembles the sound of a shoemaker cobbling on his last. The petrels breed in burrows on the higher slopes of the island, but they are normally pelagic and so are not easily observed. Every now and then one does come near the island, flying low over the tussac grass before dropping down close to their burrows. These birds can be seen on most visits to the island but are never easy to find.

The beach on the eastern side of the island is a good place to look for some of the smaller birds of Kidney Island. Dark-faced ground-tyrants and Cobb's wrens are common along the boulder beach with tussacbirds usually never very far away. Southern sea lions are not uncommon in this bay and can sometimes come up into the tussac grass to sleep. These resting places have a distinctive smell and the blades of the tussac grass are completely flattened by the weight of these huge beasts. Before descending through the tussac grass to the beach, it is a good idea to find a vantage point to check if any are visible, and to listen out for any snorting noises. Meeting a sea lion face to face, although a memorable experience, is neither to be recommended nor safe. The occasional elephant seal has been known to come ashore at this site, but fortunately they rarely move far from the top of the beach. The brown-headed gulls and South American terns are very active in defending their territories on the headlands on either side of the beach. The skuas and vultures are chased away as soon as they fly over the headland. A few black-crowned night herons can be found roosting along the northern arm of the bay. To get back to the hut there is a short but steep climb up out of the bay before heading towards the hut and on to the beach. Amid the short tussac grass, the blue form of *pratia*, some scattered specimens of Antarctic eyebright and sizeable clumps of cinnamon grass grow wherever the ground is exposed to sunlight.

In recent years southern right whales have been recorded in the deeper waters to the east of Kidney Island and in the entrance of Berkeley Sound. These whales are most often encountered by the boats working in the area, or are occasionally seen by visitors to the island. In calm weather it may be possible to circumnavigate Kidney Island before returning to Port Stanley. This gives the visitor a chance to get a close up look at the gigantic flocks of sooty shearwaters. As with any boat trip around the islands, there is always the chance of finding some of the more unusual seabirds or cetaceans that pass through the waters around the Falkland Islands.

A visit to Kidney Island is a unique opportunity to see 'original' Falkland habitat. It can be quite a tiring day, but a memorable one.

There are a three other tussac grass covered islands between Cape Pembroke and Berkeley Sound. Cochon Island is the largest, lying a mile and a half to the northeast of Kidney Island; the other two are just to the north of Cape Pembroke. All these islands are off-limits but can be viewed from the sea.

Kidney Cove
Getting there
Kidney Cove has only recently been opened up for tourists by the owners of Murrell Farm, Adrian and Lisa Lowe, in conjunction with Sulivan Shipping Services, who have been taking visitors from cruise ships to the cove. A new jetty has been built on the south side of Murrell Farm so that it is now possible to leave Stanley Harbour, cross Port William, and land at Sparrow Cove in less than 15 minutes. A new company, Hebe Tours run by Neil Rowlands, has been set up to take visitors to the penguin colonies at Kidney Cove.

Where to stay
Hebe Tours have put a cabin on the slopes of Mount Low to enable self-catering visitors to spend more time at this site. This cabin has a room which functions as a kitchen/dining-room/lounge, and two bedrooms. These have two single beds in one room and a single and a double bunk bed in the other. A modern toilet is in a separate building adjacent to the cabin. Cooking and heating in the cabin are gas-fired. Electricity for lighting both buildings is provided by batteries, which are supplemented with wind power. Water is available from a nearby spring. A radio transceiver is provided as part of the rental, so that contact can be maintained with the outside world. A small patio and barbecue area has been created for visitors to use. The views out over Kidney Island and Cochon Island to the mouth of Berkeley Sound are superb from here.

What to see
Close to this cabin are the remains of a house used during the World War II by the 16 men stationed on Look Out Hill. The base of a naval gun with which they guarded the entrance to Port William can still be seen. There is little left of the house apart from a very solid-looking fireplace, which has stood the test of time much better than the rest of the house. These men also created a garden in the shelter of the hill, traces of which are still visible today.

The trip to Kidney Cove takes about 20 minutes in a Land Rover. The headlands to the southwest of Sparrow Cove and the beaches of Kidney Cove and Mine Cove were mined extensively during the 1982 war, consequently access is no longer possible. All these areas have been fenced off and are clearly identified as being danger zones. These minefields present no obstacles to the gentoo penguins who come ashore at Kidney Cove, then walk up through the fenced areas until they reach one of the three **gentoo penguin colonies** on the grassy bank. One of these colonies has a small group of king penguins in its midst. The only other noteworthy colonies of this majestic species in Falkland are on Saunders Island and at Volunteer Point, on the northeastern part of East Falkland. Elsewhere there are a few others in smaller groups. This is definitely the nearest **king penguin colony** to Port Stanley.

The grass around the freshwater pool behind Mine Cove contains some of the many species of geese that breed on Falkland, whilst a varied selection of ducks visit the pool during the day. Magellanic penguins breed nearby on the drier slopes behind the coves, and also to the north in the turf-covered summits of the steep cliffs, which are quite a walk from the nearest beach. Further along the coast is a large rookery of rockhopper penguins, which manage to make their way up the steeper slopes. The views from here out over Berkeley Sound towards Volunteer Point are superb. To the west of Mount Low is the peak known as Twelve O'Clock Mountain. Apparently the name relates to the fact that, viewed from Port Stanley, the sun appears to be directly above this hill at noon, thus signalling time for lunch.

All of these sites can be visited on foot when staying at the Hebe Tours cabin on Mount Low, but are too much to accomplish on a day trip from Sparrow Cove. A typical day visit involves a rapid boat ride from Stanley and a journey by Land-Rover to the penguin colonies at Kidney Cove. Including boat trips, this trip can take 2½–4 hours. In the event of the weather deteriorating, it is possible to return to Port Stanley in the Land Rover. This adds quite a lot of time to the return journey and is a rarely used option. According to the visitor's wishes, an additional trip can be organised to visit the rockhopper penguin colony on the northern shore.

PORT LOUIS

The original capital of the islands in the 19th century, now a peaceful settlement, is a popular site on East Falkland.

Getting there

The road from Port Stanley was the first major road out of the city to be built after the 1982 war. This links the Mount Pleasant Airfield (MPA) with Stanley. The road leaves Stanley Common, passing Sapper Hill before continuing south of Mount William, Tumbledown Mountain and Mount Harriet. This area is one of the most heavily mined that the visitor will see but is not very extensive. In the middle of one of the fenced off areas to the south of the road is a fine example of one of the stone corrals that the gauchos built in the 1800s. Most unusual here are the road signs, 'Slow Minefield', which have been photographed many times since they were erected. Leaving the main road at the first right-hand turning, the visitor then drives through a valley across Wickham Heights, overlooked by Mount Kent on the left and the Two Sisters on the right. Once beyond the minefields, the only material evidence of the 1982 war is the wreckage of Argentinian helicopters that were destroyed by the British forces and the military establishment on the top of Mount Kent.

The dominant geographical features of **Wickham Heights** are the stone runs. These 'rivers of stone' have aroused much interest since first described in 1764 by Antoine Joseph Pernetty. He was visiting the largest of the stone runs on Falkland, a short distance from Port Louis. This four-mile, grey 'valley of fragments' was given the name 'Princes Street' by Charles Darwin when he visited the islands in 1833, as it reminded him of the cobblestones in Princes Street, Edinburgh. These features are found on the Devonian Quartzite on East and West Falkland and are most commonly seen in the Wickham Heights. Seen from the air they appear as grey patches on the slopes of the hills. They consist of many rough boulders sorted in such a way that the smaller stones are underneath the larger boulders. These stones are not stable, making it impossible to drive a vehicle or ride a horse across them. Where the road cuts across a stone run, the lower stones that have not been exposed to the elements, are quite red in colour compared to the pale grey hue of all the stone revealed to the air. Very little plant life can survive in the relatively sterile habitat in the stone run. A few native strawberries, and a type of *senecio*, are the rare plants with any colour, apart from the unique snake plant whose white flowers are endemic to Falkland.

There is a superb view northwards as the road drops down from the Wickham Heights towards the junction; to the left is Port San Carlos, to the right Port Louis. The settlement of Estancia nestles at the head of the very long inlet that enters the South Atlantic far north of here. Port Louis is only a short drive from here, past the turning to Green Patch, which in clear weather affords the visitor a wonderful view over Berkeley Sound.

History

Port Louis was the site of the first French settlement on Falkland. Antoine Louis de Bougainville left St Malo in 1763 to establish a colony at Port Louis, formally taking possession on April 5 1764. He named the islands 'Isles Malouines' from which the Argentine name 'Islas Malvinas' is derived. Captain John McBride, from the British settlement at Port Egmont on Saunders Island, informed the French of the British colony in 1766. These two colonies continued to coexist until France relinquished its claim to the Falkland Islands in favour of the Spanish. Bougainville was paid £25,000 to reimburse the expense he had incurred in setting up Port Louis. The formal transfer to Spain occurred on April 1 1767 when Bougainville passed control over to the Spanish governor Don Felipe Ruiz Puente.

The Spanish, under the command of Don Juan Ignacio de Madariaga, expelled the British from Port Egmont in 1770. The British settlement was re-established at Port Egmont in 1771, where it remained until the British departure from the islands in 1774. The Spanish remained at Port Louis, known then as Port Soledad, until 1806 when the governor Juan Crisostomo Martinez quit the islands, leaving behind a plaque claiming sovereignty for Spain. The United Provinces of the Rio de la Plata, which later became Argentina, withdrew the remaining Spanish settlers from the islands in 1811.

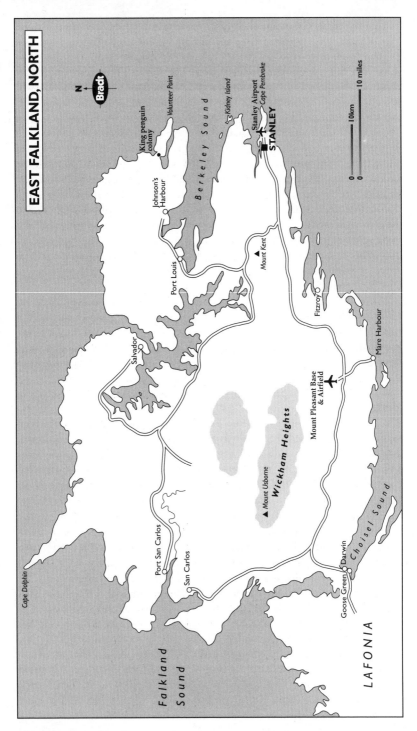

EAST FALKLAND, NORTH

In 1820 the Argentine government in Buenos Aires, having gained independence from Spain in 1816, claimed sovereignty over Falkland and sent a David Jewett, commander of the *Heroina,* to hoist a flag on the islands. Don Pablo Aregusti was appointed governor in 1823, and in this capacity he granted a concession of land on East Falkland to Louis Vernet and Don Jorge Pacheco. The first attempt at settling only lasted a year, but Vernet's second expedition in 1826 was more successful. In 1828 he was given permission to form a colony on East Falkland and was accorded fishing and sealing rights. Vernet became governor in 1829, using Port Soledad (Port Louis) as his base. He arrested three American schooners for illegal sealing in 1829, the news of which only reached the United States when one of the boats, the *Breakwater,* escaped. Another of the ships, the *Superior,* was released whilst the third, the *Harriet,* and her captain were taken for trial in Buenos Aires. The American response to this was to dispatch *USS Lexington* under Commander Silas Duncan to the islands. The ship arrived on December 28 1831 and destroyed the settlement at Port Soledad, and declared the islands free of any government. Matthew Brisbane, who had been placed in charge by Louis Vernet, was taken to Montevideo in irons.

A new governor was sent to the islands by Argentina in 1832, but was murdered by mutineers shortly after taking up his appointment. The commander of the Argentinian warship *Sarandi,* Don Jose Maria Pinedo, took charge until the arrival of Captain Onslow, with his ships *HMS Clio* and *HMS Tyne,* who had landed at Port Egmont on December 20 1832, before reaching Port Louis (Soledad) on January 2 1833. He gave Pinedo written notice that he was exercising British sovereign rights and would be raising the British flag next day. He then requested Pinedo lower the Argentinian flag and leave the islands. Pinedo protested and refused to comply with such demands. The British landed next day, took down the Argentinian flag, returned it to Pinedo, and raised the British flag. Pinedo left Falkland, taking with him all the Argentinian forces that had been stationed on the islands. Subsequently the settlement was left in the hands of William Dickson, who had been Louis Vernet's bookkeeper. Matthew Brisbane took over from him when he returned to the islands in April 1833. In August of that year, during the mutiny of a group of seven gauchos led by Antonio Rivero, Brisbane, Dickson and two others were murdered. The surviving settlers escaped firstly to Hog Island and later to Turf Island in Berkeley Sound. They were found on the sealer *Hopeful* two months later. Following the arrival of *HMS Challenger* in January 1834, the gauchos were arrested and sent via Rio de Janeiro for trial in England. This trial never took place and the men were later returned to Montevideo. The first officer of *Challenger,* Lieutenant Henry Smith, and a boat crew were left in charge of the settlement.

In the autumn of 1833, in the midst of all of this upheaval, Charles Darwin arrived in Berkeley Sound on the *Beagle,* under the command of Captain Fitzroy. He visited Port Louis and the surrounding region, collecting botanical and geological samples during his expeditions. He appears not to have liked the islands or their climate, as, for instance, he wrote on his third day in the islands, 'the whole landscape has an air of desolation'. His descriptions of the countryside and its wildlife were some of the first ever made about the Falkland Islands.

The Colonial Land and Emigration Commissioners proposed their suitability for colonisation in 1840. Two years later Governor Moody was instructed by Lord Stanley to investigate the potential of Port William as the site of a new town. Captain Ross of the Ross Antarctic Expedition collaborated in this investigation and advised that Port William was suitable. Governor Moody received instructions in March 1843 to establish a new settlement there and work began during the following July, when the move from Port Louis was initiated. Subsequently, Port Louis has derived its income from sheep farming.

Where to stay

It is now possible to stay in self-catering accommodation at Port Louis. The **Garden House** is a traditional three-bedroomed house, with two twin rooms and master bedroom. Cots and highchairs are available on request. The house has a well-equipped kitchen and central heating. All towels and linen are provided. This house, overlooking the Careenage, is the perfect base from which to explore both the Port Louis area and the abundant wildlife along the north coast. Contact Peter and Melanie Gilding, Port Louis, East Falkland, Falkland Islands; tel: 31060; fax: 31061.

What to see

The new bypass takes the road away from the settlement. Port Louis Farm, in common with all the others on Falkland, is privately owned and, therefore, permission must be sought before travelling across the land. The old road arrives from the south, passing the now redundant sheep-dip, and comes to the site of the original French settlement. A short distance from here is the indicator of magnetic north, left behind by the crews of *Erebus* and *Terror*, the ships participating in the Ross Antarctic Expedition.

Port Louis is in many ways architecturally typical of a modern Falklands settlement, but some 19th century houses bear witness to its stint as the islands' capital. The pine trees growing by the main house, in the lee of the prevailing winds, provide relatively secure nesting-sites for Falkland thrushes. At low tide, Magellanic oystercatchers and blackish oystercatchers favour the bay, whereas speckled teal and crested ducks prefer the brackish water where the stream flows into the sea.

At less than an hour's drive from Stanley, Port Louis is an ideal base to get the feel of *camp* life and to explore East Falkland.

VOLUNTEER POINT

The king penguin colony at Volunteer Point is one of the highlights of any visit to the Falkland Islands. It is the largest colony of this species on the islands and is still increasing. There are two additional species of penguin and many other birds breed in this fabulous scenery. The majority of visitors who reach this site do so via the road and track from Port Stanley, and the drive to and from Volunteer Point is an experience in itself. In the past, Volunteer Point has been visited by some of the cruise ships that pass through the islands, but as landing cannot be guaranteed this is not a regular occurrence.

History

King penguins were first recorded at this site in the late 1860s, although they were almost extinct in the islands by 1870, their feathers and their oil making them a valuable resource. A small colony was reported at nearby Cow Bay in the 1920s, with a well-established rookery at Volunteer Lagoon being noted by the early 1970s. This colony continues to grow and over 400 birds have been counted at this site in recent years. Not all these will be breeding adults but more young are being produced each year. Some of the adult birds have been found to be carrying tags put on them in South Georgia, so recruitment from this distant island is another factor in this colony's success story. The site is generally known as Volunteer Point, but in reality the point is some distance from the beach. The penguins make their nests on a grassy strip of land that separates the lagoon from the open sea, linking the headland to East Falkland. This whole area, including Cow Bay, is private land and is included in the Volunteer Point Sanctuary. Permission to access Volunteer Point must be obtained before departure from George and Jenny Smith at **Johnson's Harbour** (tel: 31398). Access may be denied if the proprietors consider the driver to be incompetent and therefore in potential need of rescuing. Every single visitor, irrespective of status, is charged £10 to enter Volunteer Point. At time of writing this farm is for sale. The above details may therefore be incorrect and should be verified.

Getting there

It is only possible to get to Volunteer Point in a four-wheel drive vehicle. Previous experience of driving over the soft boggy ground that typifies *camp* is essential, as many inexperienced drivers have realised to their cost. The route from the preceding settlement, Johnson's Harbour, to the penguin rookeries varies throughout the year, and can therefore be very difficult to locate. Although the possibility exists for the visitor to hire a vehicle for the drive to Volunteer Point, it is far more sensible to book a seat on an organised trip. Although these days out are not particularly cheap, it does mean that the visitor gets the maximum benefit from the trip, and does not have to spend the day extricating a vehicle from a muddy hole!

The penguin colony is only about 45 miles from Port Stanley using the newly created road and tracks. However, this drive normally takes $2^1/_2$–$3^1/_2$ hours, depending upon the state of the track and the route taken.

The made-up road now continues past Port Louis to Johnson's Harbour. The remainder of the drive is over white grass and diddle-dee following the many tracks. One of the side tracks before Johnson's Harbour approaches Fish Creek down a very steep incline that is not for the faint of heart. The shallow waters around the creek are full of small mullet that can be seen zooming away through the water as any vehicle approaches. The deeper water in the creek is sometimes home to silver grebes and the omnipresent speckled teal.

The old route between Fish Creek and Johnson's Harbour settlement varied according to tide. At low water it was possible to drive along the exposed narrow beach, much to the amazement of the upland geese and Falkland flightless steamer ducks. At high tide there was no beach to cross and it became necessary to use the track leading over the headland on the higher ground. This was a slower route than crossing the beach. Knowledge of the local tide times was essential to ensure that it was possible to drive all the way along the beach without getting caught by the tide.

After leaving the picturesque settlement at Johnson's Harbour, the tracks lead up the valley between Mount Brisbane and North Lookout. The view from the head of the valley, looking back over the farm across Berkeley Sound to Wickham Heights, is magnificent. In wet years the five miles between these hills and the coast can be very difficult to drive over. Many of the vehicles that have got bogged down have done so in this stretch. As a rule the shallow peaty pools hereabouts are not very rich in wildlife.

The pale blue waters of the shallow lagoon behind the penguin rookeries come into view before long. The approach to the shanty at the northern end of Volunteer beach can be tricky to negotiate due to the small streams that flow from the hills into the lagoon. Temporary bridges are used by locals to span these streams and are moved from one crossing point to another as required. Once past the shanty the abundant wildlife soon becomes evident. Upland geese and ruddy-headed geese are very common in the grassy valley that leads from the shanty to the lagoon. By late summer the small lakes contain family parties of speckled teal and crested ducks. The track heads up on to the bank that divides the lagoon from the beach and continues past all the penguin colonies towards Volunteer Point. The king penguin rookery is towards the far end of the bank. Vehicles are best parked on the open grassy area to the north. There is no shelter other than in the vehicles themselves, therefore warm clothing is essential at this site.

What to see

The main **penguin colony** does move slightly from year to year, but is always located between the valley and the southern boundary fence. These birds are used to the presence of visitors throughout the year but a distance of 7.5m must be respected. It is possible to get close views of the birds by sitting beside their main routes to the sea and waiting for them to come and inspect the unfamiliar object. The majority of the inactive birds in the main group are probably incubating their huge, single egg. This egg is sometimes visible on top of the penguin's feet, as it awaits incubation, but is hidden when the bird sits down. The penguin's stiff tail feathers help prop the bird upright when it is incubating or roosting. Penguins can also rest by lying prone on the ground but seem to prefer to remain upright, presumably as this gives a better chance of spotting any approaching predators.

The air around the rookery is full of soft piping noises through the summer. This sound is the young calling to their parents. When just hatched these youngsters are small enough to stay hidden under the folds of their parents' skin, especially on cold windy days, but as they get larger, or on warm days, their heads peep out just above the parents' feet. Chicks, which have grown too big to fit under the parent birds, still try to hide by pushing their heads into their former haven. They look a rather comical sight, only their head hidden, and the rest of the body exposed to the elements. As they grow, the chicks grow a very fluffy, brown, downy coat to protect them from the cold. Years ago they were known as 'oakum boys', as the colour of these downy feathers was reminiscent of the oakum used in caulking ships. These birds look a sorry sight when they lose these feathers and gain their adult plumage, before heading out to sea for the first time.

Adult king penguins have very rich auburn-coloured neck patches and throats. This colour is not so intense in the immature birds that are too young to breed. These birds have a singular reproductive cycle, which involves breeding early in year one, late in year two and resting for the third year; consequently the rookery contains birds of various ages. Those males that have come ashore looking to mate are the most vocal. They make themselves as tall as possible before pointing their bill up to the sky and trumpeting, finishing with a flourish before slowly subsiding to their usual height. This is always an impressive performance, although the penguin tends to sound like a trainee wind-musician. The main breeding activity takes place around the principal flock, but there are usually several smaller groups nearby. There may be some young birds in these satellite groups, but they are usually non-breeding adults. Males seeking a mate wander around the main group, adopting a very exaggerated strutting walk and batting each other with their flippers.

The majority of the birds return to the sea at Volunteer Beach. Some walk in the other direction, to the lagoon, where they can be seen washing and splashing about in the shallows. The low banks above the small beach on the edge of the lagoon make a good vantage point for observing these birds. Sometimes they can be seen swimming in the shallow water and the graceful speed of their movements is in stark contrast to their upright waddling gait on land.

King penguins constitute the main attraction of Volunteers, as the sanctuary is known on the island, but they are not the only penguins breeding prolifically on this grassy bank. Two colonies of gentoo penguins occupy the lagoon side of the bank a short walk from the king penguins. The number of colonies has varied over the years. Sometimes two groups of penguins will merge, whilst in other years they will remain apart, but the overall number of birds does not vary significantly. By late summer all the young will have been gathered into crèches in the middle of the colony for protection from predatory birds. It is quite a sight when the young race after their returning parents to beg for food. The adult's purpose is twofold: it wants to teach its offspring to feed and also wants to ensure that it is nurturing its own young and not its neighbours'. Magellanic penguins prefer the beach side of the bank where the drier sandy ground is much more suitable for digging burrows than the wet peaty ground. The bank above the beach is, therefore, riddled with used and unused penguin burrows.

After the penguin colonies have been visited there is plenty more to see. The **flora** is dominated by grasses thanks to the grazing birds and sheep. Some of the wetter valleys are full of *gunnera*, with its inedible red berries hidden under the leaves in late summer. The most colourful flower is the sea cabbage with its silvery white leaves, fluffy to the touch and topped by bright yellow flowers at the height of the summer. The seeds formed during January are a preferred food of the islands' smallest finches, the black-chinned siskins. The sea cabbage grows above the shoreline, anchoring the shifting sands. Their deep roots enable these plants to survive in what must be a very inhospitable habitat when the wind whips up the sand. In the lee of the sea cabbage, small groups of waders gather in late summer, the majority of which are white-rumped sandpipers that have come from North America to winter on the islands. The other birds are the resident two-banded plovers, which breed above the high tide mark, so it is sometimes possible to find some of the young racing from one clump of sea cabbage to the next.

Dotted along the long sandy beach are clusters of penguins, geese and steamer ducks. Magellanic, gentoo and king penguins have differing requirements as far as choosing a breeding site is concerned, but mixed flocks on the beach are nonetheless quite usual. On windy days they lie down with their backs to the wind and seem to be fast asleep, ignoring the sand drift gathering up behind them. The low elevation of the bank means that it is difficult to watch the penguins swimming to the shore. They appear as if by magic out of the surf as the waves crash upon the beach. Sea lions have been glimpsed trying to catch these birds.

The second most frequent species, after penguins, are geese. Upland geese and ruddy-headed geese frequent all grassy areas. By late summer they have gathered into large family groups. Habitually the males gather together flocks of juveniles, irrespective of their parentage or age. According to one theory, this behaviour suggests that the males use unrelated offspring as an avian shield for their own goslings, the probability being that any predator will not detect their young. The predators here are mostly avian. Turkey vultures and red-backed hawks are the most numerous and can be seen around most colonies, whilst peregrine falcons circle high over Volunteer Point Sanctuary. Antarctic skuas nest close to their food sources. The skuas that breed here are generally very tolerant of man and unfortunately have begun to scavenge from the visitors to this site. The paucity of vegetation and the natural desolation of the landscape, although ideal for penguins, are not a combination to attract many more species to this region.

A walk beyond the eastern fence leads the visitor out onto a series of headlands, some with spectacular caves. Rock shags breed on some of the headlands and night herons can often be found feeding in the pools. This walk gives another dimension to this already fascinating area

The small islets beyond Volunteer Point at the far end of the reserve are the haunts of fur seals, and visitors are not normally allowed. Elephant seals have been recorded on some of the sand beaches in the sanctuary but, in common with fur seals, they often pick sites that are not readily accessible to tourists.

SEAL BAY

This remote spot on the north coast is rarely visited but has a good range of wildlife in an attractive situation.

Getting there

The area is part of the Port Louis Farm, owned by Peter and Melanie Gilding, from whom permission must be sought before entering their land. They will occasionally undertake guided tours; otherwise the only tour operator with permission to take groups to Seal Bay is **Discovery Tours**. For details contact Tony Smith; tel: 21027; fax: 22304; email: discovery@horizon.co.fk.

Seal Bay is at roughly the same distance from Port Stanley as the king penguin colony at Volunteer Point, and consequently is a full day excursion. The route follows the main road as far as Port Louis before branching off northwards. Once again it must be emphasised that local knowledge is essential to reach this destination.

What to see

The shepherd's shanty, Seal Bay House, lies behind the beach. To the west is the Rabbit Rincon promontory, to the east past a smaller headland is the inlet of Swan Pond and, between the two, is McBride Head, the most northerly point of this part of East Falkland. Extensive rookeries of rockhopper penguins occupy the cliffs around Seal Bay. The rare macaroni penguins have been detected in low numbers in these colonies on several occasions in the past. Gentoo penguins have made their colonies where the sea is more accessible away from the cliffs. Seal Bay is a popular holiday destination for Falkland Islanders.

SALVADOR

This farm to the north of East Falkland has been in the hands of one family for five generations. The recent completion of an all-weather road has meant that it is now possible to reach Stanley in two hours. This beautiful coastline, with its abundant wildlife, has much to offer the visitor looking for somewhere away from the more popular sites.

History

Andrez Pitaluga established the farm in 1838 when he settled in the Falkland Islands. He spent many years obtaining the leases of land in East Falkland, before he set about removing the wild cattle that had been introduced by the sailors and early settlers. The farm was started in the early 1880s and named Gibraltar Station in memory of his birthplace. The fifth generation of his family farms the 50,000 acres in the traditional manner, currently producing fine wool from sheep of Tasmanian origin.

Getting there

The farm is a 15–20 minute flight from Port Stanley or approximately two hours by road. The farm owners will transport the visitor from the airstrip to the accommodation. Excursions are available in a four-wheel drive vehicle. It is hoped in the near future to be able to offer boat trips to some of the nearby islands on which there are colonies of elephant seals, southern sea lions and sundry breeding seabirds. Another option is to travel to the north coast to view the wildlife from the sea, bearing in mind that all boat trips are weather-dependent. The farm can be contacted for more up to date information.

Where to stay

The accommodation is self-catering in Salvador Lodge, which can sleep up to eight in three twin-bedded rooms and two single rooms. There are three toilets, a bath and a shower. The lodge is a relatively modern house with a solid fuel stove, which provides heating and hot water. It has a well-equipped kitchen and a lounge with TV, video and radio. A pack of tea, coffee, bread and buns is provided on arrival for each group. All other provisions must be brought with the visitor. Meat, usually mutton, is always obtainable and fresh vegetables are occasionally available. The small store has limited supplies of drinks and sweets. Depending upon the farmers' work commitments, a fully catered option may be booked for overseas groups. The lodge is closed annually between April 30 and September 15. Camping is permitted on this settlement and the charge is £5 per person per night. Contact Robin and Jene Pitaluga, **Salvador Lodge** Gibraltar Station, Falkland Islands; tel: 500 3199; fax: 500 31194.

What to see

The main attractions of this area are the penguin colonies along the northern coast. Large rookeries of rockhopper penguins mixed in with king shags are found near Cape Bougainville. A few macaroni penguins have been noted in these colonies in recent years. At Mare Rincon, a little further along the coast away from the cliffs, gentoo penguins and Magellanic penguins breed in profusion. A careful look through the gentoo penguin colonies may well reveal a few king penguins, especially in late summer when they come ashore to moult. Many species of wildfowl breed in suitable habitat along this northern coast, so the pools are worth investigating. Closer to the farm there is a small colony of gentoo penguins within easy walking distance across the creek.

The lovely coastline, with its white sand beaches stretching between jagged rocky outcrops, makes this a superb place to stay for hikers, casual walkers or wildlife enthusiasts. Local mullet can be caught in the creek just a short walk from the lodge. A further option is a walking tour of the settlement, which explains how a traditional sheep farm works.

This relatively unknown part of East Falkland is worthy of inclusion in the itinerary of a visit to the islands.

CAPE DOLPHIN

This destination entails a long drive from Port Stanley. As at Volunteer Point, the last stretch of the drive beyond the all-weather road is through difficult terrain, where local knowledge is essential and permission must be granted from the owners. Cape Dolphin is the most northerly point of East Falkland, marking the division between East and West Falkland. It is an infrequently visited site with enormous potential.

Getting there

In order to reach this distant headland the visitor must follow the main road from Port Stanley before turning north towards Port Louis, then follow the left fork at Estancia towards Port San Carlos. The Cape Dolphin track heads north from this road and then passes between West Hill and Coutts Hill.

What to see

The Cape Dolphin area is a designated wildlife sanctuary best known for its breeding southern sea lions, which still breed close to the very tip but are in much reduced numbers. Also breeding along the headland are gentoo penguins and king shags, with rock shags breeding on the cliff faces.

The largest pond in the area is Elephant Beach Pond, which is close to the dunes that lie behind Foul Bay. The other pool is Swan Pond, situated almost at the tip of Cape Dolphin. Both pools are good places to look for black-necked swans, as although this shy species does not often allow a close approach, it can quite easily be viewed at these locations. Amid the more common waterfowl, pairs of yellow-billed pintails can be found on both ponds. The only grebes that breed on these waters are the white-tufted on Swan Pond.

SAN CARLOS/PORT SAN CARLOS

The Spanish sloop *San Carlos* visited East Falkland in 1768, giving its name to the inlet and the settlements which lie on the western side of the island, 50 miles from Port Stanley. Port San Carlos is situated on the arm of the inlet that later becomes the San Carlos River, which is one of the best-known fishing sites on East Falkland.

San Carlos
Getting there

San Carlos is a three-hour drive from Port Stanley along the all-weather road, past the military base at Mount Pleasant before turning north prior to reaching the Goose Green/Darwin area. All gates in the section of road from Darwin to San Carlos should be left in the position that they are found. There is an airstrip close to the settlement, which is roughly 25 minutes from Stanley by air. It is possible, with the farmer's permission, to drive from San Carlos to Port San Carlos, but local knowledge is needed to locate the correct route.

History

Ajax Bay, opposite Port San Carlos settlement, was chosen as the site of a factory to freeze sheep carcasses for export to the UK. It was a complete financial disaster, and after wasting a great deal of time and money, it was eventually closed down in the mid-1950s. The buildings were still standing in 1982 and were used by the British Task Force as a field hospital after the landings in June that year. The television images of the Argentinian planes attacking the British Task force in San Carlos Water are some of the most dramatic of that war. The Task Force started landing troops at 02.00 on Friday May 21 1982. By the end of the day several thousand men had been landed and had established the bridgehead. During this action *HMS Ardent* was abandoned after a series of air attacks, and two helicopters were shot down. Seventeen Argentinian aircraft and four helicopters were brought down that day. The shore facilities were not attacked until May 27, by which time some of the British forces were already making their advance on Goose Green. San Carlos Water continued to be a busy port until the Argentinian surrender on June 14 1982.

Port San Carlos also made the headlines in 1982 when the 3rd Battalion Parachute Regiment landed at nearby 'Green Beach', so called because during the British-Argentinian conflict beaches were colour-coded according to their military significance.

What to see

The majority of visitors to San Carlos are interested in the military history of the area. Little remains from the 1982 war apart from the remnants of the field hospital and the memorial. The **British War Cemetery** is a short distance to the north of the settlement overlooking San Carlos Water. This well-maintained memorial is a poignant reminder of the lives lost. Another relic from the landings is the renovated missile-firing site on **Lookout Hill**, to the north of the settlement. A small, but well thought out museum to commemorate the events in **San Carlos Water** has been opened next to the Blue Beach Lodge. It contains photographs and objects from those hectic days of winter 1982. This is a branch of the museum in Port Stanley where many more relics from the 1982 conflict can be seen. The museum also contains a display prepared by Falkland Conservation about its work and about the islands' wildlife. There is also a section about rural life on the islands prior to the events of 1982.

San Carlos does not have huge colonies of seabirds near the settlement, but several species of waterfowl can be found along the shore and Commerson's dolphins are frequently seen in San Carlos Water. The scenery in this part of East Falkland is superb, from the views across Falkland Sound to the heights of Mount Usborne, the highest mountain on Falkland at 2,312ft (704m). One of the best panoramic views can be had from the pass through the Sussex Mountains. To the south, the visitor looks out over Goose Green/ Darwin to Lafonia; to the north the view takes in the length of San Carlos Water to Fanning Head.

Port San Carlos
Getting there

Port San Carlos, although only a short distance from San Carlos, is best reached from Port Stanley along the all-weather road. This journey can be achieved in just over two hours by road, or by a 20-minute flight. The drive takes the visitor through some splendid scenery.

History

William Cameron founded a farming community in 1870, which was then called San Carlos North. It stayed intact until 1989 when it was divided into five individual farms. Port San Carlos is one of the premier fishing sites on the Falkland Islands.

Where to stay

Full board and self-catering properties are available at Port San Carlos, whereas, at the time of writing, no accommodation is on offer in San Carlos.

The house called **The Pod** can sleep six adults in one double room, which contains a cot or folding bed, one triple room and one single room. There is a shower room, a bathroom and two toilets. Electricity is generated throughout the day. Tea and coffee facilities are free to residents at any time. Transport can be provided to enable the visitor to travel around this farm. A self-catering bungalow, sleeping eight in three bunk beds and a double bed is also available in the settlement. Meals can be taken at the Pod upon payment of an extra charge. Contact Patrick Bernsten and Pat Pratlett; tel: 41018; fax 41019.

The other accommodation in the settlement is fully catered at **Smylies Farm**. This farmhouse can sleep eight in one double room and two triple rooms. Contact Tony and Jenny Anderson (tel/fax: 41013).

Four miles upriver is a **'portacabin' at Blackleys**, which is situated next to the San Carlos River and is therefore popular with fishermen. It can sleep up to five in two bunk beds and one single bed. On site there are a gas cooker, toilet and cold running water. The portacabin's generator provides electricity. Contact Patrick Bernsten and Pat Pratlett at The Pod (see above).

What to see

Most of the visitors to Port San Carlos have come to fish in the San Carlos River that enters the sea a few miles from the settlement. The prime time for fishing is from the end of February to the end of April. Falkland mullet and trout can be caught in the river, and the former can also be hooked downstream in the tidal reaches of the river. The current record sea trout for the islands, weight 22lb 12.5 oz (10kg), was caught in 1992 on the San Carlos River. River permits and fishing licences can be arranged in Port Stanley.

There is plenty for the non-fishing visitor to explore. Port San Carlos is a picturesque settlement some miles inland from **Fanning Head**, which overlooks the entrance of Falkland Sound. North of the head is a rockhopper penguin colony that looks across to West Falkland. Cetaceans have been observed from this vantage point as they enter or leave Falkland Sound. The tide race carries food to the surface, therefore when the flow of water is at its greatest, the feeding frenzies of gulls, terns and other seabirds can be seen from the shore.

Paloma Beach is approximately a 40-minute drive from the settlement. The spectacular beach stretches for two miles along Middle Bay. This scenic site is home to a gentoo penguin colony that occasionally attracts some king penguins. To the west of the beach is **Smylies Creek**, which is a good location to look for some of the island's wildfowl, as are Paloma Pond and Shallow Pond which lie behind Paloma Beach. Black-crowned night herons can be seen creeping along the shallow waters of Smylies Creek. Upland geese and ruddy-headed geese are common on the grasslands inland from the beach. One of the rarest geese on the islands, the ashy-headed geese, has been recorded several times here.

Many of the species of wading birds found on the islands have been seen in the Fanning Harbour area, some five miles west of Port San Carlos. These birds regularly commute between the shore and nearby Rabbit Island.

DARWIN/GOOSE GREEN

The name Goose Green has become one of the most famous in the islands after the events of May and June 1982. Darwin and Goose Green are situated less than a mile apart on the narrow neck of land that joins the two sections of East Falkland: the low-lying land of Lafonia to the south and Wickham Heights and the Onion Range to the north. Choisel Sound opens out to the sea to the east and Brenton Loch flows into Falkland Sound to the west. Darwin is named after the famous naturalist, Charles Darwin, who visited the islands in the 1830s. There is evidence of the gauchos who once lived in Darwin. For those interested in the history of the Falklands war in 1982 there is much to see. Visitors at Bodie Creek can admire one of the most southerly suspension bridges in the world.

History

Samuel Fisher Lafone, a merchant from Montevideo, bought the region to the south of Darwin in 1846. The name for this area, Lafonia, is a corruption of his surname. He had also bought the contract to take charge of all the wild cattle in East Falkland, having made his base at Hope Place on the southern side of Brenton Loch. By the time the Falkland Islands Company bought him out five years later very few cattle remained. Hope Place was found to be unsuitable for livestock farming, and in 1859 the settlement was transferred to its present location in Darwin. The company became the most important sheep owner on the islands and by 1880 they had 100,000 sheep on East Falkland. In 1922 Goose Green was chosen as the site of an improved sheep handling operation. Wool sheds, hydraulic presses, dips and pens were moved to the settlement. Sheep were originally farmed for their meat until this proved uneconomical; thereafter wool became the islands' major export. The shearing sheds in Goose Green are some of the largest on Falkland.

The Community Hall in Goose Green, in the centre of the settlement, was to be the home of 114 people during the war. Almost a month after the initial Argentine invasion all of the residents of Goose Green and any visiting civilians were imprisoned in the hall. They were only allowed out for very short periods each day and had to endure these cramped conditions until liberated by the Second Parachute Regiment on May 29 1982. Goose Green and Darwin were garrisoned with up to 1,400 Argentinian troops. These soldiers were well entrenched and had placed hundreds of mines around the settlement. After a heavy naval bombardment the men of the Second Parachute Regiment attacked in what became the first major land battle of the war. Many men were killed, including Colonel 'H' Jones of the 'Paras' and Flight Lieutenant Nick Taylor who was shot down in his Sea Harrier over the settlement. The British men of the Parachute Regiment, who died freeing Darwin and Goose Green, are remembered by a memorial on the hill overlooking the settlements and by the memorial at San Carlos. The restoration of the settlement after the war took some time. Some buildings in Goose Green still show bullet holes and the minefields are a constant reminder of those dangerous days.

Since the war the farm has been sold to the Falkland Island Government, who set up Falkland Landholdings Ltd to run the 300,000-acre farm. Goose Green is not the thriving community it was during the 1980s and has far fewer residents nowadays. In contrast, Darwin is prospering with a recently refurbished and reopened lodge and holiday cottages.

Getting there

Darwin and Goose Green are only a 35-minute drive from the international airport on the military base at Mount Pleasant, whereas Port Stanley is over an hour's drive away. It is also possible to fly in from Port Stanley airport. The flight takes approximately 20 minutes.

Where to stay

The recently reopened lodge at **Darwin** has six bedrooms that have views over Choisel Sound, the settlement and the Wickham Heights. This well-appointed property has a lounge, conservatory and dining room. Locally grown organic produce is part of the menu. Contact Ken and Bonnie Greenland; tel: 32255; fax: 32253.

There is also the option of staying in one of the two three-bedroomed cottages, each sleeping six, in Darwin. The visitor can be completely independent or arrange to use the lodge bar and restaurant. These well-equipped cottages have all linen provided. There is a store in Goose Green for those who wish to choose their own shopping, or stores can be purchased in advance for visitors who do not wish to bring their own goods. Contact Ken and Bonnie Greenland at Darwin House (see above).

What to see

A short walk from the lodge leads to the recently renovated **corral**. The gauchos used this circular building in the 1800s for gathering cattle. Adjacent to the corral is a stone building, the **Galpon**, which was home for the gauchos and their horses. The shore and the small pond are favoured haunts of ruddy-headed geese and upland geese. Magellanic oystercatchers and blackish oystercatchers can be seen performing their display flights during the summer over the lagoon in front of the lodge.

The road from Darwin towards Goose Green cuts through the Boca Wall, a gorse-covered bank of peat which marks the division between the two settlements. The **memorial** to the 17 men of the Second Parachute Regiment who died is on Darwin Hill a little further along the track. The open grassy slopes were the sites of some of the fiercest battles including that in which Colonel 'H' Jones was killed. His memorial is a hundred yards from the road on the bank of a low hill. On the slope above this marker can be seen the remains of the foxholes that he was attacking when he died. It is not far to the grave of Flight Lieutenant Nick Taylor, which lies close to the airstrip.

Goose Green is a much larger settlement than Darwin and has a proportionately larger quay where all the wool from the farm was loaded in the past. The end of the quay is built over the remains of a boat named the *Vicar of Bray*. This is the last extant ship to have participated in the California Gold Rush. Legend has it that the *Vicar of Bray* was in San Francisco Harbour during the great earthquake of 1906, and it is now owned by the San Francisco Museum. Black-crowned night herons can be found roosting on the timbers inside this hulk. Rock shags are often quite approachable as they roost on the bollards at the end of the quay. The wreck of the *Garland* is visible from the quay, three miles across Choisel Sound. This 18th century iron ship, built in Liverpool, was wrecked here in 1911.

One of the highlights of a visit here is the **Bodie Suspension Bridge**. This involves a 15-minute drive to the south of Goose Green to the Bodie Creek. The track bends sharply before the inlet to reveal a rather magnificent bridge, built in 1824–25 to span the 400ft (122m) gap. It was built to reduce the time taken to drive sheep from the southern parts of Lafonia to the shearing sheds in Goose Green, thus avoiding an arduous detour around the inlet. This bridge is now closed but is still a superb sight, although a little incongruous in this setting with no other man-made structure in sight.

After returning to Goose Green there are two cemeteries to visit. The first, on the outskirts of Goose Green, is the disused **Darwin Cemetery**. The other is across the neck of land to the north of Darwin. This is the **Argentine Military Cemetery**, which lies on the opposite site of Choisel Sound and contains the graves of Argentinians who fell during the 1982 war.

There are opportunities to watch the wildlife of this area using Darwin as a base. Boat trips to some of the small islands in Choisel Sound can be organised by prior arrangement. Fishing, golf and horse riding are popular pastimes when staying here, or it is possible simply to relax in the peaceful atmosphere. The golf course is at Goose Green, whereas the horse riding is based at Swan Inlet near Mount Pleasant.

Darwin is being promoted as an alternative place to Port Stanley to begin and finish a trip to the Falkland Islands. The interested visitor can explore the most typical aspects of Falkland life in this region.

BLEAKER ISLAND

Lying to the southeast of Lafonia, Bleaker Island has only been on the tourist map in recent years as a stopping point for some of the cruise ships that visit the islands. The opening of self catering accommodation for the 2001–2 season will make this island available for land-based visitors. This long, thin island is over 12 miles (19km) long but is only one mile (1.6km) wide at the widest point. It is still stocked with sheep but has a very good range of wildlife including three species of breeding penguin.

Getting there

The majority of visitors who reach this island do so via the smaller cruise ships that are able to get in close enough to land people. The only other method of getting to Bleaker Island is to fly via FIGAS. The airstrip is not far from the accommodation.

Where to stay

The self-catering accommodation is situated in the recently renovated **Cobb's Cottage**. It can accommodate five people in two twin rooms and one single room. Basic foodstuffs can be provided. Food can also be arranged from the Malvina House Hotel in Stanley. There is 24 hour electricity with a gas cooker. Washing facilities include a bath and shower. The cottage is equipped with TV, radio and a hi-fi. The visitor is not alone on the island as there is a resident couple on the island. The accommodation can be booked through the

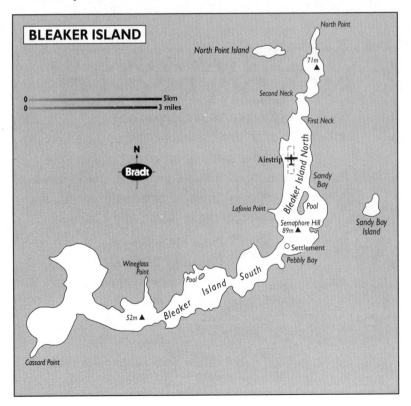

Malvina House Hotel, 3 Ross Rd, Stanley; tel: 21355; fax: 21357; email: malvina@horizon.co.fk.

What to see

The highlight of this island is the rockhopper penguin colony of some 750 pairs that is situated only a short walk from the cottage. Further south a colony of gentoo penguins can be found, along with a scattering of Magellanic penguins. The pools on the island contain both white-tufted and silver grebe, as well as many wildfowl, including the occasional black-necked swan. There is some tussac grass on the island, which is home to a population of grass wren and Cobb's wren. There are also some small tussac islands offshore which are home to some of the birds that can be seen on Bleaker Island. Birds of prey are well represented, with breeding crested caracara and the occasional striated caracara that have probably come from Sea Lion Island to the southeast. Southern sea lions can often be seen hauled out on the rocks but do not breed on the island. Up to 40 have been seen at any one time.

There are miles of open country for walking and long sandy beaches for those that like to potter along the strand line.

For those who have visited most of the more commonly visited sites, this new venture offers a chance to be a little different.

West Falkland 6

West Falkland is generally more rugged than East Falkland, the highest point being Mount Adam at 2,297ft (700m). The three main hilly areas are the Mount Robinson/ Mount Adam range which runs east to west ending at Byron Heights, the Hornby Mountains which run parallel to Falkland

Sound to the west of Port Howard, and the high ground in the Port Stephens area. West Falkland is mostly composed of Palaeozoic sedimentary rocks, quartzite, sandstone and shale. Some of the higher peaks show signs of glaciation during the Pleistocene period. The eastern coast along Falkland Sound is very linear, whilst the coastline to the west is deeply indented. Rugged cliffs reaching 700ft (213m) dominate western coasts. There are many shallow lakes and streams. The habitat is mostly grasslands in the wetter areas, described as oceanic heath formations, but this gradually changes as the ground dries into diddle-dee/blechnum fern heaths. In these two habitat types a range of other plants occurs, depending upon the soil type and the amount of water present.

The main settlements are Port Howard, Fox Bay and Fox Bay West, Port Stephens, Chartres, Hill Cove and Roy Cove. Flying over West Falkland, a scattering of shepherds' huts can be seen away from the main settlements. A recent programme of road-building means that it is now possible to travel from Port Howard to Chartres, Fox Bay or to turn north to Hill Cove. Thanks to this road, journeys that used to take the best part of a day can now be completed in a matter of hours. Although not as rich in wildlife as some of the smaller islands, there is still plenty to see. Port Howard is one of the main fishing centres on Falkland.

PORT HOWARD

The settlement is situated at the base of Mount Maria (2,400ft) at the head of its own sheltered harbour. It is one of the most picturesque settlements, especially when the gorse is in full bloom in springtime. The only accommodation was the farm manager's house until a few years ago. Port Howard is one of the few remaining large farming settlements in the islands. The farm is some 200,000 acres which supports 47,000 pure bred Corriedale sheep.

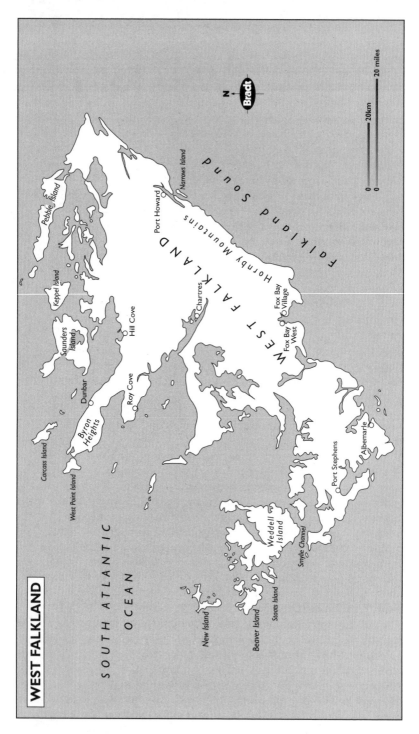

WEST FALKLAND

Some of the outlying islands may have a greater variety of wildlife in a small area than Port Howard but the potential of this area is very great. The varied day trips, and the comfort and welcome at the lodge, make this an essential stop on a tour of the islands.

Getting there

There are two airfields serving Port Howard, the nearest of which is only a few minutes walk from the lodge, on the other side of the bay. The other airfield is a ten-minute drive from the settlement at Purvis Pond. Both are used by FIGAS to get the visitor to the settlement. The flight from Port Stanley usually takes approximately 30 minutes depending upon wind strength and direction.

It is also possible to arrange a transfer from one of the settlements on East Falkland, but this is usually for a special event and as such, rather rare. Visitors may also drive from one of the other settlements on West Falkland, the majority of which are serviced by their own airstrip, or arrive by boat on the *Tamar*. Vehicle hire can be arranged from Port Howard Lodge.

Where to stay

The lodge has seven rooms, all en suite. There is also one separate bathroom and one public toilet. Other public areas include dining room, lounge, bar and conservatory. The lodge is well known in the islands for its food and hospitality. Hattie Lee is justifiably regarded as one of the best cooks on Falkland. Breakfast and dinner are taken in the dining room. A packed lunch can be made ready for any excursions. A very relaxed atmosphere makes this an extremely comfortable place to stay.

Port Howard Lodge Port Howard; tel/fax: 42187; guest phone: 25125; email rlee@horizon.co.uk.

What to see

There are a variety of things to do whilst staying at the lodge. During the season, fishing is very popular. There are many different birds to be seen around the settlement and the possibility of seeing even more on excursions. There is a nine-hole golf course, Clippy Hill, which is free to visitors, and a putting green at the lodge.

Port Howard was occupied by approximately 1,000 troops during the 1982 war with Argentina. Much of the equipment left behind after their departure has been placed in a small museum beside the lodge. The collection gives an idea of what life must have been like during the occupation. Guided excursions take visitors to some of the sites that figured in the war. At the edge of the settlement there are some well-marked minefields remaining from the war.

Many walks start from the lodge, whereas a Land Rover is needed to reach the other sites of interest. Maps of suggested walks are available in the lodge. The sheltered gardens of the lodge are a good place to look for some of the smaller birds and are a suntrap. The harbour is only a ten-minute walk from the lodge through the settlement. The bridge and ford in the middle of 'town' are a good

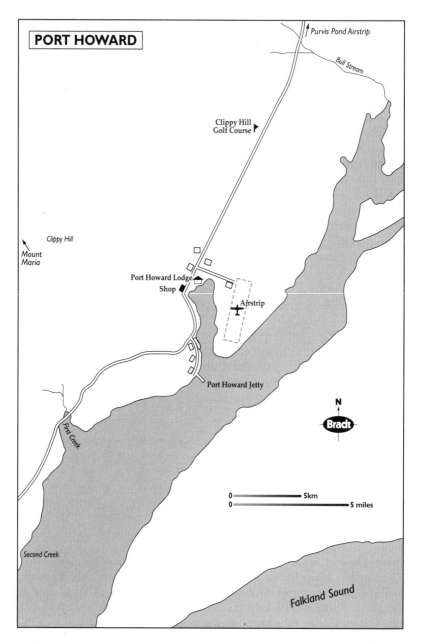

place to look for black-crowned night herons feeding in the stream. Small groups of black-chinned siskins can be seen in the low bushes on the slope above. Where the stream enters the inlet, a flock of speckled teal are usually feeding in the shallows. The track winds past the shearing shed to the quay. The shearing sheds are used several times during the summer, so it is often possible to see how the wool is processed. Walking up over the airport and along the inlet eventually leads to the cemetery in which can be found the grave of Captain Hamilton, who lost his life during the Argentinian occupation in 1982. Bull Stream flows from this inlet, helping to make a very rich area botanically.

The main channel to the south is reached by a short walk or drive from the settlement. Magellanic oystercatchers and blackish oystercatchers feed along the shore, along with a scattering of two-banded plovers. It is sometimes possible to observe Commerson's dolphins cruising in the shallows, whilst further out there are southern giant petrels zooming low over the water. **Double River** enters the sound in a broad expanse of stone and mud. The views from here are fantastic, looking out through the entrance channel into Falkland Sound. On the return trip, a detour up to **Freezer Rocks** on the side of Mount Maria is well worthwhile. The views from here are amazing on a clear day. All of this can be reached by Land Rover or included in a day's walk from the lodge.

EXCURSIONS FROM PORT HOWARD
A variety of sites can be visited from Port Howard using the new roads.

Fox Bay
The trip to Fox Bay can take only an hour or so. However, there are many places to visit on the way. A short drive from Port Howard takes one past a small quarry in which red-backed hawks have occasionally nested. A little further down the road are the old peat diggings. The settlement does not use much peat in modern times, but the scale of the diggings can still be perceived there. On the opposite side of the road, towards Fox Bay, there are the remains of two of the aircraft shot down during the war. There are eight or nine wrecked planes on Port Howard land. It is a good place to see Falkland pipits, and yellow orchids have been found here recently. The road then continues past Harps Farm. Crested Caracara have been seen along the ridges that border some of the streams in this area.

The road continues for a while though fairly level ground before descending on a steep bend. Just beyond the stream is the lay-by created by the road crew when they extracted the hard core necessary for building the road. This is a wonderful site for geologists or, indeed, anyone with an interest in fossils. The broken rock towards the rear edge of the flattened ground is full of trace fossils. There have been at least three species of *trilobite* and five species of *brachiopod* and *crinoids* found here. The rock is part of the Fox Bay Formation, which is early Devonian in age (Emsian period), some 385–390 million years old. As these stops can occupy most of the morning, it is just as well that there is a good lunch spot not too far away at Hawk's Nest Ponds. The road crosses the Chartres River either by ford or a narrow bridge. This scenic spot often has a good number of waterfowl on the river.

The two **Hawk's Nest Ponds** are well worth looking at. They are only a short distance from the road on the east side of the road. Care should be taken when approaching the northern pool, as the track can be rather wet, making it easy to get bogged down here. The track leads to the reed bed at the northern edge of the pond. A good variety of wildlife can be found feeding along the edge of this reed bed, especially if the ground behind is flooded. Although this is primarily a good site for waterfowl, this flooded area can be good for wading birds. The reed beds have occasionally held a few black-crowned night heron. Close to the edges of the pool it is possible to see speckled teal, silver teal and white-tufted grebe, whereas the flock of chiloe wigeons are usually found out in the middle. Among the most attractive water birds on Falkland, the black-necked swans breed on both of the Hawk's Nest Ponds. After Christmas their young are quite well grown and can be seen following their parents across the pool. These are very shy birds and will not allow observers to approach closely. As with any patch of water on Falkland, there is always the chance of an unusual bird turning up; for example an ashy-headed goose has been seen in with the flocks of upland geese in recent years. The southern pond also has reed beds. In this case two small areas of reed on the west and south side of the pool are worth investigating. This pool is much wider and therefore is more favoured by the flying steamer duck. This species can be difficult to see on a visit to the islands. In recent years at least one pair have bred on this pond. Although there are fewer water birds in number on this pool, there is a greater variety of species. Yellow-billed pintail is another species that has recently favoured the southern pool. The white grass around the pool is a good place to see Falkland pipits. As this species breeds here, their tuneful song can be heard on sunny days in the spring. Although called Hawk's Nest Ponds, birds of prey are not common here. It would, however, be an unusual visit that does not discover at least one red-backed hawk quartering the ground in the far distance.

The drive from the pond to Fox Bay passes through some of the wettest areas on West Falkland. Although the habitat seems ideal for a range of waterfowl, there is usually very little worth stopping for apart from some very tame rufous-chested dotterels that often feed right beside the road. The last mile before reaching the settlements at Fox Bay provides some of the more spectacular scenery of the trip. Shortly after the road forks to the left is Fox Bay East, the other fork leading to Fox Bay West. In the bay between the two settlements are a small number of tussac grass islands. Magellanic penguins can be seen gathering on the rocky ends of these islets. The shallow bay here is a good site for observing Peale's dolphins. They can be seen cruising around the edges of the bay or playing in the kelp around the main bay.

Just inland from the quay is the **wool mill and museum**. The latter, although only a small part of the building, is full of photos and artefacts from the early settlers and the first days of wool farming on Falkland. There is also a chance to buy some of the latest T-shirts and hats that have been made here. The wool mill is a fascinating building with all sorts of fearsome-looking machinery that turns the raw wool into the finished product used in making the jumpers at Port Howard, amongst other places.

The track beyond the mill leads through a series of gates (which should be left in the position you find them) out into a long passage between fields. At

Above New Island (WW)

Left Native strawberry (WW)

Below left Falkland thrush and gorse, Carcass Island (WW)

Below right Lady's slipper, Carcass Island (WW)

Following page Rockhopper penguins, Kidney Island (HB)

the end of this passage, bear right around the bay, skirting the minefield until on the south facing cape called **Kelp Point**. Park here and walk onto the slight rise. The sights and sounds should lead you to the gentoo penguin colony. This colony moves slightly every year. The old breeding sites can be seen by locating the bright green circles of enriched grass. As with all colonies, a safe distance must be kept from the birds. It is preferable to ensure that one is not blocking the birds coming to and from the colony by standing on their track to the sea. By following the birds back to the beach, many more can be seen on the rocks where they come ashore. They often stand around here for a while when preening, moulting or just resting having come in from the open sea. The occasional king penguin has been seen here, coming ashore to moult. If unable to find their own species for company, king penguins will make do with the next best, which is often a gentoo penguin colony. A pair of red-backed hawks has nested in this area most years. They will usually let you know if you are too close to the nest site by screaming and making their presence felt. If the wind is from the south, black-browed albatrosses can be seen zooming over the water. In springtime southern fulmars have been seen feeding in the bay prior to their move down to the Antarctic to breed. The main bird activity in the bay involves large numbers of rock shags and king shags. On the rocks below the low cliff, small groups of snowy sheathbills can be found, in amongst large numbers of Falkland flightless steamer ducks and kelp geese. In good visibility the scenery here is superb. One of the most unusual gentoo penguin colonies can be seen on the hill to the south of Fox Bay West. The penguins are only visible with a fairly powerful pair of binoculars or a telescope, as they trudge their way up to the colony at the top of the hill. The late afternoon light on the Hornby Range gives the visitor driving back to Port Howard a quite different sensation from that experienced in the morning.

Hill Cove, Main Point and Turkey Rocks

The other recommended full-day excursion from Port Howard initially follows the same route until the right turn towards Hill Cove is reached. This track follows the lower slopes of Mount Adam over Teal River before rising up over the valley between Mount Adam and Mount Fegan. To the southwest, the settlement of Roy Cove, which was founded in 1872, and George Bay can be seen. Cresting the rise above Hill Cove, the view looking north is spectacular. On a clear day Saunders Island and Carcass Island can be seen across Byron Sound, whilst over the top of Shallow Bay House, Keppel, Goulding and Pebble Islands are visible. It is only a short distance down the hill to the Hill Cove 'forest'. This impressive stand of trees was originally planted in the 1880's but was substantially enlarged in 1925. These trees are amazingly tall and healthy compared to those seen elsewhere on Falkland. The whole area is full of birds, mostly black-chinned siskins and Falkland thrushes, flying around and calling. The far side of the forest contains some smaller trees, including some apple trees, and there is also a small cemetery. The road continues past the settlement to the east of the trees. Before the road follows the edge of Byron Sound, it passes the marker which commemorates the completion of 80km of road. Beyond this is Shallow Bay House and then Main Point House where the road finishes. This farm is home to the only British miniature horses on Falkland. Permission is needed to continue past this point over their land to make a round trip back to Port Howard.

There is no easily defined route between Main Point House and Turkey Rocks along the edge of River Harbour. A driver with local knowledge is essential in these parts. The drive gives wonderful views out towards Pebble Island and the many smaller islands beyond River Harbour. **Turkey Rocks** is a valley that divides two escarpments of sheer rock and has a stone run through the middle. The area is called Turkey Rocks on account of the turkey vultures that breed on the crags on either side. Red-backed hawks and peregrine falcons are also seen in this area on a regular basis. This is an excellent site for a picnic. In late summer small numbers of native strawberries can be found on the western flanks of the valley. The return trip to Port Howard descends some rather steep slopes and crosses through the Warrah River before rejoining the main road.

Narrows Island

The third option for a day out while based at Port Howard is to spend some time on Narrows Island. This thin island on the western edge of Falkland Sound is just over one mile (1.9km) long and up to 240 yards (220m) wide. The boat ride is an amazing experience, especially during the summer months, as it is at that time of year that many Commerson's dolphins come into the shallow waters at Port Howard. As soon as the engine is started, they approach the boat and then accompany it all the way on the short ride to Narrows Island. As the boat goes through the Narrows, many more dolphins come to play in the bow wave or alongside the boat. Landing on the island is by means of a pallet left on the beach for that purpose.

Although it is a small island, the best part of a day can be spent exploring the wide range of wildlife found here. The flora on this island is much more diverse than many of the other islands in Falkland Sound, as it has not been seriously overgrazed. There are a great variety of habitats, from diddle-dee heath to stands of tussac grass. So far 63 species of plants have been recorded; of these six are only found on the Falkland Islands. These are Falkland cudweed, coastal nassauvia, snakeplant, smooth ragwort, woolly ragwort and Falkland rock cress. This is the only site where snakeplant is found on West Falkland. The tussac grass at the northern end of the island is a favoured resting site for southern sea lions, although they can occasionally be found on some of the beaches. Some of the largest balsam bogs on Falkland occur on the slope just above the landing point. The Falklands' more flamboyant flowers can be found here during the spring and summer months, including lady's slipper orchid, almond flower and thrift.

There are 18 species of breeding bird on Narrows Island. The eastern coastal cliffs have a small colony of rock shags tucked out of the wind. On the top of the island, in one of the two colonies of kelp gulls, a small group of dolphin gulls also have their nests. The Antarctic skuas breed on the higher slopes, keeping a watchful eye on the gull colonies for any unattended young. As there are many species of bird nesting on the island the visitor has to be careful not to tread on any nests. Magellanic oystercatchers and blackish oystercatchers nest at the top of the beach on the open shingle areas whilst the two-banded plovers nest in the more open, sandy areas. The breeding waterfowl tend to hide their nests in the thicker banks of diddle-dee and grass. In late summer, after the young have fledged, the used nests are more visible when the down has been blown about by the wind. There are no penguins nesting on Narrows Island, although they can often be seen fishing offshore, as can a few black-browed albatrosses. On calm days the Commerson's

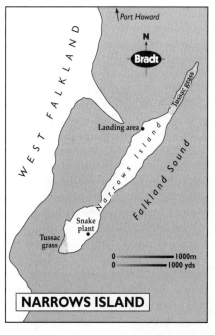

NARROWS ISLAND

dolphins can easily be seen from the island. Other cetaceans, including killer whales, have also been seen in recent years, but are a rare event.

Gladstone Bay

A new visitor site has been opened up in the 2000–1 season. Getting there involves an hour or so drive north past Many Branch Farm before climbing the slopes of Mount Jock. The views from here are superb, looking back to Port Howard and Falkland Sound to the south and over Purvis Harbour out to Pebble Island to the northwest. There are some small examples of stone runs on the higher slopes. This new track runs down to the shore of Purvis Harbour. A colony of gentoo penguin and large numbers of waterfowl frequent Gladstone Bay, with colonies of king shag and rock shag along the low cliffs to the west. Black-crowned night herons breed in the small clumps of tussac grass that cling to the sides of the cliff. Southern sea lions can sometimes be found on the flat rocks on the point to the west of the beach.

FISHING

Port Howard is one of the main centres for fishing in Falkland. The fishing season runs from the beginning of September until the end of April. The licence required is £10 per annum. The two most popular species of fish with anglers in Falkland are the resident brown trout and the Falkland mullet. The former is found in the freshwater rivers, whilst the mullet is found in tidal waters, often following the tide as it comes in over shallow ground. The most frequently fished rivers are the Warrah and the Chartres. The Warrah is a 12-

mile trip from Port Howard. It is also possible to fish in its main tributary, Green Hill Stream, or a little nearer to the lodge in Many Branch Creek. The Chartres River is about 90 minutes' drive along the new road from Port Howard. It can be fished from Little Chartres Farm onward. Sea trout can also be caught in some of the creeks around Port Howard.

OTHER ACCOMMODATION ON WEST FALKLAND

It is possible to stay on some of the other farms on West Falkland in either full board or self catering accommodation.

Full board can be obtained at Hill Cove for up to five people in the home of Peter and Shelly Nightingale. This active sheep farm also has a nine hole golf course, fishing, a variety of wildlife and plenty of beach combing. It is sometimes possible to participate in the farm work at certain times of year. Contact Peter and Shelly Nightingale, **West Lagoons Farm** Hill Cove, West Falkland; tel/fax: 41194.

Self-catering accommodation can be had at Crooked Farm Inlet. This cottage has two double rooms and two twin rooms and has been recently modernised. While staying in this sheltered inlet the owners offer guided fishing, horse riding and Land Rover hire (the availability of the latter depending upon farm work). Contact Danny and Joy Donnelly, **Crooked Farm Inlet**, West Falkland; tel/fax: 41102.

Camping is possible at several of the farms on West Falkland. At Bold Cove opposite Port Howard, one of the most scenic areas on West Falkland, there is a cairn to commemorate the 300th anniversary of the first sighting of the Falkland Islands. This farm has fishing nearby and a vehicle available for hire. Some basic groceries are available, more with prior notice. Baths are available in the farmhouse nearby. Contact Jimmy Forster, **Bold Cove Farm**, Bold Cove, West Falkland; tel: 42178; fax: 42177.

Further west camping is also allowed at Port Stephens. As there are no facilities all campers must be self sufficient, and as there are restrictions on the airstrip all must arrive by land or sea. All arrivals must inform the farm beforehand and obey the local farm rules. Contact Peter and Ann Robertson, **Port Stephens Farm**, West Falkland; tel: 42307; fax: 42304.

Spring Point can also only be approached by road or by sea. Contact Ron and Fiona Rozee, **Spring Point Farm**, West Falkland; tel: 42001. This area is a popular holiday destination with many islanders. The mixture of white sand beaches and rugged coastline make for an attractive mix. A good variety of wildlife can be seen in this area. Some stores are always available whilst others can be organised by prior arrangement.

Magellanic penguins

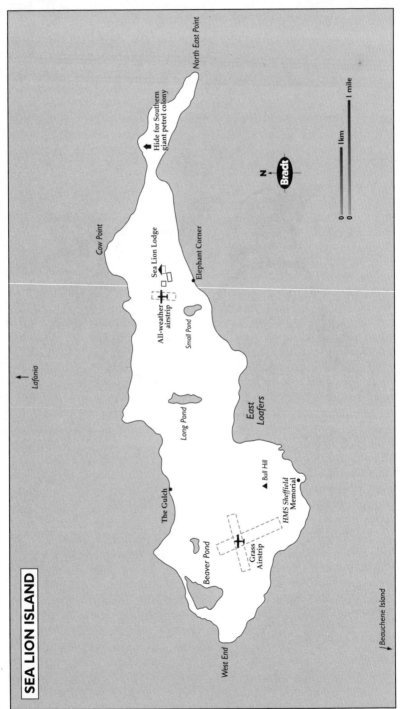

SEA LION ISLAND

Sea Lion Island

Sea Lion Island, one of the smallest islands in Falkland, is one of the most popular destinations for visitors. Lying eight miles from East Falkland, this island forms a plateau rising to approximately 100ft. It is five miles long and just over a mile at its widest point. From Bull Hill, at the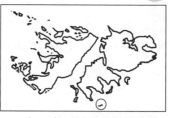
western end, the island slopes gently down eastwards to the open sandy beaches. There are a number of pools on the island. The tussac grass extends around some of the coast away from the cliffs, whilst inland the habitat is short-cropped turf. This island has the most accessible breeding colonies of southern sea lions and southern elephant seals. It also has one of the highest densities of breeding birds on the islands. It is one of the best places to see one of the most endangered birds of prey in the world, the striated caracara, locally known as the 'Johnny Rook'. There are many small birds on the island in the absence of any ground predators. In early and late summer there is the chance of seeing killer whales close inshore. The abundant wildlife makes this island ideal for photography. Many of the published photographs of Falklands wildlife have been taken on Sea Lion Island. Even on a short holiday in the Falklands, the sheer abundance of wildlife in such a small area makes Sea Lion Island a must on any itinerary.

HISTORY

This is the most southerly inhabited island in the group. The original settlers built their house on its present site on the slight rise so that it would be possible to signal to passing ships or to the settlements on the mainland from near their house. A system of bonfires, used to signal to the mainland, was used in Falkland until the arrival of radio. Three fires in a row meant that help was needed. This low-lying island is difficult to see from the mainland, so the effectiveness of this system must be in some doubt, as was shown in 1929. When a Frenchman employed on the island, one Alexander Douglas, committed suicide, his work mates decided that the authorities on the mainland should be informed. The lack of a boat on the island meant that one of the men, Benny Davis, built a raft from wooden barrels and set off through the surf towards the mainland. He launched this boat just after dark and reached Speedwell Island, nearly 30 miles away, roughly 12 hours later. It is said that he simply headed west until he could smell the seabirds on Annie Island.

The island was actively farmed until recently and has been home to the Falkland Islands' stud sheep flock. Commercial farming no long takes place. The hardship caused by this geographical isolation cannot be underestimated. Until the introduction of the inter-island floatplanes in the 1950s, the only connection with the rest of the islands was one or two visits a year by ships calling in to pick up wool and to leave mail and provisions. Since 1982 things have changed dramatically; boats now call in three or four times a year and Islander aircraft fly in and out almost daily during the summer. The lodge was purpose-built in 1986, adjacent to the existing farm buildings. A new hard surfaced airstrip close to the lodge has now largely superseded the grassy runway at the western end of the island. The grass strip is still used in certain winds. The island was not greatly involved during the Argentine occupation of 1982. There is a memorial to those killed on HMS Sheffield on Bull Hill. The ship was hit on May 4 1982 but did not sink until May 10, when it was under tow to a safe anchorage in South Georgia. The grave near the garden is of Mrs Susan Whitley, one of the three Falkland Island civilians in Port Stanley killed on June 11 1982.

GETTING THERE

The majority of visitors arrive by plane on the 35-minute flight from Port Stanley or from other places on Falkland. These local flights operate daily on demand. It is possible to book a place on the freight boat *Tamar* and thus arrive by sea, although as schedules are finalised a few weeks prior to departure, booking passages can be difficult. Landing can be problematic, so there is no guarantee of getting ashore. This boat delivers freight throughout Falkland and calls in at Sea Lion Island every six weeks or so. Occasionally cruise ships visiting the archipelago include a stop at the island in their itinerary. These are weather-dependent and therefore cannot be confirmed in advance. Those arriving on a cruise ship are usually welcomed in the lodge and then left to explore. Those arriving by air are met and taken to the lodge. The visitor is given a short time to settle in and is then taken on an introductory guided tour which points out the main areas to be visited and what to look out for.

WHERE TO STAY

The only place to stay is **Sea Lion Lodge** (tel: 32004; fax: 32003; email: sealion_lodge@horizon.co.fk). The lodge has six twin rooms, one double room, and two single rooms. All twins and doubles are en suite with a shower, sink and toilet. The two single rooms have access to a shower/toilet. There are also two public toilets. The lodge is centrally heated throughout. Three meals a day are provided. There is the option of taking a packed meal or coming back to the lodge at lunchtime. The superb views from the bar allow guests to watch elephant seals at all times of the day and, in the evenings, Magellanic and gentoo penguins can be seen arriving in great numbers.

WHAT TO SEE

Walking around Sea Lion Island on the open, grassy turf is fairly undemanding but, as everywhere, there are some essential ground rules. Some of the grassy slopes above the cliffs at the western end of the island can get very slippery in wet weather. In the Bull Hill area in particular, the cliffs themselves are steep, so care is needed in windy weather. Tussac grass can be very thick and is often above head height making progress and orientation difficult on occasion.

In sheltered spots there is also the chance of meeting sleeping sea lions or elephant seals. Upon arrival the visitor is usually given a rough map of the island, on which one area, East Loafers on the southern coast, is marked as being out of bounds. This is the main breeding area for the southern sea lions, hence the warning sign at the top of the cliff, 'BEWARE OF LIONS'. These are dangerous animals and are best viewed from the top of the cliff. Southern elephant seals are a different matter as they are less aggressive. However, one must keep a respectful distance from them – the standard advice is to remain at least one of their body lengths from them, and to make sure that they always have access to the sea, never getting between them and the water. Despite their size they can move very quickly and with very little warning. The map also shows the few fences that remain on the island and, more importantly, the gates in these fences, some of which are electrified. At the lodge, or on the introductory tour, advice is given regarding the ground rules for the welfare of the wildlife. This enables the visitor to approach both animals and birds in safety, without causing the wildlife any distress.

Of the 50-plus species of birds in the Falklands archipelago, two deserve a special mention. The Antarctic skua can be very energetic in defence of its territory. Most of the skuas nest in the open grass at the western end of the island, with a few nesting just off the main track from the lodge towards the eastern end of the island. These large birds can be seen on the nest and are best admired from a certain distance. The other species is the striated caracara. They are very inquisitive birds and have a strong liking for shiny or brightly coloured objects. When these beautiful birds of prey are in the area, it is a good idea to keep a close eye on one's possessions.

Although Sea Lion Island has the best reputation for seeing killer whales on Falkland, they are by no means guaranteed. They are most often seen at the eastern end of the island, usually cruising past where the gentoo penguins come ashore or where the elephant seals have their pups. They can also be seen near the sea lion colony at East Loafers. Keeping an eye out to sea is essential, especially if there is any disturbance of gulls, terns and shags at the edge of the kelp. These birds often follow the killer whales in the hope of some scraps.

Walks

This small island offers a wide variety of walks. It is possible to walk around the whole coast in one day, however this would mean missing many of the spectacular sights that make this island so unique.

Cow Point, North East Point and Elephant Corner

The closest beach can be reached by cutting across the field to the north of the lodge and continuing down a shallow valley through the tussac grass towards the sand. Many Magellanic penguins nest in this area, including one pair often seen using a burrow almost under one of the stiles. At the western end of the beach a few elephant seals can be seen, hauled out above the tide line, when they come ashore to moult at the end of the breeding season. A walk along the beach should find upland geese and kelp geese, as well as several noisy groups of Magellanic oystercatchers. After Christmas many of these have young and are often to be seen in small family groups along the water's edge. There is no safe access to the western end of the island from this beach.

Turning east one can walk along the sand towards **Cow Point**. The sand does disappear in places and it becomes necessary to walk over flat rocks. Two stretches of large boulders are not so easy to walk over. This area has many small birds, including rock wrens, popping in and out of the stones at one's feet, whilst elegant dark-faced ground-tyrant catch flies at the top of the beach. From Cow Point small numbers of gentoo penguins can be seen porpoising their way back to the shore through the banks of offshore kelp. These penguins are making their way to the long sandy beach that stretches eastwards from here. The flat area between the north and south beaches is regularly swept over during the winter gales. Breeding gulls and terns often use the higher ridges; therefore it is preferable to keep at a reasonable distance from these areas. The large gentoo colony is a dominating presence at the top of the beach and is clearly designated, a wire fence ensuring that the penguins are not disturbed. It is always worthwhile looking at this colony to see if there are any king penguins present. Up to five birds have been noted in recent years.

Many small wading birds can be found feeding in the shallow pools behind the sand beach. Along with the two-banded plovers, there are often many white-rumped sandpipers that have come here from their North American wintering grounds. At the far end of the beach there is a hide from which good views of the small colony of southern giant petrels can be obtained. These are shy birds and are very easily disturbed. The hide should be approached in such a way that the hide is always between the visitor and the birds. The area between the hide and the **North East Point** is dominated by clumps of tussac grass growing in fine loose sand. There is usually one pair of striated caracara in this area and a strong possibility that one of the resident peregrine falcons might pass overhead. If time is limited, there are more rewarding areas to explore on this island.

Heading west again, the beach on the south side of the island is another favourite haul-out site for elephant seals. Both Magellanic oystercatchers and blackish oystercatchers can be found nesting at the top of the beach here. As their nests are well camouflaged, walkers must watch out for displaying adults and thus avoid the nesting sites. The end of the beach is by far the best place to watch elephant seals.

Next is a small bay, the aptly named **Elephant Corner**, behind which is a path leading onto a low promontory in the middle of the cove. The elephant seals can be viewed in safety from this excellent spot for photography. The fence line along the edge of the tussac grass behind Elephant Corner is a good site to watch some of the smaller birds, especially in springtime. It has also been the temporary home to several vagrant birds over the years. The grassy bank between the flat sand beach and the lodge is a super place to watch both upland geese and ruddy-headed geese. It is possible to explore this eastern end of the island before lunch.

Long Pond, Bull Hill and Beaver Pond

The western tip of Sea Lion Island is much further from the lodge. It may be possible to get a lift to the Bull Hill area and walk back, or to take a packed lunch and explore the whole area on foot. The garden is a short walk from the airstrip. The hedges shelter a good variety of small birds and protect all the vegetables grown by the lodge. Turkey vultures are often found sitting on the higher hedges at the back of the garden. Between the airstrip and the gardens are the remains of the 'triworks' – the brickwork is all that remains of the site where penguins were rendered for oil. Each penguin rendered approximately half a pint of oil, which was used for lighting. Hundreds of penguins were 'taken' for this purpose.

The first pool is tucked away in the tussac grass on the southern side of the island. This pool is home to several species of duck such as chiloe wigeon and speckled teal. It is also a great place to watch Magellanic penguins zooming through the shallow water, as they are not this easy to observe when in the sea. The overhanging tussac often hides a few black-crowned night herons. Snipe can be found feeding in some of the wetter grass. In springtime, grass wrens and black-throated finches can be heard singing from their elected song posts. Outside of the breeding season the grass wrens are hard to find, unlike the rock wrens that advertise their presence with frequent chattering. Among the species seen on this pool are the elegant silver grebes. Although these can be seen on many of the pools on Falkland they are much closer to the observer at this site. On the seaward edge it is a good idea to listen out for any snorting or snoring as elephant seals can often be found asleep, hidden in the tussac grass.

By following the fence line on the inner edge of the tussac grass it does not take long to reach a low cliff from where the southern sea lions can be viewed on their breeding beach down below. During January and February pups can be seen with their mothers at the top of the beach. The 'beach master' males are very aggressive in protecting their harems from the younger males who wait their chance in the shallow water just off the edge of the beach. It is at this time of year that killer whales can occasionally be seen patrolling the shores. This grassy slope can be dangerous in high winds or when wet. On walking past the fence the visitor is usually accompanied by Falkland thrushes and tussacbirds.

The next pond, **Long Pond**, is much more open, the only shelter being a narrow strip of reeds on the western bank. It is on the borders of these reeds that most wildfowl tend to congregate. At first glance, there may appear to be very little bird life on the pond but, in fact, a good variety of water birds breed here. The grassy banks are one of the favoured areas of upland geese and ruddy-headed geese. The open heath in this area is a good site for rufous-chested dotterels and Falkland pipits. If the wind is from the north, there are some nice sheltered areas to have lunch in the next area of tussac grass overlooking East Loafers. It is always advisable to have a look around for dozing sea lions before settling down to eat!

The most visited sites on this end of the island are the **memorial to *HMS Sheffield*** and the nearby rockhopper penguin colony in the Bull Hill area. After following the fences from East Loafers past the end of the grass airstrip, the visitor needs to be on the lookout for nesting skuas. The corrugated iron shack is the fire control point for the airport. The memorial is high on the hill overlooking the area in which *HMS Sheffield* was lost. Although the rockhopper colony behind the cross is not as large as in former times, it is still an impressive sight. Mixed in with the penguins are a large number of king shags. The sights, sounds and smells make this a memorable place. Due to the high number of breeding birds here, many scavenging species are also present, including striated caracara and the ever-present tussacbirds, and this is one of the best places to see snowy sheathbills.

Offshore, many black-browed albatrosses pass the island on windy days. These breed on the island of Beauchene, which can be seen on the horizon on clear days. Large numbers of sooty shearwaters arrive during the breeding season in order to breed here and, probably, also on the offshore tussac islands such as Sea Lion Easterly. The far west of the island has a few more king shag colonies but little that cannot be seen elsewhere.

On the northern shore, **Beaver Pond**, so called after the Beaver float planes that landed here from the 1950s until they were replaced by the Islander aircraft during the early 1980s, is worth investigating. This peaty pool has good numbers of geese nearby and often has breeding gulls and terns along the boulder beach on the seaward side. The grassy slopes to the east of here are populated with many breeding pairs of Antarctic skuas. On returning to the lodge along the northern side of the island, it is best to avoid the tussac grass, as this can be impenetrable in places. There is one track leading through the tussac grass to the gulf where all the island's freight is landed. Many birds can be seen feeding along the edge of the tussac grass, perching on the wire fence. It is important to locate the gates on the way back to the lodge, as there is a boggy area between the garden and new airstrip that is best avoided unless one is looking for the snipe which like to frequent this area.

Two-banded plover

Pebble Island

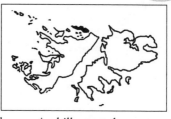

Pebble Island is one of the larger outlying islands and is situated to the north of West Falkland. It is some 24 miles long and about six miles at its widest point. The landscape varies greatly, from large ponds and moorland, to long sandy beaches and high cliffs. The majority of the wetlands are on the eastern part of the island and the three major hills are at the western end. The island gets its name from the semiprecious stones which are found along the coast. The settlement and the airstrip are at the narrowest part of the island. Comprising 22,000 acres, Pebble Island has operated as a sheep farm since the early 1800s and came to international prominence in 1982 when the SAS raided the island during the Argentinian occupation. The hotel was the farm manager's house before its conversion and is the largest building in the settlement. For the naturalist, Pebble Island is a superb place to watch the greatest concentrations of wildfowl and wading birds on the Falklands. It also has four species of breeding penguin most summers. In recent years, a few king penguins and the very rare erect-crested penguins have been observed here. This island's location – it is one of the closest in the Falklands archipelago to South America – earns it a good track record as the temporary home to many rare birds.

Pebble Island has something for everyone. The visitor can spend days exploring the spectacular scenery with its abundant wildlife, or just relax in the easy-going atmosphere of the comfortable lodge. An island not to be missed on any visit to Falkland!

HISTORY

John Henry Dean bought Pebble Island, along with the nearby Goulding, Middle and East Islands, in 1846 for the grand sum of £400. The sheep farm, which he established, is still run as an active farm today, with some 13,500 sheep, nearly all purebred Corriedale stock famous for their high quality wool. The quality of the grass means it has one of the highest stock ratings on the islands, grazing one sheep to every 1.5 acres.

During the Argentinian occupation of 1982 a number of Pucara and Mentor ground attack aircraft were based on the airstrip, this being one of the better strips on Falkland. The Argentinians changed the name of the island to Isla

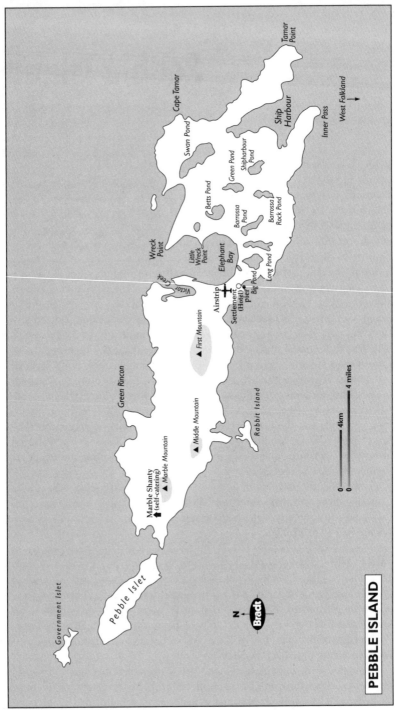

PEBBLE ISLAND

Bourbon and garrisoned several hundred troops here to protect the airstrip. Eleven of these aircraft and their fuel dumps were destroyed during a daring night raid on May 15 1982 by the SAS, under cover of naval gunfire. The people of Pebble Island were then imprisoned in the farm manager's house, now the hotel, shortly after this attack and remained there for the duration of the war. The remains of some of these aircraft can be seen beside the runway. There is also a small memorial to this assault at the eastern end of the airstrip. The other major action during the conflict near Pebble Island was the sinking of HMS Coventry by Argentinian aircraft on May 25 1982. There is a memorial to HMS Coventry on the shoulder of First Mountain, overlooking the settlement. The other memorial on the island is at the western end of the island, not far north of Marble Mountain. This commemorates the Argentinian Learjet that was shot down by HMS Exeter, killing all its crew.

GETTING THERE

The airstrip, only a five-minute walk from the hotel, is one of the best grass landing strips on the islands. In wintertime, the long sandy beach close to the settlement, Elephant Beach, doubles up as a landing strip when conditions permit. It is also possible to book passage on the inter-island freight boat the Tamar. Sailing schedules are only fixed a few weeks in advance, so available berths can be very difficult to reserve.

GETTING AROUND

Big Pond, Long Pond, Elephant Beach and First Mountain are all only a short walk from the settlement. Otherwise, although fairly easy walking, most of the other sites of interest on Pebble Island are quite a distance from the hotel. It is possible to take a packed lunch and spend several days hiking around the island. Another option, particularly for a visit to the penguin colonies at the western end of the island, is to book a tour in one of the four-wheel drive vehicles at the hotel. Weather permitting, boat trips can be arranged to visit some of the closer islands. There are also interesting cruises to discover which seabirds or cetaceans are feeding nearby. The hotel is a departure point for some very varied excursions.

WHERE TO STAY

The majority of visitors stay at the Pebble Island Hotel (tel: 41093; guest pay phone: 25127), although there is also self-catering accommodation at the shanty at Marble. The manager is Jennifer Hill. The hotel has six en suite twin rooms and two single rooms, which share a bathroom. All rooms have tea and coffee-making facilities. There is one public toilet. The large lounge has an open peat fire and bar with views across the island to Elephant Beach and Wreck Point. Home cooked meals are eaten in the separate dining room. The hotel is centrally heated throughout.

The self-catering accommodation at Marble contains four double bunks and basic cooking facilities. Contact Raymond Evans, Pebble Island, West Falkland; tel: 41098; fax: 41099.

The whole of the western tip of the island is known as Marble and lies in the shadow of the mountain. The shanty here is roughly an hour's drive away from the main settlement.

Do not forget to lay in an adequate stock of provisions, as the only small store is at the settlement.

WHAT TO SEE

Pebble Island has so many different sites of interest that a stay of several days is needed to explore them all. The hotel provides a map, which indicates the main areas and the layout of the fences on the island. The deeper ponds on the eastern half of the island are home to large numbers of waterfowl, whilst the wading birds prefer the shallow pools and the sandy expanses of the four-mile long (6.5km) Elephant Beach. Some of the more spectacular scenery is to be found in the western half of the island. Driving here requires a high degree of concentration to avoid the softer patches in which it is easy to get 'bogged'.

The largest building in the settlement is the hotel. Nearby is the farm manager's modern house. The other houses are used by visiting sheep-shearers and school staff, as there have been very few islanders living on Pebble Island in recent times. The shearing sheds and associated gathering-pens are near the quay, as are the main farm buildings. Migrant gangs of shearers who visit each island in turn during the summer months carry out shearing. The island's power is provided by the oil-fired generator situated towards the quay. The hotel does have its own generator to supply electricity during the main part of the day. Water is obtained from the streams that run down from First Mountain. During the shearing period, large numbers of sheep are being driven to and from the gathering-pens, so this area is best avoided at that time. Horses and cattle are on the large grass fields near the settlement and do not usually take any notice of the visitor. It is advisable to keep away from the pig fields to the north and west of the settlement. The island's graveyard is between the western end of Elephant Bay and the end of the airstrip.

Walks and excursions
Elephant Beach and Big Pond
In order to reach Elephant Beach, the visitor must follow the track leading from the gate beside the sheepdog pens some 100yds from the hotel, cross the field past the aero-generator and the pig fields, before heading towards the gap in the dunes behind the small pond. Walking east towards Big Pond behind the sand dunes, this first pool is usually home to a pair of flying steamer ducks along with the more expected speckled teal and crested ducks. The short turf around this small pool, and around most of the ponds on the island, is cropped short by the upland geese and ruddy-headed geese that prefer these areas. The grassy track between this pond and Big Pond is a good place to look for long-tailed meadowlarks feeding in the rough grass. The red-breasted males are surprisingly difficult to see at first but are worth the search. Red-backed hawks can often be found perched, tucked out of the wind, high up on the bigger

dunes. **Big Pond**, as the name suggests, is one of the largest on the island. It is also quite deep, which favours diving birds such as the many white-tufted grebes and the occasional rare species such as great grebe. The shallow waters behind the dunes are the best location if looking for chiloe wigeons among the numbers of grazing geese. These very wary birds do not usually allow close approach, especially if the red-backed hawk is nearby. The small promontory on the western side of the pond has a profusion of almond-flower blooms in midsummer; both white and blue colour forms can be found here. The remains of the small jetty are left over from the one used in the days of the Beaver float planes that landed on Big Pond before the airstrip was constructed. To visit all the other ponds by foot is rather impractical as they are spread over a wide area. It is possible to get dropped off by Land Rover to explore these areas before being collected later in the day.

Fish Creek, Shag Point and Sturgess Point
There are two other walks that start from the settlement. The first leads through the farm and out along the shore. The two jetties are ideal places to look for black-crowned night herons. The latter can be easily overlooked, as they remain motionless for so long whilst waiting for fish to swim by. The path follows the coast past Fish Creek, before climbing the slope that leads to Shag Point and then Sturgess Point. The views back westwards over the settlement or out over West Falkland to the east are superb on a clear day. This is a good site to sit for a while, in calm weather, and look for any passing cetaceans. Commerson's dolphins are the most likely but Peale's dolphins are also possible.

Extension to Phillips Cove and Ship Harbour Pond
For those wanting a much longer walk (or drive), the track continues along past three more fences. The track at times becomes rather difficult to follow but eventually leads to the scenic beach at Phillips Cove. The steep sides of this site mean that it is often more sheltered than some of the more open beaches. The stream and small pool behind the shingle beach contain a variety of waterfowl. In the past king shags have nested on the low cliff to the south side of the beach. The track continues from Phillips Cove around to Ship Harbour Pond, where black-necked swans can usually be found along with a few ducks, before leading into the main track near Ship Harbour.

Victor Creek
The second area within walking distance, although a little further from the settlement, is Victor Creek. To reach this site, follow the tracks up and over the airport, bearing right through a gate on the north side towards Victor Creek. This passes some of the fir trees that have been planted in recent years. The headland that forms the eastern arm of the creek is full of Magellanic penguin burrows. At low tide, the shallow creek is a good place to look for Magellanic oystercatchers and lots of two-banded plovers. The latter can be found roosting at the top of Victor Point. The strand line back towards Elephant Bay is full of all sorts of odds and ends, from relics dating from the

1982 war to huge bones belonging to some very large whales that stranded many years ago. Some of the rib bones are so old that they look like lengths of curved timber thrown up by a recent gale.

Betts Pond, Green Pond and Swan Pond

For the birdwatcher, Betts Pond and Green Pond have the greatest variety of species, including both white-tufted grebes and silver grebes along with most of the ducks that breed on Falkland. One of the specialities of Pebble Island is the large quantity of black-necked swans that breed here. They breed on many of the more suitable ponds, so that by Christmas many small cygnets can be seen following their parents in the middle of the ponds. Once these have reached maturity, they gather in large flocks, which can number over one hundred by the end of the season. By midsummer large numbers of wading birds have reached Pebble Island. At that time of year some of the pools are rather shallow, which suits the shorter legged species, such as white-rumped sandpiper and the occasional rarer species, such as Baird's sandpiper. A day can easily be spent visiting all the pools between Ship Harbour and Wreck Point. Pebble Island has a well-deserved reputation for attracting some of the rarer species of bird from South and North America. In recent years these have included white-winged coots, pectoral sandpipers and one rosy-billed pochard. Swan Pond, despite its name is not always one of the best places to see swans on the island. Good numbers of wildfowl can be seen along the sheltered edges of this pond, the largest on the island, but it does not generally have as much to see as some of the smaller ponds.

Tamar Point, Cape Tamar and Wreck Point

The habitat beyond Swan Pond changes to a drier diddle-dee heath as it climbs to form the sea cliffs in the Cape Tamar area. This is much to the liking of the many Magellanic penguins whose burrows are everywhere. There are several sites worth visiting along this rocky coastline. By following the track from the southern end of Swan Pond towards Tamar Point, along the eastern edge of Ship Harbour, large numbers of Falkland flightless steamer-ducks and a scattering of Magellanic oystercatchers can be seen. Once past the next fence, there is a small rockhopper penguin colony at the edge of the cliff. A little further along the track there are more impressive colonies to be seen, which soon become visible on the next headland. Almost every year there are two colonies of rockhopper penguins at this site, and large numbers of king shags also nest here. The king shags tend to move from colony to colony, so that they are in slightly different sites each summer. The presence of these breeding birds attracts scavengers such as dolphin gulls, kelp gulls, Antarctic skuas and turkey vultures. This is a place of constant activity. By late afternoon many of the king shags are coming back to the colony, so there is a constant stream of birds coming in to land. By sitting on the small outcrop close to the rockhopper penguins, the visitor can watch them come ashore and then hop their way up the cliff. Small groups of penguins can be seen swimming around beyond the outer edge of the kelp beds that fringe the coast, before diving and reappearing at the base of the cliff. The small crags on the seaward side of the colony are a favourite haunt of peregrine falcons and crested caracara, although both species are rather shy and are not easy to see when perched. If the wind is onshore, good views can be obtained of black-browed albatrosses and sooty shearwaters as they pass by. In spring and autumn a wider range of seabirds can be seen from here in favourable conditions. In late summer there is the chance of seeing some of the few royal albatrosses that visit the region at this time of year. Becalmed, these mighty birds dwarf their nearest neighbours.

The track to Tamar Point is difficult to follow due to the large numbers of Magellanic penguins that have burrowed into the peat. Tamar Point is a low headland looking across to West Falkland. The tidal stream can reach ten knots between these two points. This attracts large numbers of birds and the occasional southern sea lion. King shags and rock shags feed in large flocks when the tidal stream flows fastest, with black-browed albatrosses and sooty shearwaters skimming low over the water. With luck, prions or diving petrels can sometimes be observed in the rougher water. A telescope is very useful here.

Returning through the gate and following the rather vague track to Cape Tamar brings the visitor out on to the headland. Falkland thrift flowers in profusion most years along the cliff top. This is an excellent site to watch southern sea lions. They are viewed from the ledges in the tussac grass above the rocky outcrop where they come ashore. It is not an easy scramble to the ledge above them, and should not be attempted by those who do not like heights. The sea lions haul themselves out on some sloping flat rocks close to the base of the cliff. Between these rocks and the cliff is a shallow pool in which they are often seen playing. These lumbering beasts on land are transformed into lithe, agile predators in the water. The steep rocks to the left of the viewing ledge harbour a small colony of rock shags. By late summer the wheezing calls of the young can be heard as their parents bring food to their growing brood. More black-browed albatrosses can be seen passing close by, especially in an onshore wind.

It is possible to take a different route back to the settlement by following the track out past Wreck Point, although this is not an easy track to use as it crosses a shingle. Between Wreck Point and the top of Elephant Beach are a large number of cetacean skeletons. These are the remains of pilot whales that were washed ashore, or 'wrecked', in the early 1980s. White-rumped sandpipers and two-banded plovers prefer the small pools in the rocky shore along this section of beach. The journey back to the settlement along the hard sand of Elephant Beach is the easiest driving on the island. There are some small, sharp rocky outcrops, and many birds use this beach, so it is still advisable to drive carefully. Flocks of Falkland flightless steamer ducks and kelp gulls are often found along the upper beach with Magellanic oystercatchers and blackish oystercatchers along the water's edge. The gap in the dunes back to the hotel can be difficult to see at times, as sand occasionally obscures the entrance.

The west of the island
Northern coast

The northern coast to the west of the settlement is typified by rocky headlands and white sandy beaches as befits such an exposed landscape. The first stop when heading west is on the shoulder of First Mountain where the memorial to HMS Coventry is situated. In clear weather, this vantage point gives a superb view back over the settlement and then on out to West Falkland. In late spring and early summer several of the small, berried plants are in bloom at this site. One of these, the native strawberry, has edible fruit, which can be picked in late summer. The landscape on the western half of Pebble Island is much more arid than that on the east; there are no large pools, only small streams running towards the coast. It is the latter that can be difficult to ford without getting bogged.

The headlands on the northern coast can be worth a visit. The local race of peregrine falcon, Cassin's falcon, favours these rocky outcrops. Often the only sign that a bird is present are the plucking posts where they have removed the feathers from their latest catch. Many small birds feed alongside the track, including black-throated finches, Falkland pipits, and if one is lucky, a grass wren or two. By mid-morning the visitor will have reached the large colony of gentoo penguins situated to the north of Middle Peak, just inland from the headland know as Green Rincon. The track to this site heads towards the coast just beyond the long fence running north south. The birds make their nests on the level ground at a short distance from the beach to the east of the headland. They have moved their nesting site several times over the years, but still follow the same route back to the sea. The present colony is surrounded by lush green circles of vegetation, which have prospered as a result of guano being dropped on the site, thereby enriching the soil below. When seen from the air these could be interpreted as Falkland's first crop circles!

Green Rincon

There is much activity in the vicinity of Green Rincon, making this an ideal place to break the journey. On the eastern slopes of the first beach is a small colony of southern giant petrels. These birds should not be approached as the adults are very shy and will leave the nest at any sign of man; their young are then left at the mercy of the weather and any predators that happen to be in the area. The adults usually move away to sit on the sea and wait there until the cause of their panicked flight has moved on. It is possible to walk out to the headland behind these birds by keeping below the skyline on the east side of the cape. There is a small colony of rock shags tucked away on the lower cliffs and a pair of red-backed hawks is often in the area. The easiest way onto the beach is to follow the small valley at the eastern end of the beach. The worn track in the middle of the beach is the 'runway' that the gentoo penguins use on their way to and from their colony. There are usually a good number of birds loafing on the sand at the water's edge, some asleep, others preening ready to go back to sea. There are always a few birds moulting. These are the immature penguins that change their feathers in the summer, earlier than the breeding adults, ready for the rigours of winter. Falkland flightless steamer-ducks are also found along the shining white sand along with a scattering of Magellanic penguins and a few Magellanic oystercatchers. All these birds are potential prey for sea lions, which can occasionally be seen cruising through the shallows hunting for any unwary bird. Their presence is usually signalled by a small mob of gulls and shags that tag along behind hoping for any leftover scraps. Green Rincon, the headland, is a good spot for a picnic, with several rocky outcrops providing shelter and superb views over the island. Crested caracara can sometimes be seen around this headland along with the occasional juvenile striated caracara that have left their breeding grounds on the Jason Islands to the northwest.

Around Marble Mountain

The track west from here drops down onto the beach for a while before climbing back up onto the plateau. Some of the bright green slopes near Marble Mountain are very wet and, therefore, can be very difficult to cross in a vehicle. The track passes a small memorial situated behind some white fencing. This has been recently refurbished and marks the crash site of an Argentinian Learjet that was shot down during the war in 1982.

The largest rockhopper penguin colony on the island is on the coast to the north of Marble Mountain. By following the right hand fork in the track, the visitor rounds a small hill to find a mass of birds on the grassy slopes at the top of a rocky headland. Although the cliff is not as high as the site this species of penguin uses near Cape Tamar, it is still a difficult climb for these charismatic birds. It is possible to sit at various points around the colony to watch all the comings and goings. As with the other colonies, there are many different scavenging birds present. The turkey vultures, for instance, take off when man approaches, whilst others, such as kelp gulls and dolphin gulls, just keep a wary distance. Many penguins can be seen at the bottom of the cliff using the pools as a communal bath.

In recent years at least one pair of macaroni penguins has been breeding in this colony. They are slightly larger than their rockhopper cousins but the best features to look for are the thicker, brighter bill and the distinctive orange-yellow crests, which meet above the eye. The crests of the rockhopper penguins are thinner, more yellow and do not meet above the eye. They have tended to use the same area in the colony, furthest away from the main access path to the sea. This species breeds in small numbers in the Falkland Islands and, therefore, is never easy to see. This has been the most reliable visitor site for macaroni penguins during the 1990s. This island has also been the summer home of an erect-crested penguin since 1997. This much rarer species of penguin is normally found on the subantarctic islands of New Zealand and is probably only the third record for Falkland.

Some of the best pebble beaches are at the far western end of Pebble Island. These can be reached by rejoining the main track near the rockhopper penguin colony and heading west. As the track bends around Marble Mountain, there is a faint track towards a gate on the slight rise to the right. By following this track along the valley below, the visitor comes to a small pool, which can be a good site for speckled teal and the usual scattering of upland geese and ruddy-headed geese. There is no defined path through to the beach, and beyond this point there are several wet areas to be avoided before reaching the shore. The shingle beach changes profile after each storm. This constant movement results in very rounded pebbles, some of which are very attractive and well worth searching for, provided that they are then left for others to admire. Southern sea lions can be seen in the distance on the shores of Pebble Islet. The gap between the two islands is a favoured shortcut for rock shags and king shags. Magellanic penguins nest in the drier ground between the valley and the beach; the burrows often undermine what looks like firm ground, making walking a little treacherous at times.

The only building at the far end of the island is the self-catering shanty. The gorse bushes that have been planted here sometimes harbour some of the smaller birds, for example black-chinned siskins and black-throated finches. The track then follows the contour of Marble Mountain back towards the settlement.

Southern shore

The tracks on the southern side of the island tend to be more braided than those on the northern side of the three hills. This is often due to sections becoming too wet to get through, so that alternative routes have had to be created. It must be emphasised that it is still important to keep to the paths. Visitors must leave all gates in their original position in accordance with the farmer's wishes. Time and weather permitting, it might be worth visiting the area around Rabbit Island, on the south side, which can be a good site for ducks, geese and the occasional flock of waders. The southern side of Pebble Island is much more sheltered than the north shore, and therefore has more sandy or muddy bays with a greater variety of marine life than could survive on the more exposed coasts. It is in these bays that kelp geese and black-crowned night herons can be found, along with several pairs of blackish oystercatchers.

The drive back to the settlement takes over an hour from the Marble end of the island. The views to the south from this route back are spectacular; on a clear day Saunders Island can be seen beyond the nearest island Keppel.

Sporting activities

For those wanting some exercise, there is a nine-hole golf course with its own unique Pebble Island rules. Clubs can be hired from the hotel, although it must be said that, at the time of writing, the golf course is in need of some attention. If weather conditions permit, sand yachting can be tried along the four-mile long Elephant Beach. This is also a super beach for beachcombing.

Carcass, West Point and New Island

These three islands, lying to the west of West Falkland, are some of the most remote inhabited islands in Falkland. All three are privately owned. Only Carcass takes in staying visitors on a regular basis, but an ever-larger number of tourists call at each of the islands every year on cruise ships. These 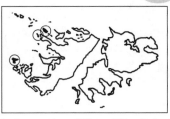 are rather mountainous islands with some very impressive cliffs on West Point and New Island. These cliffs are the ideal breeding grounds for large numbers of black-browed albatross and have extensive penguin rookeries. Carcass and New Island are home to large numbers of small birds, as neither cats nor rats have become established here.

CARCASS ISLAND

This island lies at the outer end of Byron Sound opposite West Point, to the northwest of West Falkland. The nearest inhabited settlements are West Point some seven miles away, Dunbar on West Falkland and Saunders Island to the east. The island lies roughly northwest to southeast. The rounded hills extend along almost all of the five-mile length of the island, sloping down to beaches on the western shores and to a low cliff on the northern side of the island. This is one of the most picturesque islands in the Falklands group. The present owners, Rob and Lorraine McGill, have two cottages, which they let as self-catering accommodation for Falkland Islanders or as fully catered for overseas visitors.

The abundance of songbirds, the luxuriant growth around the settlement and gently rolling landscape give this island a very difference ambiance to any other in the Falklands.

History

The island is named after *HMS Carcass*, a Royal Navy ship under the command of Captain Pattison, which reached the Falkland Islands in 1766. The island has only had three owners in 100 years of inhabitation. Charles Hanson, a Dane, leased Carcass, the Jasons and some of the smaller islands nearby in 1872. Hanson and the subsequent owners managed the island without introducing cats or rats, so that the island now abounds with many small birds. The tiny settlement has well-established hedges and trees giving it an atypical appearance for the Falklands. The oldest house is Valley Cottage, which was built in the

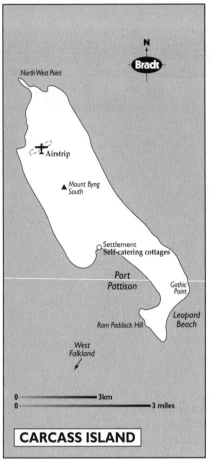

CARCASS ISLAND

1870s. This is now used as one of the self-catering properties.

Getting there

The airstrip used by the Falkland Island Government Air Service is at the north of the island, a 20-minute drive from the settlement. Transport to the airstrip is arranged with local proprietors using their Land Rovers. The small jetty at Port Pattison is used by the inter-island boats when landing goods for the settlement. The majority of visitors who come to Carcass Island arrive as passengers on the cruise ships that visit Falkland. Some tourists use the jetty but the majority land on the beaches in their inflatable dinghies. Visitors to the settlement land in Port Pattison, whilst those wanting to visit the large penguin rookeries at the south end of the island can land on Leopard Beach, or on the sand beach the other side of Gothic Point Paddock. Visitors particularly appreciate the tea and cakes served in the main house at the end of their stay. A very welcoming atmosphere prevails.

Accommodation

For those wishing to stay on the island, two cottages are available for rent. **Valley Cottage** sleeps six, **Rose Cottage** sleeps four. Bed linen is usually provided, apart from towels. Both cottages are heated and have well-equipped kitchens. There is a licensed bar in the main house, and a store with a good stock of dried and tinned food. Visitors should bring their own fresh produce, although the owners can provide milk and mutton. For visitors originating from beyond the Falklands, it is possible to book a fully catered stay. Contact Rob and Lorraine McGill, Carcass Island, West Falklands; tel: 41106; fax: 41107.

What to see

This island does not have the dramatic cliffs of certain of the other western islands, but does have many beautiful sandy beaches situated below the gently rolling hills. The luxuriant growth of fuchsia, gorse and cypress around the settlement attracts many small birds. Black-chinned siskins, Falkland thrushes and Cobb's wrens are present in great number, all making use of the hedges and trees to build their nests. The famous colony of black-crowned night herons, located in the trees around the main house, has diminished in recent years, but the birds can still be seen roosting on or near the jetty, a short walk from the settlement. The striated caracaras, locally known as Johnny Rook, are very much in evidence around the settlement. They often perch high up in the cypress trees, keeping an eye open for any chance of a quick meal. The cottage gardens are a spectacular sight when in full bloom; the yellow of the gorse in springtime can be seen many miles away on West Falkland. The sheltered gardens have been temporary home to all kinds of tired vagrant birds blown in from the South American continent.

The hill behind the settlement gives a commanding view across Byron Sound to West Falkland. The military base on Byron heights is one of the few man-made structures visible from here. Looking back down into Port Pattison, Peale's dolphins can sometimes be seen playing in the beds of kelp that fringe the bay.

South end

One of the most popular sites on the island is the **penguin colony** at the south end. An hour's walk from the accommodation takes in the track that runs out through the paddocks around the houses, before continuing along the base of the hills towards Gothic Hill paddock. From the path, many ducks and geese can be seen feeding along the shore at low tide. Tussacbirds, intent on finding whatever food is disturbed as one walks, sometimes accompany walkers. As the track reaches the last hill, it climbs slightly around a bank of tussac grass that has been protected from the sheep by a wire fence. After the first gate, the first gentoo penguin rookery is soon visible on either side of the fence. Why some of these birds choose to nest on one side and not on the other is a mystery. Some birds situate their nests higher up the hill. The combination of grass and tussac is a prime habitat for large numbers of upland geese and smaller numbers of ruddy-headed geese. Late in the summer the upland geese gather into large flocks on the short grass for safety whilst they moult their flight feathers. On the slightly higher ground many Magellanic penguins and their burrows can be seen. The wet areas in the middle of this site can be deep enough to hold small numbers of duck, including the elusive yellow-billed pintail. The flora of this area is typical of boggy ground on Falkland but does include some nice pink-flowered pimpernel along with the more easily found *pratia*. In the early summer the scattered clumps of tussac grass make good singing perches for the displaying black-throated finches.

There is a gap in the dunes on the south side of this meadow leading out onto a white sandy beach. There are invariably small groups of Falkland flightless steamer ducks and both Magellanic penguins and gentoo penguins clustered on the sand. There are no southern sea lions breeding on Carcass Island, but they can occasionally be seen swimming through the shallow water close to the shore, on the look out for an unwary penguin returning to its breeding site. The rocky crag, known as Ram Paddock Hill, is a favoured roost site for the crested caracara, although this shy species rarely allows a close approach by man. The far side of this paddock has some good stands of tussac grass above some low cliffs, upon which there are some small colonies of rock shags and yet more tussacbirds. Black-browed albatrosses and southern giant petrels can be seen gliding low over Byron Sound. The first section of the walk back can be taken over the flat sandy beach before climbing up to the track leading back to the settlement.

North end

It is possible to walk around the island in one day, although this does not give the visitor a lot of time to explore properly. To visit the north end of Carcass Island, it is a good idea to get a lift to the north end beyond the airport and to walk back. Beyond the fence that marks the northern limit of the grazed land are some narrow bands of tussac grass. The striated caracara have been known to nest on the small rocky outcrops in this area, so it is advisable to keep a look out for any birds on sentry duty near the nest, as they can be quite aggressive when defending their eggs and young. The flat grasslands before the fence make a good nesting site for Antarctic skuas, birds that have a well-deserved reputation for defending their nest sites. However, the skuas tend to ignore the visitor as long as a respectful distance from the bird is maintained.

There is one large shallow pool at this end of the island along with some smaller pools in the tussac grass. This large pool has a good population of geese and other wildfowl including silver grebes and white-tufted grebes. The arrow-leaved marigold, with its large white-green flowers, can be found in the marshy areas near the pool. The grassy bank at the top of the beach on the seaward side of this pool is the breeding ground for many kelp gulls. The flat grass is the ideal site for the displaying Magellanic oystercatchers in the early part of the breeding season. Along the rocky shore Falkland flightless steamer ducks are common, along with a scattering of brown-hooded gulls and a few white-rumped sandpipers, the latter present from late summer into early autumn. Nearly every pool in this area has good numbers of waterfowl. Snipe can often be found in some of the more marshy ground.

The top of the beach is a beachcomber's delight, with all sorts of flotsam and jetsam piled up by the latest gales. This beach is popular with both Cobb's wrens and grass wrens. In late summer this end of the island is one of the areas favoured by elephant seals when they come out of the water for a few weeks to moult. There are plenty of pleasant sites out of the wind suitable for picnic lunches. Striated caracaras soon find out when food is in the offing and come to investigate. Anything left unattended, including cameras and binoculars, is liable to be snatched for investigation. Many other birds will come to inspect who has invaded their territory. The small lump of tussac grass a short distance offshore is often used by a small group of black-crowned night herons as a roost site around high tide. These can be seen flying in from all directions as the tide comes in.

There are two main routes back to the cottages. It is possible to follow the northeastern coast for a while before crossing back to Port Pattison. However there are better routes to follow as, apart from views over towards Saunders Island and a few rock shag and king shag colonies, there are more interesting possibilities elsewhere. The same views can be had from climbing the most northernmost hill and following the ridge back down the island. From the highest point on **Mount Byng** (875ft, 304m), it is possible on a clear day to see as far as the Jasons and Pebble Island on one side and away to New Island on the other. The drier ground along the summits produces a different flora with many more of the berried plants such as tea berry, mountain berry and diddle-dee. Tucked away in the rocks on the higher slopes, yellow daisy and lady's slipper can be found during late spring and summer. There are not as many birds on the higher slopes as there are lower down, but rufous-chested dotterels like to breed in this habitat. Red-backed hawks and the occasional peregrine falcon can be seen on some of the steeper crags.

The other major route back is to continue around the lower slopes of the hills for a while before following the major valley up to a saddle between two hills. Scurvy grass grows in profusion at the base of the first hill, whilst dark-faced ground-tyrants appear to be perched on every tall rock. The track then crosses a west-facing valley before descending to the settlement. For the energetic visitor it is not too far, merely steep, up to the highest point on the island from the saddle at the end of the first valley. The view is definitely worth the effort of the climb.

WEST POINT ISLAND

The island is renowned for huge colonies of black-browed albatrosses on some of the most spectacular cliffs in the archipelago. West Point is not a big island, but there is more than enough for the walker and naturalist to see. The area around the small settlement is at its most colourful in springtime when the densely flowered gorse is in bloom. Some 1,500 sheep are kept on this 3,630-acre farm. The highest point on the island, Mount Misery at 1,211ft (369m) on the western side of the island, is above some nearly sheer cliffs that run most of that side of the island. The channel between West Falkland and West Point, Wooly Gut, is strongly tidal. The name 'wooly' refers to a sudden down-draught from the nearby cliffs, which in days of sail was a great threat to the safety of the boat.

History

West Point Island was originally known as Albatross Island and has belonged to the same family since the 1860s. It was first part of the Shallow Bay Estate on West Falkland before being set up as a separate farm in 1879 by Arthur Felton, the great uncle of the present farmer, Roddy Napier. From the 1700s onwards many penguins were killed on West Point for their oil, each penguin yielding about a pint. When meat and fur were among the islands' major exports, sealers came here on a regular basis.

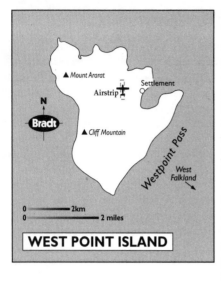

Mount Ararat

Settlement

Airstrip

N

Brandt

Cliff Mountain

Westpoint Pass

West
Falkland

0 ———— 2km
0 ———— 2 miles

WEST POINT ISLAND

Getting there

This popular island is on many a cruise ship itinerary. It does have an airstrip, but that is small and difficult to use, making visits by air impractical for any holidaymakers on the islands. It does, however, have a very good anchorage at West Point Harbour just below the settlement. The track from the jetty leads up to the farmhouse, which is tucked in amongst some very healthy trees. For many years the visitor was taken across the island to the seabird colonies in a single-decker green bus. This incongruous machine lasted some time but is now no longer used. A sturdy Land Rover does the job nowadays. As on the neighbouring island of Carcass, the welcome and the afternoon tea are some of the highlights of a visit to West Point. Hundreds of visitors must have passed through these two lounges over the years. One gets the impression that every subject under the sun has been discussed on these two far-flung islands. The owner, Roddy Napier, has a great knowledge of the island and its wildlife going back many years.

What to see

The bird life of West Point, although not as varied as that on Carcass Island due to the presence of cats, rats and mice, is still very interesting. It is now believed that cats have been successfully eradicated. The result of these predators having been introduced to the island many years ago is a general lack of small birds. Some, such as black-chinned siskins, Falkland thrushes and grass wrens have survived and can be heard singing on a spring morning. The lush garden and vegetable patch are good places to see some of these small birds. The male long-tailed meadowlarks, known locally as military starlings, look particularly fine when perched on a flowering gorse bush. Their red breasts stand out from a long way off.

The major attraction of this island is the impressive **black-browed albatross colony** on the western side of the island. It is about a five-minute drive across the island or a walk of approximately 30 minutes. The track takes the visitor up out of the settlement through a series of fields before reaching the inner edge of the tussac grass that grows on the island's periphery, at a safe distance from the local sheep. A path leads through the tussac grass out on to a point overlooking the sea in a small valley, which contains many hundreds of black-browed albatross nests. This species is thought to have doubled in number in the last 40 years on this island. These birds situate their mud-pot nests on the top of the slope, so that they can land and take off without too much difficulty. With a wingspan of over seven feet (2.13m) they need plenty of room to get to and from their nest site in safety. Also nesting here are rockhopper penguins, who make their way up the steep cliff face using only their sharp claws to hang on. The guttural cries of a returning penguin greeting its mate, combined with the eerie sounds that albatrosses make, create a unique atmosphere. For the observer at the sidelines of this impressive seabird colony it is difficult to know what to look at next, as there is always something happening. In the past some of the albatrosses in this colony have been ringed. This work was done to try to determine the longevity of this species, where the albatrosses went after leaving the island and if they returned here to breed. It seems that this species may live for 50 years or more in favourable conditions, and that they often return to the breeding grounds of their birth. Although noisy when greeting each other on the nest, they are generally silent in flight, often gliding past at a short distance from observers, heads turned ready to scrutinise before heading back out to sea. This mass of birds attracts the usual predators including turkey vultures, Antarctic skuas and striated caracara. This latter, ever vigilant, species is one of the rarest birds of prey, but it is a forgivable mistake to imagine that they are common here, as they appear to be everywhere.

The waters around the island are favoured haunts of Commerson's dolphins. They follow many of the boats into the beach, often playing in the bow wave as the ship enters the harbour. From the westward side of the island it is possible to see the occasional fur seal swimming close inshore, and on very calm days some of the great whales have been seen from this island.

NEW ISLAND

New Island has been described as one of the most scenic of the Falkland Islands. It is the most southwesterly island of the group and is located over 150 miles from Port Stanley; its nearest neighbour is Beaver Island only a few miles to the west. New Island is about eight miles (13km) long and half a mile (800m) at its widest point.

The highly indented coastline runs for 52 miles in total. The cliffs on the western side of the island rise to 600 feet (183m) whereas the eastern shores gently slope into the sea. The highest point of the island is South Hill at 743feet (226m). There are several bays on the eastern side of the island, one of which is Hookers Harbour, now known as Settlement Harbour, site of the small jetty where the island's goods are unloaded. The large bay to the south, South Harbour, was the site of the whaling station established in 1908. This island is best known as the home of one of the world's most spectacular seabird colonies, which accommodates large numbers of black-browed albatrosses and rockhopper penguins. There are no lodgings for visitors on the island, but it is a popular destination for the many tourists who come ashore from passing cruise ships attracted by the birds and some of the most photogenic scenery in the Falklands.

History

It is thought that American whalers and sealers, who were then starting to exploit the South Atlantic, first visited the island in the late 1700s. One of these

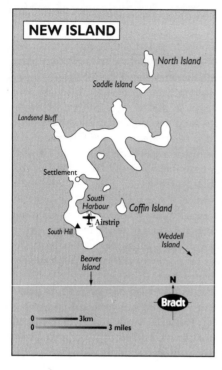

NEW ISLAND

North Island

Saddle Island

Landsend Bluff

Settlement

South Harbour

Coffin Island

Airstrip

South Hill

Weddell Island

Beaver Island

N

Bradt

0 — 3km
0 — 3 miles

men, Charles H Barnard, from New England, reached New Island in September 1812. He used the island as a base whilst catching seals around the archipelago in his ship, the *Narnia*. In April 1813 he came across the survivors of the shipwreck of the *Isabella*, which had run aground some nine weeks earlier. By June they were sheltering from bad weather at New Island. Barnard and three of his crew rowed to Beaver Island in search of provisions, leaving one man behind. They returned to find that their ship had disappeared. They searched the outer islands in vain and finally returned to New Island. Thereupon the crew promptly abandoned Barnard for two months. In the interim he built himself a small shelter and survived on a diet of whichever seabirds he could catch. When reunited the five men lived on New Island, enlarging the original shelter, until finally rescued by the British ship *Indispensable* in November 1814. Barnard returned home two years later to Hudson, New England, alive but penniless. In 1823 a Captain Weddell visited the island to replenish his ships' stocks. He and Barnard wrote detailed descriptions of the island, which have survived to this day, enabling historians to compare those times with now.

In the early 1850s a Captain Campbell, owner of a ship named *Levenside*, thought that the guano on the island was worth collecting. He obtained a licence from the Falkland Island Government. However the low value of the guano, and the sinking of his ship at the entrance of Port William on East Falkland, put paid to his venture.

Between 1851 and 1860 a French ship, the *Victor*, came to the islands to collect 'trypots'. These three-legged pots were used to render penguins for their oil. There are stone-corrals near the penguin rookeries where these birds must have been caught.

The island was leased in 1860 by the Smith Brothers, who were based in South America at Montevideo. This was the first time the island had been leased. The brothers also wanted to exploit the deposits of guano that generations of seabirds had laid on the islands. This was the last time that anybody attempted to make money from these worthless deposits. The Smith Brothers also established a settlement on New Island. A small human population had settled here by 1861, as well as 500 sheep and a small number of cattle. This was the first attempt at introducing sheep to the island, although pigs and rabbits had been brought in during the 1820s. Sheep numbers peaked in the late 1970s when some 3,300 were grazing on the island. During the latter part of the 1800s and the early 1900s sheep farming was the main source of income. The only exception was in 1893–4 when Edward Nilsson, the owner of the island at that time, had a licence to cull 10,000 penguins for their oil. This was the last record of penguins being taken for oil on the islands.

In the early 20th century the southern oceans witnessed the swift expansion of the whaling industry. The first Falkland licence was granted to Alexander Lange, who operated out of New Island in the summer of 1905–6. During that season Lange and his men managed to catch 125 whales. In 1908 a whaling station was set up by Salvesens of Leith in a 30-acre site on the south side of South Harbour. It was ready for operation in January 1909 and its first whale was caught soon after. Four catchers operated out of this station. These boats at first doubled up as mail and passenger boats around the islands, before being replaced by an inter-island boat, the *RMS Columbus*. The products from this whaling operation were used to make margarine, soap and bombs, whereas the whale bones were ground down and used as fertiliser. By 1916 some 1,188 whales had been caught and processed here. The station's activities were eclipsed by the company's much more profitable operations in South Georgia, with the result that in 1916 the New Island Whaling Company station was closed, the equipment was dismantled and shipped to South Georgia. South Harbour developed into a busy port, with its own Post Office and customs officer, when it became a Port of Entry for the islands. The post office closed in 1917, by which time, owing to the general decline of the industry in Falkland itself, the number of boats calling into New Island had decreased significantly. All that remains today are some of the boilers and some rusty metal.

New Island was purchased in 1971 by the New Island Preservation Company with the aim of establishing the island as a nature reserve. This state of affairs continued until 1977 when the company was dissolved, and the island became two properties, New Island North and New Island South. New Island North is run as a private nature reserve, owned by Tony Chater since 1985. New Island South is run as a reserve by its owner Ian Strange, who encourages students and scientists to come to the island to study the wildlife on a long-term basis. In 1988 the New Island South Conservation Trust was set up as a registered charity with the aim of promoting the study and appreciation of ecology and conservation. New Island South was recognised as a wildlife sanctuary by the Falkland Islands government in 1993.

Getting there

There is a grass airstrip on the island, but as there is no accommodation for most visitors, the majority who visit New Island during the austral summer come from the cruise ships that visit Falkland. Researchers studying the island's wildlife use the only accommodation. Permission to land on this reserve must be obtained in advance.

What to see

Nowadays the settlement is a collection of modern houses overlooking a picturesque bay. The walk from the jetty towards the most accessible **seabird colony** leads from the jetty past the house with the blue roof towards the head of the bay. In this bay lies the wreck of the *Protector III*, which was beached here in February 1969, having originally been brought to the islands to be used as a sealer based at Albemarle in West Falkland. The shed was built towards the end of the 1800s for dealing with sheep and for storage. The gorse bushes that flank the path from the settlement are a superb sight in springtime and are home to many of the small birds, which breed here. The path then crosses a grassy valley, which has been cropped short by generations of rabbits, before gradually climbing up to the higher, western, side of the island. Once past the stile, the tussac grass increases in density as it reaches the cliff edge. The sounds of the colony greet the visitor before the colony itself is visible. The cliff is not very high at this point but is chock full of birds. This colony is a real mixture with black-browed albatrosses, king shags and rockhopper penguins all jumbled together. The albatrosses and shags tend to be right at the top of the cliff, and even though some penguins do nest with these other species, they also have their own rookeries slightly further inland, in the heart of the tussac grass. Some of these birds are part of the long-term studies and, therefore, their nests may well have individual markers. The study areas are clearly marked out with wooden pegs. It is very important that these pegs are not displaced. By following the path that leads to the south side of this bay, it is possible to get to a good observation point without disturbing the birds. This spectacular site has so much going on it is difficult to know where to look next. This is definitely one of the most photographed areas on the islands. Birds are coming and going all the time: the albatrosses glide by with a serene grace, the shags all hustle and bustle as they crash-land next to the nest, whilst the penguins porpoise their way through the sea to the base of the cliff before living up to their rockhopper names as they clamber up the cliff to their rookery. Above all this, the scavengers keep an eye out for an opening. Turkey vultures and Antarctic skuas are the most noticeable and dolphin gulls the most vocal of the scavengers. The striated caracaras create the most havoc as they glide over the colony. Only the albatrosses seem unperturbed by this ace scavenger.

The other popular visitor site is the **fur seal colony** that lies to the north of the settlement. The track leads from the valley behind the bay upwards past Rookery Hill to Landsend Bluff. This is roughly an hour's walk from the jetty. Approximately 500 fur seals come back to breed each year on the flat rocky ledges. The bulls are the first to return in November, the females following a few weeks later once the bulls have laid claim to their patch of rock. Each male then tries to keep 'his' females in his harem until the pups have been born and the females have been mated again. These animals were hunted almost to extinction during the 1800s and were not finally fully protected on the islands until 1921. It is not possible or advisable to get down to the colony. The seals can be viewed in safety from the tussac grass at the top of the cliff. There is always something going on in this colony, whether it is the males defending their territory, the females tending their pups or the non-breeding animals playing in the beds of kelp a few yards offshore. Elephant seals do not breed here, but occasionally one or two can be found hauled up on the beach when they have to come ashore to moult. Southern sea lions can also be seen almost anywhere on the island, but usually in small numbers.

One of the most numerous birds on the island is the thin-billed prion. As the visitor approaches the island by boat, these grey and white seabirds can be seen flitting low over the waves close to the shore. This bird spends most of its time at sea, only coming ashore after dark to elude its predators. Some do not escape, and their corpses can occasionally be found near the narrow burrows in which they have laid their eggs. The peregrine falcons that live on this island appear to have learnt how to catch these elusive birds.

The sheltered eastern side of the island is more to the liking of the Magellanic penguins and the gentoo penguins. The former make their nests in loose colonies along the shore, avoiding the wetter areas. The gentoo penguins on New Island have large colonies at the north and south end of the island. These are not generally visited by humans but can easily be seen from the boat. The occasional king penguin will join with the gentoo colonies when they come ashore to moult.

The largest pool on the island is beyond Coffin Bay at the southwestern end of the island. This is the best place to look for any wildfowl on the island. There is a sizeable gentoo penguin colony on the side of the small hill behind the shallow pool. A partially albino bird was present here during the summer 1999/2000. As on the other islands to the west of Falkland, there is always the chance of vagrant birds reaching these shores.

The rich marine life around New Island supplies food for all of these seabirds and mammals. Southern right whales have been seen from boats and from the shore on several occasions in recent years, as have the more common Commerson's dolphins and Peale's dolphins.

Silvery grebe

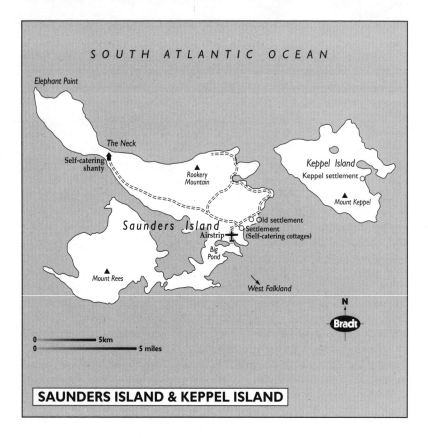

SAUNDERS ISLAND & KEPPEL ISLAND

Saunders Island and Keppel Island

These two mountainous islands are situated to the north west of West Falkland. Keppel Island is no longer inhabited and allows no access to visitors, whilst Saunders Island is an active sheep farm with self-catering accommodation used throughout the year. Both islands have black-browed albatross colonies along with colonies of rockhopper, gentoo and Magellanic penguins. It is only possible to reach Keppel Island by boat, as there is no airstrip, unlike Saunders Island, which has one of the best airstrips away from the major settlements.

SAUNDERS ISLAND

This island comprises 30,000 acres, lying three miles off the northwest coast of West Falkland, and is operated as one farm. It is historically important in the islands as it was the site of the first British settlement in 1765. The present day settlement is situated at the base of a range of hills, the highest of which is Rookery Mountain (1,384ft, 422m). The high cliffs to the north of this range are home to many breeding seabirds. These hills are separated from the highest peak on the island, Mount Harston (1,431ft, 436m) by a sandy isthmus known as the Neck. The southwestern part of the island reaches 1,220ft (371m) at the summit of Mount Rees. The lower land between the settlement and Mount Rees has some pools and is the site of the island's airstrip. In recent years the island has become well known as being home to one of the most accessible black-browed albatross colonies on Falkland situated on the northern coasts. However, Saunders Island has much else to offer, the Neck area in particular having a diverse selection of breeding seabirds, including a small colony of king penguins. The only accommodation is self-catering, either in the settlement or out at the Neck.

History

The first British base on Falkland, about 30 minutes' walk along the coast from the present day settlement, was set up at Port Egmont in 1765 by Commodore John Byron, who was in command of the British expedition to explore Falkland. A British Captain, John McBride, established a proper settlement there on January 8 1766. This settlement was attacked and put to rout by a

Spanish force commanded by Don Juan Ignacio de Madariaga in 1769, after which the British returned home. (The British military forces on Falkland have recently restored the graves of the Royal Marines killed during this battle.) After lengthy negotiations – under the threat of war – between Britain and Spain, an agreement was signed on January 22 giving Port Egmont back to the British. The Spaniards surrendered possession on September 15 1771, passing control of the settlement to Captain Scott who was commanding the frigate *Juno*, the sloop *Hound* and the store ship *Florida*. The British withdrew from Falkland in 1774, leaving behind a flag and a plaque that claimed ownership of the islands. The island has continuously been an active sheep farm since the 19th century. There was no direct action on the island during the war in 1982. The island has widened its economic base by opening up to tourism, with the provision of the three self-catering cottages and in welcoming the visits of the cruise ships that visit Falkland.

Getting there

As with the other outlying islands, there are only two ways for tourists to reach Saunders Island. It is possible to book a passage on the inter-island freight boat, the *Tamar*, but as this is an infrequent service, it is not a practical way for the visitor to visit the island. The majority of visitors get to the island by air using FIGAS (Falkland Island Government Air Service), booking seats on its daily service around the islands. The visitor will be met at the airstrip, one of the best on the outer islands, and taken to the reserved accommodation. The two self-catering houses in the settlement are only a five-minute drive from the airstrip, whereas the property on the Neck is a good hour's drive away. There is superb walking in the vicinity of both cottages. It is possible to book Land Rover excursions from the settlement but not from the Neck. At busy times of year on the farm, for instance during shearing periods, these trips may be slightly curtailed.

Another option is to visit Saunders Island on a day trip from one of the other islands. This is most frequently done from Pebble Island, a 15-minute flight away. This method does mean that the visitor is at the whim of the very changeable weather on Falkland and also that time on the island may be limited by the variable FIGAS work commitments on any given day. It is rare, therefore, to get enough time to visit the wildlife sites at the Neck but, nonetheless, the black-browed albatross colony on the northern coast is within easy range of a day trip. For those not wishing to do any self-catering, or not wanting to keep packing and unpacking, it is a way of seeing one of the wildlife spectacles of Falkland and experiencing another aspect of the *camp*, the local word for the Falklands countryside.

Where to stay

The accommodation on the islands was originally used by the British military as rest and recuperation centres for the Falkland garrison. This has since been modernised and is open for all visitors. There is a small store, dealing in pounds sterling, at the settlement where food can be bought, although bread will have to be brought by the visitor. The farm can usually provide milk and eggs but it is a good idea to check before departure. The farm animals are quite inquisitive about any visitors on the island. It is not unusual to find a horse looking in the sitting-room windows!

Of the two self-catering cottages, the larger can sleep ten people in three twin rooms, one single room and one triple room. There is central heating in all the main rooms and four bedrooms, shower room, bathroom and toilet. There is a well-equipped kitchen and a sitting room with television and radio. Bed linen is provided although towels are only provided for overseas visitors.

The other property in the settlement, **Stone Cottage**, was originally built in 1875 overlooking the harbour. It has been extensively modernised to enable it to sleep eight. It has one double room with double bed and two single beds and two twin rooms. Only the two upstairs bedrooms have central heating. It has a well-equipped kitchen, toilet and bathroom (bath, shower and toilet). Television and radio are provided. As with the larger cottage everything is provided with the exception of towels, which are only provided for overseas visitors.

The ten-mile drive from the settlement to The Neck takes an hour or so depending upon conditions. The accommodation here is of a fairly basic nature in a two-room 'portacabin', which is capable of sleeping six. One room has two sets of bunk beds and there are two single beds in the kitchen. The building is carpeted throughout and has a gas-cooker, heater and gas-powered water-heater. At the time of writing the toilet facilities are primitive, but a shower and flushing toilet are planned. Visitors wishing to stay at the Neck should check at the time of booking. It is quite probable that the visitor will see no one else whilst staying here. A small radio transceiver is available on request. There is an ordinary radio provided to enable the visitor to listen to the daily flight announcements, news etc. The wildlife in this area is superb, the majority of which is within easy walking distance of the portacabin. For those wanting longer walks, there are elephant seals and spectacular scenery at the far northwest end of the island at Elephant Point.

For all accommodation contact David and Suzan Pole-Evans, Saunders Island; tel: 41298; fax: 41296; email: davidpe@horizon.co.fk.

What to see
Black-browed albatross colony
The main attraction of Saunders Island for the wildlife enthusiast is the large **colony of black-browed albatrosses** that breed along the cliffs on the north coast below Rookery Mountain. The drive out to the colony takes the visitor out through the gathering-pens on the edge of the settlement before climbing some rather steep slopes, through some of the largest areas of *Blechnum magellanicum*, the tall fern, on Falkland then descending to the coast. Depending upon the state of the tide, the track either follows the coastal route or crosses a stream and continues along the beach for a while. On the rather low-lying land between this beach and the next, the visitor starts to see penguins for the first time. Small numbers of Magellanic penguin nest on the

more arid slopes whilst gentoo penguins have a small colony a short distance back from the second beach. They can often be seen gathering on the beach in small parties. If time permits during the visitor's stay on the island, this rather scenic part of the island can provide an interesting stop.

After climbing the steep track at the far side of the second beach, it is only a drive of approximately 45 minutes before the black-browed albatross colony is reached. The visitor is usually allowed to remain for a couple of hours or more at this spectacular site. A diddle-dee heath runs down from the top of Rookery Mountain to the edge of the cliff. Small clumps of tussac grass occur on the steeper sections of cliff where they are out of the reach of grazing sheep. The high cliffs drop straight into the sea and are therefore particularly dangerous on windy days. There are very many wet patches where water runs off the hill out to the sea. These can be rather boggy and slippery. There is a narrow channel of clear water between the kelp beds that surround most of Falkland's shores and the cliff edge.

The albatross colony is situated along the coast on the top section of the cliff. The adults are present between September and April, the eggs are laid during October and fledged young leave the nest between mid March and early April. The ideal conditions for observing these birds are bright sunshine and an onshore wind. There is then ample opportunity to try and take the ultimate flight shot of these elegant birds as they cruise low over the cliff top. It is possible to sit a few yards from the colony with birds passing low over visitors' heads. As with all wildlife, it is advisable to keep a good distance away from these birds, so that they are not disturbed and therefore allowed to behave naturally. During the incubation period, the colony is relatively quiet after the noise of the courtship displays at the beginning of the season. The only sounds are the greetings of these giant birds to each other as they swap over incubation duties. When the young birds are big enough to be left, both parents fly out to sea, gathering food such as lobster krill and squid. These fluffy white young creatures are a comical sight on the mud pot nests. As some of these nests have been used over many years they have been built up into quite substantial structures. Many of those birds that are not occupied around the actual breeding site can be seen at sea beyond the distant kelp beds. There is constant movement of albatrosses in and out of the colony throughout the day. They have been studied in recent years as part of a project to discover more information about these long-lived birds. This is why some birds will be noted as having metal rings on their legs, thus enabling the researcher to identify individual birds.

As with all seabird colonies, scavengers are ever present. In this case, the scavengers are usually turkey vultures, southern giant petrels and the occasional stray immature striated caracara later in the summer. There is also a constant stream of rock shags and king shags flying past as these birds also have colonies nearby. The main king shag colony is to the southwest near the Neck, whilst small groups of rock shags breed on many of the cliffs in the vicinity. Small birds are not common on this exposed site apart from the ubiquitous dark-faced ground-tyrants, which seem to be able to survive in almost any habitat on Falkland. They are usually seen flitting around on the cliff face below the nesting albatrosses.

The flora is not very varied at this site, although small clumps of pratia, *Pratia repens*, can be found along with pig vine, *Gunnera magellanica*, in the short grazed turf.

This albatross colony stretches along the coast until it reaches the Neck in the far distance. By walking along in this direction for half an hour or so, the visitor comes across a colony of rockhopper penguins scattered in three or four satellite sites. All of these birds use the same path to get back to the sea. By remaining discreetly to one side, it is possible to watch these tough little birds porpoising their way through the surf before leaping ashore to begin the arduous climb up the cliff to reach their nest. Many can be seen to have black or red stains on their otherwise gleaming white front. This colour comes from the lobster krill (red) or squid (black) that they have been catching. They are very inquisitive birds and will often come over to investigate anyone or anything unusual near the track. Rockhopper penguin colonies are rather raucous places, as each bird greets it mate on its return from the sea. This din, when combined with the cries of the young, is unforgettable. A lone macaroni penguin was seen at this site on several occasions during the 2000/2001 summer season.

The narrow channel between the cliffs and the kelp is occasionally used by Peale's dolphins. Fur seals and southern sea lions have also been seen swimming along this channel.

The return trip to the settlement can either follow the same route, if time is limited, or can follow the coastal track past the beaches and around a headland to the original location of the Port Egmont settlement. The most visible feature above this shallow valley is the site of the newly restored graves of the five Royal Marines killed at the end of the 1700s. The largest edifice on the other side of the valley is the remains of a large, stone-built structure lying parallel to the shore. Close by is the plaque marking the historical importance of the site. The little valley, where these original settlers obtained their water, is a good place to look for *fachine*, one of the few native bushes on Falkland.

The Neck

The drive out to the Neck, one of the Falklands' best wildlife sites, takes an hour or so along a track that can be rather rough depending upon the recent weather conditions. This isthmus is only a ten-minute walk from one hill to the other and takes about five minutes to cross. The whole area can be visited during the day if the visitor is staying at the settlement, but is not an easily practicable destination for an excursion from another island. The low sandy bank between the hills has been scoured by the wind over many years, making this an ideal breeding site for gentoo penguins and Magellanic penguins. The gentoo penguins have at least nine satellite sites for this extended colony. Birds seem to be coming and going from either beach. During the late 1990s a lone chinstrap penguin was occasionally seen mixing with the gentoo penguins. It was a rather shy bird and would soon disappear upon the arrival of humans.

This flat land is also popular with large numbers of roosting gulls, and small flocks of waders have been noted at times. There is very little variation in the flora due to the sand blasting that occurs during the frequent gales. However, there are some nice clumps of sea cabbage and some of the oreob family are represented on the banks at either end. The grassy banks are home to the small colony of king penguins, which started to breed here in the late 1980s and have slowly been increasing over the years. The largest number as yet recorded here has been 22 birds. As it is a very new colony disturbance must be kept to a minimum. It is requested that everyone stay outside the markers, which have been placed around the colony.

There is no obvious path beyond the king penguins' territory along the north west coast. It is worth persevering over some wire fences before reaching a large rockhopper penguin colony on the steeper slopes. As with all grassy cliffs on Falkland, this can be dangerous in wet or windy weather. In the past this colony has contained a small number of macaroni penguins. Large numbers of king shags nest in with the rockhopper penguins, so that apart from the coming and goings of the penguins along their track to the water, there is a constant aerial passage of shags dropping in and taking off from the colony. Throughout the breeding season the shags bring back seaweed to use in nest building, with the constant problem of neighbouring birds stealing much of the material for the nests. The result is a very vigorous colony. Only a short distance away is the start of the elongated colony of black-browed albatrosses, which extends all the way to the foot of Rookery Mountain. The majority of these birds tend not to fly over the Neck itself but to keep out over the open sea. Consequently, although it is still easy to watch the birds on the nest, there are not so many birds to be observed flying by at close range.

Walks from the Neck

For people staying at the Neck, with more time at their disposal than those arriving on a day trip, there are many enjoyable walks. Elephant seals can be found at **Elephant Point**, which is the furthest point of the island from the settlement. There are some small pools just inland from Elephant Point, which have harboured a variety of wildfowl, including the odd scarce species coming in from South America. Not all the burrows here belong to Magellanic penguins, as rabbits are also found in this area.

From the top of **Mount Harston** on a clear day one can see across to Carcass Island and West Point Island and over to the Jasons away on the horizon. In calm weather cetaceans such as Commerson's dolphins have been seen close inshore, whereas southern right whales have been noted in deeper waters and have even been seen from the settlement in recent years.

The southwestern parts of the island tend to be the least visited. The pools have sheltered both silver grebes and white-tufted grebes, a variety of ducks and the occasional black-necked swans. In 1984 the largest of the pools, **Big Pond**, accommodated the largest ever flock of cinnamon teal that the islands have ever seen, when around 20 birds were present. It was thought that they bred there that year. There are no large colonies of seabirds in these parts other than a few Magellanic penguins and some rock shags. Waders make their nests along the shores and some of the islands' songbirds can be found in the more sheltered places. A few South American terns nest near the airstrip most years. They make a terrific din, driving away marauding Antarctic skuas from their breeding grounds.

KEPPEL ISLAND

At present it is not possible to visit this island, although some of its seabird colonies can be seen from the air. It has a unique history in the islands due to the establishment of the South American Missionary Society on Keppel Island in the mid 1800s. The present owner runs it as a nature reserve. The island is slightly nearer to Saunders Island than to Pebble Island and extends over approximately 9,600 acres, reaching a peak of 1,122ft (342m) on Mount Keppel. The southwestern part of the island is much higher above sea level than the low-lying land to the northeast. It is in the latter area that any pools are to be found. The settlement is situated on the flatter southeastern side of the island.

History

Allen W Gardiner, who was the son of the founder of the South American Missionary Society, leased the island in 1885. It has been described as the first established farm on West Falkland and soon became a very profitable business. The island was to be a base from which the society could then voyage to Tierra del Fuego to try to Christianise the native inhabitants, the Yaghan Indians. The idea was that the Yaghans were to be brought to the island to be taught and trained. This mission continued as a farm and training centre for Yaghan Indians and as a base for missionary work in Tierra del Fuego and Patagonia until the death of the then superintendent, Thomas Bridges, in 1898. During that time the farm had prospered, so that by 1877 it was bringing in £1,000 per annum from its sheep, cattle and extensive vegetable gardens. The remaining Indians were taken to a new mission on the South American mainland, which resulted in the closure of the Keppel Mission.

The island continued as a farm until 1911 when it was sold to the Dean brothers who also owned nearby Pebble Island. The island was sold again in 1988, the farm continuing to be used until the island was cleared of stock in 1992 to become a nature reserve. One of the largest buildings in the settlement is the farm manager's house and another is the chapel, which was converted into a shearing shed in the early 1900s.

What to see

The only chance the visitor has of viewing the wildlife on the island is at a distance, usually from the windows of the plane on the flight between Pebble Island and Saunders Island. The northwestern end of the island has a low cliff along which there is a linear colony of black-browed albatrosses and some colonies of rockhopper penguins. Those islanders who worked on the island have described the settlement and its gardens as a good place for the smaller birds of the islands, although the reported presence of feral cats means that there are unlikely to be a wide range of the smaller seabirds nesting nowadays. The flight between the islands can also be an opportunity to look for any cetaceans that happen to be swimming in the shallow water.

Keppel Island has many interesting features and figures in the formative history of the Falkland Islands. Seen from the air or sea it is an intriguing island.

Crested caracara

Weddell, Staats and Beaver Islands

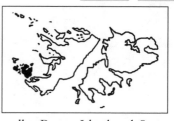

These three islands, the nearby smaller islets, rocks and New Island, form an archipelago in miniature at the southwestern tip of the Falkland Islands. Weddell Island is by far the largest of this group, with an extremely indented coastline and the highest peak in the area, Mount Weddell, at 1,256ft (383m). The smaller Beaver Island and Staats Island lie to the southwest of Weddell Island. All three of these islands, like many others to the west of Falkland, are much more arid than those to the east, having appreciably less rainfall. There are settlements on Weddell and on Beaver Island with shepherds' shanties on Staats and on nearby Tea Island. The larger islands have been farmed whilst some of the smaller islets are still covered in tussac grass, never having been grazed. The coastline in the northwest can generally be described as relatively level with few high points. The southwestern coastline is very different, characterised by lofty sea cliffs and precipitous rocky islets. Of this group, Weddell Island alone offers accommodation for the visitor. Compared to other sites in Falkland these areas are relatively lacking in wildlife, although there are the ubiquitous penguin colonies. Some of the smaller islands are richer in wildlife.

WEDDELL ISLAND

Weddell Island, comprising some 63,000 acres, is the third largest island in the archipelago. The southwestern coasts are much higher than the low-lying area to the west of Mount Weddell and are bisected by Chatham Harbour. There are some buildings on the edge of this natural harbour, but the main settlement is on the east side of the island near a smaller, more sheltered bay. The airstrip is only a short drive from this settlement.

History

The island has been an active farm for many years. The owner of the island in the 1930s, John Hamilton, was responsible for importing many exotic animals and birds to Weddell and to the neighbouring Staats and Beaver Islands. During his period of tenure, Hamilton brought in parrots, skunks, ibis, rheas, Fuegian otters, Patagonian foxes and guanacos. Only the latter two have definitely survived on certain islands. The possibility that Fuegian otters have

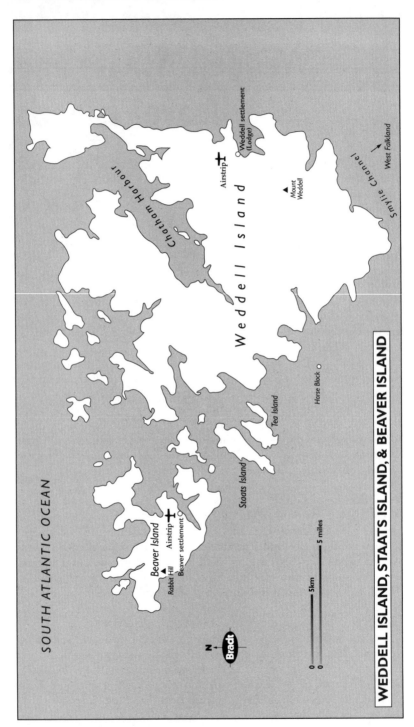

WEDDELL ISLAND, STAATS ISLAND, & BEAVER ISLAND

survived on some remote islands cannot be excluded due to the presence of so much suitable habitat.

Where to stay

The accommodation available is self-catering or fully catered with a licensed bar in the main house. There are two houses used for visitor accommodation; both are open all year and have 24 hour electricity. Information packs and hikers' maps of the island are available. **Mountain View House** sleeps ten guests in five twin bedrooms, and has one bathroom and two toilets. It has a fully equipped kitchen and a large lounge that has excellent views from its patio. All linen is provided, although towels will only be provided on request. The smaller property, **Hamilton Cottage**, sleeps seven or eight in three bedrooms with a combination of single and bunk beds. Two rooms have three or four beds, and there is one single room. There is one bathroom, plus a washroom with shower. There is a fully equipped kitchen-diner. Pillowcases are provided and bed linen and duvets are available on request, but visitors normally bring their own. Contact Karen Taylor, Weddell Island; tel: 42398; fax: 42399.

What to see

The extensive gorse hedges that mark out the edges of the fields around the settlement are a splendid sight in springtime. These lines of yellow are visible from some distance away. The trees, which surround the houses in the settlement, have been home to a small colony of black-crowned night herons in the past. The narrow harbour at the settlement is a reliable place to look for Commerson's dolphins, which can often be seen moving slowly through the shallow water or playing out in the middle of the bay. There are no large numbers of geese on this island due to the presence of Patagonian Foxes. These predators are well camouflaged, as the colour of their coat matches the white grass. The island has large numbers of gentoo penguins, to the extent that gentoo penguin eggs used to be harvested from here in large numbers many years ago. The only other penguin that breeds here is the Magellanic penguin. There are no big breeding colonies, but many seabirds can be watched from the shore when they are feeding in the strait between West Falkland and Weddell Island. This strait is called Smylie Channel and has one of the strongest tidal currents in Falkland. This fast flowing water brings food for a variety of birds close to the surface. Where the channel opens out at its southern end, many sooty shearwaters and black-browed albatrosses gather in small flocks. Prions can be seen flitting in around the waves in rough weather. In spring and autumn southern fulmars and pintado petrels join in with this seething mass of birds. Rock shags and king shags feed in the calmer water at the edges of the channel. This can also be a good area for cetaceans, but the disturbance of the water caused by the strong current means that it is rarely calm enough to see them.

The scenery on the southern and western edges of the island is spectacular, with many interesting rock formations. One of the more unique lies a mile or so southwest of Pillar Bluff. This is Horse Block, a rugged lump of rock some 67m high which at close range appears to have four 'legs', looking for all the world as though it is standing on the water.

At the eastern approach to Smylie Channel is **Sea Dog Island**. This is thought to be one of very few islands in the archipelago that has never had sheep, or even been landed on, owing to its rocky cliffs. It is thought to be home to many of the smaller seabirds, such as prions and petrels, which can only breed in the absence of any small ground predators such as rats.

STAATS AND BEAVER ISLANDS

These two islands cannot be landed on without the permission of the owners, Jerome and Sally Poncet. Despite the lack of visitor accommodation on Staats or Beaver Islands, they are worthy of a visit as representatives of the southwestern facet of the Falklands archipelago.

Staats Island

Staats is a narrow island with some very impressive cliffs on its southwestern side. The only safe landing-point is on the northeast bay below the small shepherd's shanty. The island does not have a great many breeding birds owing to the presence of the Patagonian Foxes that prey on any ground nesting birds. The complete absence of trees means that the only survivors are those big enough to defend their burrows, for example the Magellanic penguins, or those able to nest on the cliffs, such as the rock shags or dark-faced ground-tyrants. Apart from the foxes, this island is best known for the colony of guanacos that was introduced in 1937 and which survives to this day. They can be easily seen from the sea as they feed in the valleys, often observed in small groups, their eerie whinnying cries echoing across the valleys.

To the east of Staats Island is **Tea Island**, a smaller version of Staats with another small shanty. Having been grazed in the past, Tea Island is not renowned for its wildlife.

The trip by boat from Staats Island to the anchorage at Beaver Island takes the visitor past **Coffin Island** and **Stick in the Mud Island**. These are typical tussac grass islands with their original bird populations undisturbed by man. Southern sea lions can often be seen basking on the flat rocky ledges at either end of the island. There is a very strong current flowing past Stick in the Mud Island, making observation difficult.

Beaver Island

The anchorage on Beaver Island is on the northern side of this highly indented coastline. A series of low hills traverses the island. The settlement with its sheltered gardens is on the western side of the harbour. In the hinterland most of the habitat is a mixture of grass and diddledee with a scattering of gorse bushes. There is a grass airstrip not far from the settlement.

This island has a much more varied selection of wildlife than the previous two. Assuming permission to land has been granted, the visitor lands on the eastern arm of the bay from where it is only a short walk to a large gentoo penguin colony, which extends around the side of a small valley. Many birds, including crested duck and the occasional goose, can be seen on the shore or splashing in the shallows. This island had a population of feral cats until they were eradicated in 1993; the owners are now trying to remove the Patagonian foxes that were introduced during the 1930s. If the foxes can be completely eradicated, then the wildfowl of the island should have greater success in breeding. The lack of any sizeable ponds or lakes means that there are very few freshwater ducks on the island. The south and western coasts provide useful opportunities for watching seabirds at sea, especially the black-browed albatrosses that breed on nearby New Island. These coasts are home to large numbers of Falkland flightless steamer ducks and kelp geese. The two species of caracara, crested and striated, are often observed here, as are peregrine falcons. The proximity of this island to the South American mainland has resulted in many vagrant birds being found on this island, usually discovered in sheltered spots around the settlement. Fur seals congregate on the ledges at the base of the western cliffs. From time to time they can be seen from other parts of the coast.

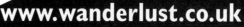

Pintado petrel

Appendix

SELECTED FLORA AND FAUNA
Birds
king penguin (*Aptenodytes patagonicus*)
gentoo penguin (*Pygoscelis papua*)
erect-crested penguin (*Eudyptes sclateri*) *
rockhopper penguin (*Eudyptes chrysocome*)
macaroni penguin (*Eudyptes chrysolophus*)
Magellanic penguin (*Spheniscus megallanicus*)
white-tufted grebe (*Rollandia rolland*)
silvery grebe (*Podiceps occipitalis*)
royal albatross (*Diomedea epomophora*) *
black-browed albatross (*Diomedea melanophris*)
southern giant petrel (*Macronectes giganteus*)
southern (Antarctic) fulmar (*Fulmarus glacialoides*) *
Cape (Pintado) petrel (*Daption capense*) *
broad-billed prion (*Pachyptila vittata*)
thin-billed prion (*Pachyptila belcheri*)
white-chinned petrel (*Procellaria aequinoctialis*)
great Shearwater (*Puffinus gravis*)
sooty shearwater (*Puffinus griseus*)
Wilson's storm-petrel (*Oceanites oceanicus*)
grey-backed storm-petrel (*Garrodia nereis*)
black-bellied storm-petrel (*Fregetta tropica*)
common diving-petrel (*Pelecanoides urinatrix*)
rock shag (*Phalacrocorax magellanicus*)
king shag (*Phalacrocorax atriceps*)
black-crowned night-heron (*Nycticorax nycticorax*)
black-necked swan (*Cygnus melanocorypha*)
feral domestic goose (*Anser anser domesticus*)
upland goose (*Chloephaga picta*)
kelp goose (*Chloephaga hybrida*)
ashy-headed goose (*Chloephaga poliocephala*)
ruddy-headed goose (*Chloephaga rubidiceps*)
flying steamer-duck (*Tachyeres patachonicus*)
Falkland flightless steamer-duck (*Tachyeres brachypterus*) #
chiloe wigeon (*Anas sibilatrix*)

speckled (yellow-billed) teal (*Anas flavirostris flavirostris*)
(Patagonian) crested duck (*Anas specularioides*)
yellow-billed pintail (*Anas georgica*)
silver teal (*Anas versicolor*)
cinnamon teal (*Anas cyanoptera*)
red shoveler (*Anas platalea)*
turkey vulture (*Cathartes aura*)
red-backed hawk (*Buteo polysoma*)
striated caracara (*Phalcoboenus australis*)
crested caracara (*Polyborus plancus*)
peregrine falcon (*Falco peregrinus*)
blackish oystercatcher (*Haematopus ater*)
Magellanic oystercatcher (*Haematopus leucopodus*)
two-banded plover (*Charadrius falklandicus*)
rufous-chested dotterel (*Charadrius modestus*)
Magellanic snipe (*Gallinago paraguaiae*)
white-rumped sandpiper (*Calidris fuscicollis*)
snowy sheathbill (*Chionis alba*) ★
Antarctic skua (*Catharacta antarctica*)
dolphin gull (*Larus scoresbii*)
kelp gull (*Larus dominicanus*)
brown-hooded gull (*Larus maculipennis*)
South American tern (*Sterna hirundinacea*)
barn owl (*Tyto alba tuidara*)
short-eared owl (*Asio flammeus*)
tussacbird (*Cinclodes antarcticus*)
dark-faced ground-tyrant (*Muscisaxicola macloviana*)
barn swallow (*Hirundo rustica*) ★
Chilean swallow (*Tachycineta leucopyga*)
Falkland pipit (*Anthus correndera*)
grass wren (*Cistothorus platensis platensis*)
Cobb's wren (*Troglodytes aedon musculus*) #
Falkland thrush (*Turdus falcklandii*)
long-tailed meadowlark (*Sturnella loyca*)
black-chinned siskin (*Carduelis barbata*)
black-throated finch (*Melanodera melanodera*)
house sparrow (*Passer domesticus*)

Mammals
southern right whale (*Eubalaena australis*)
killer whale (Orca) (*Orcinus orca*)
long-finned pilot whale (*Globicephala maleana*)
Peale's dolphin (*Lagenorhynchus australis*)
Commerson's dolphin (*Cephalorhunchus commersonii*)
cottontail rabbit (*Sylvilagus floridanus*)
European hare (*Lepus europaeus)*

house mouse (*Mus musculus*)
brown rat (*Rattus norvegicus*)
black rat (*Rattus rattus*)
Fuegian marine (sea) otter (*Lutra felina*)
Patagonian fox (*Dusicyon griseus griseus*)
southern sea lion (*Otaria flavescens*)
South American fur seal (*Arctocephalus australis australis*)
southern elephant seal (*Mirounga leonina*)
leopard seal (*Hydrurga leptonyx*)
guanaco (*Lama guanicoe*)

Flowering plants and ferns
small fern (*Blechnum penna-marina*)
tall fern (*Blechnum magellanicum*)
curled dock (*Rumex crispus*)
sheep's sorrel (*Rumex acetosella*) †
field mouse-ear chickweed (*Cerastium fontanum*) †
arrow-leaved marigold (*Caltha sagittata*)
silver-leaved ranunculus (*Hamadryas argentea*) #
Falkland rock cress (*Arabis macloviana*) #
native stonecrop (*Crassula moschata*)
native strawberry (*Rubus geoides*)
oval-leaved prickly burr (*Acaena ovalifolia*)
prickly burr (*Acaena magellanica*)
native yarrow (*Acaena lucida*)
gorse (*Ulex europaea*) †
white clover (*Trifolium repens*) †
hop trefoil (*Trifolium campestre*) †
red clover (*Trifolium pratense*) †
scurvy grass (*Oxalis enneaphylla*)
native/yellow violet (*Viola maculata*)
field pansy (*Viola arvensis*)
teaberry (*Myrteola nummularia*)
pig vine (*Gunnera magellanica*)
clubmoss azorella (*Azorella lycopodioides*)
cushion azorella (*Azorella selago*)
balsam bog (*Bolax gummifera*)
Falkland lilaeopsis (*Lilaeopsis macloviana*) #
wild celery (*Apium australe*)
mountain berry (*Pernettya pumila*) †
diddle-dee (*Empetrum rubrum*)
dusty miller primrose (*primula magellanica*)
native pimpernel (*Anagallis alternifolia*)
Falkland thrift (*Armeria macloviana*)
Antarctic bedstraw (*Galium antarcticum*)
changing forget-me-not (*Mysotis discolor*) †

lady's slipper (*Calceolaria fothegillii*)
native boxwood (*Hebe ellipitca*)
Antarctic eyebright (*Euphrasia antarctica*)
Moore's plantain (*Plantago moorei*) #
creeping berry-lobelia (*Pratia repens*)
Falkland false plantain (*Nastanthus falklandicus*) #
European daisy (*Bellis perennis*) †
marsh daisy (*Aster vahlii*)
hairy daisy (*Erigeron incertus*) #
Christmas bush (*Baccharis magellanica*)
fachine (*Chilliotrichum diffusum*)
clubmoss cudweed (*Gnaphalium lycopodioides*) #
Falkland cudweed (*Gnaphalium affine*) #
yarrow (*Achillea millefolium*) †
sea cabbage (*Senecio candicans*)
woolly Falkland ragwort (*Senecio littoralis*) #
smooth Falkland ragwort (*Senecio vaginatus*) #
groundsel (*Senecio vulgaris*) †
coastal nassauvia (*Nassauvia gaudichaudii*) #
stone run plant (Snake plant) (*Nassauvia serpens*) #
vanilla daisy (*Leucheria suaveolens*) #
Falkland lavender (*Perezia recurvata*)
Antarctic hawkweed (*Hieracium antarcticum*) †
orange hawkweed (*Pilosella aurantiaca*)
dandelion (*Taraxacum offininale*) †
soft camp bog (*Astelia pumila*)
almond flower (*Luzuriaga marginata*)
pale maiden (*Sisyrinchium filifolium*)
native rush (*Juncus scheuzerioides*) †
Fuegian rush (*Rostkovia magellanica*)
basket rush (*Marsippospermum grandiflorum*)
tussock grass (*Parodiochloe flabellata*)
mountain blue grass (*Poa alopecurus*)
Yorkshire fog (*Holcus lanatus*) †
white grass (*Cortaderia pilosa*)
cinnamon grass (*Hierochloe redolens*)
California club rush (*Schoenoplectus californicus*)
yellow orchid (*Gavilea littoralis*)
dog orchid (*Codonorchis lessonii*)

Appendix 2

FURTHER READING
Books

Chater, T *The Falklands* Penna Press, November 1993. An annotated pictorial guide.

Davis, T H and McAdam, J H *Wild Flowers of the Falkland Islands* Bluntisham Books/Falkland Islands Trust, 1989. An illustrated identification guide to the main breeding flowers on Falkland.

De la Pena, M A and Rumboll, M *Birds of Southern South America and Antarctica* HarperCollins, 1998. An illustrated field guide to the birds of the region.

Strange, I J *A Field Guide to the Wildlife of the Falkland Islands and South Georgia* HarperCollins, 1992. A field guide to the birds, flowers, animals and selected other families of wildlife occurring in the area.

Woods, R W and Woods, A *Atlas of Breeding Birds of the Falkland Islands* Nelson 1993. A species by species account of the birds that breed on Falkland.

Woods, R W *Native Plant Survey* Falkland Conservation, 1998. An illustrated guide to 26 native plant species.

Woodward S and Robinson, P *One Hundred Days* Harper Collins, 1997. The commander of the British naval forces' account of the Falkland War 1982.

Brochures

The Falkland Islands: Travel Information, Falkland Island Tourist Board, 2000

The Falkland Islands: Visitor accommodation guide, Falkland Island Tourist Board, 2000

Stanley, Falkland Island Tourist Board, 1999. Sponsored by Cable & Wireless

a Checklist of Falkland Island Wildlife, Falkland Conservation, 2000

Spruce, J *Stanley: A guide for visitors* FITB, 1999

Maps

Falkland Islands Scale 1:250,000, 1996, Ordnance Survey

Stanley minefield and area clearance situation map Scale 1:50,000, 1990

Camp minefield situation map, 1994

Both minefield maps available from the Joint Services EOD office in Stanley.

Websites

Chronicle of the Falklands/Malvinas History and War of 1982

www.yendor.com/vanished/falklands-war.html

CIA -The World Factbook - Falkland Islands
  www.odci.gov/cia/publications/factbook/geos/fa.html
Falklands Conservation www.falklands-nature.demon.co.uk
Falkland Islands Development Corporation www.fidc.org.fk
Falkland Islands Government www.falklands.gov.fk
Falkland Islands Tourist Board www.tourism.org.fk
Falkland-Malvinas Forum www.falkland-malvinas.com
Falkland Islands history and other information www.geocities.com./little_chay/
The South Atlantic Medal Association 82 www.sama82.org.uk

CD-Roms
Microsoft Encarta Encyclopaedia 99

Other sources
A Tour Guides Manual Falkland Islands Tourist Board with Falkland
  Conservation, 1991
Falklands Conservation Newsletter 1999-2000
McAdam J (Editor) *The Falkland Islands Journal* vol 7 (part 4)
The Warrah, Falkland Conservation Magazine 1994–2000
A Visitor's Guide to the Falkland Islands Falkland Conservation, to be published
  end of 2001. A site by site guide, available in the UK and in Falkland.

Index